Thomas ap Catesby Jones

LIBRARY OF NAVAL BIOGRAPHY

THOMAS AP CATESBY JONES

COMMODORE OF MANIFEST DESTINY

Gene A. Smith

NAVAL INSTITUTE PRESS
Annapolis, Maryland

Naval Institute Press
291 Wood Road
Annapolis, MD 21402

Library of Congress Cataloging-in-Publication Data
Smith, Gene. A., 1963–
        Thomas ap Catesby Jones: commodore of Manifest Destiny / Gene A. Smith.
            p.   cm.— (Library of naval biography)
        Includes bibliographical references (p.) and index.
        ISBN 1-55750-848-8 (alk. paper)
            1. Jones, Thomas Ap Catesby, 1790–1858. 2. United States—History, Naval—To 1900.
        3. United States. Navy—Officers—Biography. 4. Ship captains—United
        States—Biography. 5. United States—Territorial expansion—History—19th century.
        I. Title. II. Series.

        E340.J7 S65 2000
        359'.0092—dc21   99-053750
        [B]

Printed in the United States of America on acid-free paper ∞
07 06 05 04 03 02 01 00   9 8 7 6 5 4 3 2
First printing

Frontispiece courtesy of the U.S. Naval Academy Museum

For my wife, Tracy

❧ *Contents* ❧

⊸ Foreword ⬿

Thomas ap Catesby Jones is not one of the best-known naval officers of the early nineteenth century, but he is one of the most fascinating. When Jones entered the navy in 1805, the vast majority of Americans inhabited a few states bordering the Atlantic Ocean. When he retired half a century later, the United States had spread westward to cover the North American continent to the Pacific Ocean. The story of this expansion, of America fulfilling its "manifest destiny," is often depicted in territorial terms as a steady progression from sea to sea. In fact, the movement was neither steady nor dictated exclusively by events occurring on land.

The United States Navy matured as the nation expanded, and Thomas ap Catesby Jones was among a small group of officers who contributed to both the advancement of the navy and the expansion of the nation. Though only fifteen years of age when appointed a midshipman, Jones was older than the service he entered. He had missed the navy's baptism of fire in the Quasi-War against France and the Mediterranean Barbary Wars, but he had certainly heard of the exploits of Thomas Truxtun, Stephen Decatur, and others. President Thomas Jefferson purchased Louisiana from France in 1803; Jones reported for duty at Norfolk, in his home state of Virginia, in 1807; and a decade later he commanded the flotilla of gunboats assigned to defend New Orleans and Louisiana during the War of 1812. At the Battle of Lake Borgne, British invaders captured Jones and swept his paltry force aside, but not before they had bought time for Andrew Jackson and his army to prepare for their stunning victory at the Battle of New Orleans three-and-a-half weeks later.

After a year spent recovering from his wounds, including three months as a British prisoner of war, Jones, now a lieutenant, served for three years in the Mediterranean, then transferred to ordnance duty in Washington.

He would devote much of the next decade and a half to inventorying, inspecting, and improving the cannon of the navy. During the 1820s he commanded the sloop of war *Peacock* on a Pacific Ocean voyage during which he spent three months in Hawaii negotiating conflicts concerning trade and debts, countering British influence in the islands, and trying to improve relations between American missionaries and other residents. From the mid-1830s to mid-1840s, and again in the late 1840s, Jones would return to the Pacific serving as commander of all U.S. naval forces in the region. During one such tour of duty he believed rumors that war had erupted between the United States and Mexico and acting with speed and alacrity occupied the city of Monterey in California (then part of Mexico) in October 1842. Learning that no such war existed, Jones withdrew his forces, but it was too late: a series of events was set in train that would cloud the rest of his career and lead to a long and controversial court-martial.

The life of Thomas ap Catesby Jones provides a window through which to view the development of the United States Navy as it was transformed from a small, coastal, defense-oriented gunboat force in 1805 into a sail-and-steam service capable of projecting American power around the world only fifty years later. In addition to illustrating how the U. S. Navy fought, Jones's career provides insight into the nation's expansion across the continent.

Gene Smith is well-prepared to write this first scholarly biography of Thomas ap Catesby Jones. The author of the standard study of Thomas Jefferson's gunboat policy, Smith has also edited one of the most important firsthand accounts of Louisiana during the War of 1812 and co-authored a study of American expansion into Spanish territories bordering the Gulf of Mexico. In this biography, Smith both captures the character and life of his subject, Thomas ap Catesby Jones, and shows how the U.S. Navy developed into a force capable of winning the Civil War, which erupted shortly after the death of Jones—a slave-owning planter from Virginia.

The Library of Naval Biography provides accurate, informative, and interpretive biographies of influential naval figures—men and women who have shaped or reflected the naval affairs of their time. Each volume will explain the forces that acted upon its subject as well as the significance of that person in history. Some volumes will explore the lives of individuals who have not previously been the subject of a modern, full-scale biography, while others will reexamine the lives of better-known individuals adding new information, a differing perspective, or a fresh interpretation. The series is international in scope and includes individuals from several centuries. All volumes are based on solid research and written to be of interest to general readers as well as useful to specialists.

With these goals in mind, the length of each volume has been limited, the notes restricted primarily to direct quotations, and a Further Reading section provided to assess previous biographies and to direct readers to the most important studies of the era and events in which the person lived and participated. It is the intention that this combination of clear writing, fresh interpretation, and solid historical context will result in volumes that restore the all-important human dimension to naval history.

James C. Bradford
Series Editor

~~≥ *Preface* ⩗~

I first encountered Thomas ap Catesby Jones when I was a graduate student searching for a thesis topic. At that time I was interested in the navy and its role in California affairs, and I soon learned that in October 1842, Jones, as commander of the Pacific Squadron, had seized Monterey, California, thinking that the United States and Mexico were at war. This dramatic episode provided the topic for my first scholarly article and put me on course to become a professional historian. I moved away from California topics when I began my dissertation research, only to have Jones cross my path again. My dissertation examined the Jeffersonian gunboat program, and much to my surprise I discovered that a young Lieutenant Jones commanded the gunboat flotilla at the Battle of Lake Borgne in December 1814. Once I completed my graduate work, I sought a new topic that combined my interest in the U.S. Navy, the War of 1812, and national developments during the early republic, and once again Jones reappeared.

After some preliminary research I discovered that the only major treatise on Jones was a doctoral dissertation written by Udolpho Theodore Bradley in 1933; it was dated and in need of serious revision. Given Jones's notoriety, I was surprised and elated that he had not been studied. But as I began to explore his life I quickly learned why no one had undertaken such a project—there exists no single sizable collection of personal papers that detail his life or provide insight into his character. In other words, I had to spend years searching various archives and combing collections for traces of his personality and life.

Jones was one of the most colorful and controversial figures in the nineteenth-century U.S. Navy, yet he is often overlooked or even confused with his nephew Catesby ap Roger Jones, who commanded the CSS *Virginia* (formerly the USS *Merrimac*) in its battle against the *Monitor*. A

xv

surprising number of authors have made that mistake. Those who have
heard of Jones most likely know about his mistaken seizure of Monterey
in October 1842, one of the most memorable events for the antebellum
U.S. Navy. Despite even this notoriety, however, Jones seemed to be lost
in the shadows of the past.

According to his first biographer, Jones was a "contentious commodore" who contributed little to the navy. Yet I wondered if that assertion was completely accurate. I quickly learned that Jones was not a main
actor in the great drama of American naval development, as I had hoped.
Instead, I found that he was a transitional figure who contributed significantly as the country recast the small, defensive, gunboat-oriented navy
of the Jeffersonian period into a seagoing force that eventually depended
on iron and steam and projected American power across the earth's
oceans. Although he was active in naval diplomacy, ordnance development, and promoting the use of technology and education, Jones is not
remembered for his important contributions in any of these areas. In fact,
Jones is a good representative of the successful, dedicated type of officer
who composed the American naval patriarchy in the age of sail—he was
mariner, diplomat, warrior, scientist, and bureaucrat, and along with his
brethren he helped lay important foundations for future change.

Jones was also a slaveholding plantation owner and a devout Christian.
Yet he found nothing contradictory in Christianity and slavery. He even
made sure that his slaves went to church and learned to read and write
so that they would be better Christians. A very successful farmer, Jones
employed the most modern techniques of scientific farming to transform
his once-barren acreage into a lush paradise. In doing so he overextended his family's finances, which created new problems that prompted
Jones to make dubious decisions while a squadron commander. Ultimately, his family's financial needs brought about his downfall.

I have incurred many debts to individuals and institutions in writing this
book. My colleagues in the profession have been extremely generous
with their time and advice. I have profited from the reading and helpful
suggestions made by Christopher McKee, John Schroeder, Craig
Symonds, Bill Trimble, Spencer Tucker, Ken Stevens, Don Worcester,
David Coffey, and Bruce Elleman; their recommendations have greatly
strengthened this book, and I am truly appreciative. I am also indebted
to Montana State University at Billings (formerly Eastern Montana Col-

lege) and Texas Christian University for releasing me from teaching and for other support. Without the generous financial support of two TCU Research Grants, an EMC Foundation Grant and EMC Research Grant, the Vice Admiral Edwin B. Hooper Research Grant of the Naval Historical Center, a Virginia Historical Society Mellon Research Fellowship, and a Mayer Fund Fellowship from the Henry E. Huntington Library, I could not have finished this book, especially the research.

Many public and private institutions have been gracious in allowing me to use their records and in affording me welcomed assistance. I am very grateful to the staff members at the National Archives (especially Becky Livingston and Barry Zerby), the Naval Historical Foundation, and the Manuscript Division of the Library of Congress, all in Washington, D.C. Many departments of archives and history on the state level offered invaluable assistance, Hawaii, North Carolina, and Virginia in particular. I am also in the debt of staff members at the university libraries and special collections at Duke University, the University of Michigan, Princeton University, the University of Virginia, Yale University, the College of William and Mary, the United States Naval Academy, the University of North Carolina, and the University of California at Berkeley. The Historic New Orleans Collection (especially Alfred Lemmon and Pat Brady), Virginia Historical Society (Nelson Lankford and Sara Bearss in particular), Fairfax County Court Archives (Connie Ring), New-York Historical Society, Hagley Museum and Library, Massachusetts Historical Society, Henry E. Huntington Library, Historic Society of Pennsylvania, Franklin D. Roosevelt Library, and Frank Gapp of the Lewinsville Presbyterian Church in McLean, Virginia, deserve special thanks. The Naval Historical Center; the U.S. Naval Academy Museum; the Lewinsville Presbyterian Church; the Fairfax County, Virginia, Public Library; and the U.S. National Archives graciously allowed me to use illustrative materials.

I greatly appreciate the interest of James Bradford, the editor of the Library of Naval Biography Series; Paul Wilderson; and the staff members of the Naval Institute Press. I owe thanks to Mindy Conner for lessons in copyediting. I am most indebted to my family and friends for their constant encouragement during this task. Finally, my wife, Tracy, to whom I dedicate this work, has endured my fascination with this figure of the past; she may know little about Thomas ap Catesby Jones, but she knows much about me, and her support and encouragement have enabled me to finish this book.

Chronology

24 Apr. 1790	Born at Hickory Hill, in Westmoreland County, Virginia
22 Nov. 1805	Appointed midshipman, U.S. Navy
30 May 1806	Granted furlough to gain sea experience aboard a merchant ship
Aug. 1807–Jan. 1808	Service aboard gunboats at Norfolk, Virginia
Jan. 1808–July 1815	Service aboard gunboats on New Orleans station
Oct. 1808–Mar. 1809	Flag lieutenant of the New Orleans station
Mar. 1809–Nov. 1811	Commander of gunboat *No. 25* in Gulf of Mexico
Nov. 1811–Dec. 1814	Commander of gunboat *No. 156* in Gulf of Mexico
24 May 1812	Promoted to lieutenant, U.S. Navy
13–14 Dec. 1814	Commander of gunboat squadron that confronted British on Lake Borgne; wounded during action
Dec. 1814–Mar. 1815	Held prisoner by the British
July 1815–Jan. 1816	Granted leave to recover from wound
Jan. 1816–Nov. 1816	Service onboard ship of the line *Washington* in Mediterranean
Nov. 1816–Oct. 1817	First lieutenant of frigate *Constellation* in Mediterranean
Oct. 1817–July 1818	First lieutenant of frigate *United States* in Mediterranean
Jan. 1819–Apr. 1822	Assigned to Ordnance Service at Washington Navy Yard

28 Mar. 1820	Promoted to commander, U.S. Navy
Apr. 1822–Apr. 1824	Inspector and superintendent of ordnance for Washington Navy Yard
1 July 1823	Married Mary Walker Carter
23 Aug. 1824	Meriwether Patterson Jones, first of four children, born
Apr. 1824–Apr. 1825	Inspector and superintendent of ordnance for U.S. Navy
Apr. 1825–Oct. 1827	Commander of sloop *Peacock* in the Pacific Ocean
Nov. 1828–June 1829	Commander of South Pacific Exploring Expedition that never sailed
17 Mar. 1829	Promoted to captain, U.S. Navy
June 1829–Apr. 1834	Inspector and superintendent of ordnance for U.S. Navy
Apr. 1834–June 1836	On leave
June 1836–Dec. 1837	Commander of South Pacific Exploring Expedition
Dec. 1837–Apr. 1841	On leave due to poor health
Sept. 1841–May 1844	Commander of the Pacific Squadron
20–21 Oct. 1842	Captured Monterey, Alta California
May 1844–May 1845	Awaiting duty
May 1845–July 1845	On committee to determine site for a naval academy
May 1846–Oct. 1847	Inspector and superintendent of ordnance for U.S. Navy
June–Aug. 1847	President of second Board of Examiners for Midshipmen at Naval Academy
Oct. 1847–Dec. 1850	Commander of the Pacific Squadron
16 Dec. 1850–1 Feb. 1851	Court-martialed; suspended for five years
23 Feb. 1853	Sentence remitted by President Millard Fillmore; awaiting orders
13 Sept. 1855	Placed on Reserve List by Retirement Board
30 May 1858	Died at Sharon in Fairfax County, Virginia, of natural causes

·⚡ I ⚡·

IMPROVING YOURSELF IN YOUR PROFESSION

The Early Years, 1790–1807

Sixty-five-year-old Capt. Thomas ap Catesby Jones was enraged, hurt, and bitter. His country, he believed, had forsaken him, forgotten his gallant and patriotic deeds, and ignored his forty-plus years of dedicated service. He had been slighted, and he wanted his honor restored. Although he was seething, he could do little more than protest the perceived injustices to Secretary of the Navy James C. Dobbin. And even then, what hope had he that anyone would listen to an angry old man?

On a late October day in 1855 Jones sat in the study at Sharon, his Fairfax County, Virginia, farm, and drafted perhaps the most important letter of his career. Only days before, he had received news that a Navy Department board of fifteen officers had placed him and two hundred other officers on the navy's reserve list. Jones responded to this unprecedented forced retirement with a detailed memorial to the secretary of the navy and Congress asking for relief from the "injustice" and monetary loss the board's decision had caused. Jones wrote to protect his reputation, his career, and his financial livelihood. From between the lines of his letter emerges the story of a flamboyant and often controversial officer, yet one whose attitude toward his obligations and responsibilities in many ways represents the generation of officers who served between the Barbary Wars and the Civil War. As such, Jones's struggle was not only the most important battle of his life—and, ultimately, one he could not win—it also represents the struggle of a forgotten generation who, after many years of useful service, had been trimmed away like excess fat.[1]

In his letter Jones unabashedly told the story of a career that began in 1807 and spanned four decades. Discarding all modesty, he asserted that "a bare enumeration of all the remarkable incidents of my naval service, on shore and afloat, would fill many pages." Jones insisted that his service along the Gulf of Mexico between 1808 and 1815, "in the suppression of piracy, smuggling, and the slave trade, and in the enforcement of our neutrality laws, would alone form a volume of thrilling interest."[2]

In the next several pages he elucidated on his three deployments with the Pacific Squadron, two as its commander. Throughout he was quick to remind readers of the sacrifices he had made for his country. While maintaining his loyalty to the department, he also insinuated that the time had now come for his nation to provide its thanks. Near the letter's end Jones stressed that he "had to *work* [his] way to the honorable and enviable position in the Navy . . . through wars, pestilence, famine, floods, tempests, shipwreck, and fire." He hoped that the recipient of his letter would realize that his appeal was directed against the commission of junior officers who had unjustly attacked him, not the U.S. Navy.[3]

A month later, in another letter, Jones repeated his arguments in an even more emotional fashion. He insisted that he had "been deprived of the high and honorable position . . . won by years of faithful service." He had been denied "his right to be enrolled among those to whom his country is willing to confide the protection of her interests, as well as the honor of her flag, in whatever sea or clime the enterprise of her citizens may have penetrated." Sadly, Jones concluded that he had "been deprived of all chance of future distinction" and would "never again . . . indulge in that hope."[4]

In those two passionate letters Jones proudly extolled the service he had rendered to his country, but he did not discuss his family pedigree. Yet that, too, was something in which he took inordinate pride. He also did not mention why he joined the navy or provide information about his formative years, his family, or how a young man from a moderately influential Virginia family had taken to the sea. Jones most likely felt that these issues were not pertinent to his claim, but they nonetheless provide insight into his enigmatic character and help to explain the personality and development of this influential naval officer.

Thomas ap Catesby Jones was born at Hickory Hill, his mother's family home in Westmoreland County, Virginia, on 24 April 1790. It was spring in Virginia's Northern Neck, and the wildflowers, honeysuckle, and dogwoods were in bloom, an auspicious beginning for the second son born to Maj. Catesby and Lettice Turberville Jones. The family took great pride in its heritage, as evidenced by Thomas being given the designation "ap," a Welsh prefix meaning "son of"—thus Thomas "son of" Catesby Jones. The boy's first name, Thomas, was the name borne by his paternal grandfather and great-grandfather, neither of whom he ever met. Like many of the Virginia elite, the Jones family perpetuated the tradition of naming children after prominent members of the family. Catesby and Lettice's oldest son, Roger, born in 1789, was named after Roger Jones, the first member of the family to emigrate to Virginia.[5]

Roger Jones arrived in Virginia during the 1680s. Commissioned an army captain during the reign of Charles II, he may have come over when Lord Thomas Culpeper assumed the governorship in 1680. At that time Virginia was reeling from the tremendous discord produced by Bacon's Rebellion of 1676. The political and economic struggle between the Tidewater patricians, who generally supported the Crown, and frontier plebeians demanding reform had ended some years earlier, but its ramifications continued throughout the 1680s. Near the end of the decade the low price of tobacco exacerbated already high tensions and prompted some colonists to destroy their crops in the fields rather than accept the depressed prices. The resultant Tobacco Rebellion of 1688 forced Lord Culpeper to return personally to Virginia with troops to assume active leadership of the colony. More likely Roger Jones came with Culpeper at this time to suppress the rebellion. In any case, this former Nottinghamshire resident, who reportedly introduced the Welsh bloodline into Virginia, had served in both the English army and navy. During the mid-1680s he also had served the Crown in such exotic lands as Surinam and Antigua. This Roger Jones remained in Virginia only a few years before returning to England, where he died in 1701 at his home in Stepney (then a suburb of London). Two of his sons, however, remained in North America. Frederick, the oldest boy, moved to North Carolina while Thomas stayed in Williamsburg, Virginia.[6]

Thomas Jones apparently benefited from his father's close association with Lord Culpeper and moved within the social circles of the Virginia elite. In the early years of the 1700s Thomas received a sizable land grant from Lieutenant Governor Alexander Spotswood, who was also his business partner. Between 1713 and 1731 Colonel Jones, as he was called, acquired more land and several houses and lots in Williamsburg, where he resided, and became an influential tobacco planter who possessed several farms and eighty slaves. In February 1725 he married Elizabeth Catesby Pratt, the widow of William Pratt and niece of the famed naturalist Mark Catesby. Not the least of Elizabeth's attractions for the land-wealthy farmer were her extensive political connections. Her father, Dr. William Cocke, had been secretary of state of Virginia and a member of the King's Council before he died, and her stepfather, John Holloway, was speaker of the House of Burgesses. These familial connections helped bring Jones, his wife, and their ten children prosperity.[7]

Thomas and Elizabeth's oldest child, Thomas Jr., Thomas ap Catesby's grandfather, was born on Christmas Day in 1726. Although little is known about his formative years, he became the well-paid clerk of Northumberland County in 1749, and shortly thereafter he married Sally Skelton, daughter of James and Jane Meriwether Skelton. The couple prospered in Northumberland County during the twenty-eight years Thomas Jr. held the position of clerk. In 1757 he assumed the role of family patriarch when his father died; Jones inherited Spring Garden, the family home in Hanover County, as well as responsibility for his mother and younger siblings. Between 1761 and 1771 Colonel Thomas Jones, as he was known after his father's death, purchased Mt. Zion plantation at Cherry Point Neck, Northumberland County, where he built a stately two-story brick home with a detached brick smokehouse and kitchen and acquired a gristmill, a storehouse, a barn and stable, and several corn cribs; this estate ultimately symbolized the quintessential eighteenth-century Virginia plantation.[8]

Colonel Jones provided well for his family, giving his children the best that money could buy. Moreover, the family home was exquisitely furnished and adorned with paintings by distinguished artists. Jones hired Scottish scholar John Warden to tutor his children and his siblings. Warden had come with worthy endorsements from Thomas's brother Walter, who was then completing a medical degree at Edinburgh College. But this life of ease apparently gave Jones's two oldest sons, Thomas ap Thomas and Catesby, a false sense of superiority. In 1771 Warden reported that the two boys were completely disrespectful. They constantly denigrated him, called him an indentured servant, and ridiculed him because he was poor and worked for others. Ironically, Warden became a distinguished, successful, and prosperous Virginia lawyer while the two boys experienced continual economic setbacks as adults.[9]

Although not a major figure in the events of the Revolution, Thomas Jones did support the cause. He signed a petition against the Stamp Act of 1765, served as colonel of the volunteer Lancaster District Battalion in 1775–76, and enlisted about five hundred men from Lancaster, Northumberland, and Richmond Counties for the Virginia militia, which, along with other Virginians in July 1776, confronted Lord Dunmore's British fleet off Northumberland County. The colonel's oldest son, Thomas ap Thomas, became a recruiting officer during the war, while Catesby, the younger, served as a lieutenant. The Jones family's service did little to change the course of revolutionary events, but their efforts instilled pride and patriotism in the family, and those ideas would not be forgotten.[10]

In 1778 twenty-two-year-old Catesby Jones assumed the Northumberland County clerkship; married Miss Lettice Corbin Turberville, daughter of John and Martha Corbin Turberville of Hickory Hill; and soon thereafter took control of Mt. Zion. Unfortunately Catesby was not the astute businessman his father and grandfather had been. When he moved to Mt. Zion the plantation comprised about seven hundred acres and twenty slaves. Yet Catesby's fortunes were to be inextricably linked to those of the new nation. In the war's aftermath the country experienced a short-lived economic boom, but by 1784 the market for agricultural produce appeared to be flooded, prices had fallen, specie had become scarce, and credit had been overextended. In short, America experienced its first economic depression. Even Virginia's valuable tobacco crop fell on hard times as prices dropped and yields declined because of depleted soils. Farmers seemed helpless to escape this downward spiral, and Catesby Jones was no exception.[11]

Jones attempted to modernize and diversify his farming operations. He contracted for an iron plow that could turn up the more fertile subsoil, operated a state-approved inspection site and warehouse for grading tobacco, and brokered tobacco for others. He acquired additional slaves and lands in nearby Westmoreland County, and he managed part of his father-in-law's business. Jones also unsuccessfully ventured into new businesses to provide for his growing family, which numbered seven children before the end of the 1790s. Compounding his financial woes was a recurring sickness, probably gout and pleurisy, which left him incapacitated for months at a time. By 1798 the family's finances had fallen into disarray, and Catesby Jones had to mortgage to his brothers Jekyll and Skelton the Mt. Zion estate, slaves, and livestock.[12]

Catesby Jones died on 23 September 1801 at the age of forty-five, leaving his family in a precarious situation. The once vast estate had dwindled away, and Lettice, his widow, faced dim prospects. The home property of Mt. Zion had an outstanding lien with little prospect of the family being able to pay it. Moreover, there were six children to be fed, clothed, and educated. As was common among Americans at this time, the children were taken into the households of other family members, and in many instances they were treated as part of the core family. Roger and Thomas ap Catesby fell under the care of their uncle Meriwether Jones, who resided in Richmond.

Eleven-year-old Thomas ap Catesby was not allowed to enjoy the affluent childhood his father had known, with its tradition of social prominence, influence, and wealth. While Catesby Jones had worn silk stockings and silver buckles and had been tutored on the family estate, Thomas ap Catesby received much of his early education at nearby Cherry Point Church under the guidance of Rev. John Seward. This childhood of relative poverty left an indelible mark on the young boy's psyche. He had looked on while his father worked incessantly at his official or private businesses, suffered sickness, and dragged the family into financial ruin. Family stories that recalled the more conspicuous lifestyle of earlier generations perhaps created a feeling of insecurity in the young man that he carried into adulthood, when he would try unsuccessfully to restore the family's lost affluence.[13]

Meriwether Jones exerted an important influence over his young nephew. As a brash seventeen-year-old Meriwether had eloped with and married fourteen-year-old Lucy Franklin Reed. The adult Meriwether appeared to have outgrown his impetuous reputation; he trained as a lawyer, founded and edited the *Richmond Examiner,* and became a political power broker in the state's Republican party. Despite his apparent stability, however, Meriwether was quick to take offense and gained a reputation for duelling. Even so, he was a positive role model for the young Jones boys, for he was outspoken, held firm to his beliefs, lived up to his obligations, and exhibited an intense loyalty to allies, family, and friends—attributes that would mark the naval career of his nephew Thomas ap Catesby as well.[14]

Meriwether made arrangements with William and Mary law professor St. George Tucker for Thomas and Roger to attend the boarding school at the college soon after their father's death. Although tuition and accommodations in Williamsburg were not cheap, he saw this as an investment in the boys' future and an opportunity for them to associate with Virginia's patrician elite. The school had an enrollment of about sixty students, which meant that all the young men probably knew one another well. The William and Mary campus had completely succumbed to the liberal republican philosophy that was engrossing the nation. Students virtually canonized President Thomas Jefferson and addressed one another as "Citizen." During their studies in Latin, Greek, rhetoric, and mathematics, Jones and other students became acquainted with not only the works of Cicero, Virgil, Herodotus, Homer, and Shakespeare, but also the writings of Paine, Locke, Rousseau, Montesquieu, Hume, and Adam Smith. Yet Jones concluded that he was "unfit" for a career in law, medicine, politics, or natural philosophy; instead he wanted to study mathematics and navigation. Before the end of 1802 he had left William and Mary for Hickory Hill, his maternal grandfather's estate in Westmoreland County, where for the next two years he studied with the distinguished mathematician David Wardrope.[15]

Any sense of stability Jones may have felt at Hickory Hill was short-lived. His mother, Lettice, became increasingly ill during his stay. She died in mid-December 1804, and at age fourteen Jones became an orphan. He did not receive much inheritance because the family's estate was still in debt, and thus as a teenager he had to rely on others. Only months before her death, perhaps even knowing her time was near, Lettice sent Thomas back to Richmond to stay with his uncle. Meriwether again assumed responsibility for Thomas and Roger and this time enrolled them in James Ogilvie's Richmond Academy.[16]

Ogilvie had become a renowned educator since coming from Scotland to America in 1794. He originally opened a school in Albemarle County under Jefferson's patronage but found the life of a country teacher too difficult. He then moved to Richmond, where he attracted more students and enjoyed far greater success. Ogilvie unquestionably had a gift for teaching, but perhaps even more significant was his flair for oratory, which some called pompous and inflated. Years later Commodore Jones would be derisively accused of those same traits.

Ogilvie's academy emphasized history, geography, literature, and grammar through the innovative lecture, or "expostulatory and explanatory," method. Ogilvie required senior students to write original essays to be presented orally at a semiannual public exhibition. On 6 July 1804 Jones presented his first essay on "Happiness," one of Ogilvie's favorite topics, at the Virginia capitol in Richmond. Other subjects Ogilvie commonly assigned included political economy, history and moral fiction, and social topics such as gaming and duelling, which became particularly important to Jones when his uncle Meriwether died from injuries suffered in a duel. It is not surprising, therefore, that in his later years Jones took a strong stand against duelling.[17]

Studying in Richmond also offered Jones many educational opportunities outside of school. During the spring of 1805 Aaron Burr, charged with treason, appeared before Supreme Court Chief Justice John Marshall sitting on the circuit court bench. The notoriety of the case brought to Richmond the country's most distinguished lawyers and speakers, including William Wirt, Luther Martin, George Hay, and Benjamin Botts, and many of Ogilvie's students attended the daily proceedings.

While Ogilvie's academy offered the best education available in Richmond, it, too, was very expensive. Meriwether's finances were strained because he was sending his nephews Roger and Thomas ap Catesby and Thomas Monroe there as well as his own son Walter. Eventually the tuition created a financial burden the newspaper editor could not sustain, and in the spring of 1805 Meriwether informed his dependents that he could no longer afford to send them to Richmond Academy. But he did offer the young men the opportunity to continue their training with other instructors. Meriwether suggested that the younger boys could live at home and study science and education with a Mr. Wood, while the older boys (presumably Roger and Thomas ap Catesby) could pursue other occupations.[18]

Meriwether certainly recognized his familial obligation to provide for Roger's and Thomas's future, but his own financial situation forced him to rely on his extensive political connections to do so. As an influential Republican newspaper editor he had cultivated a long list of political confidants, and he had used his paper to support his allies, including law professor St. George Tucker, James Monroe, and President Thomas Jefferson. If Meriwether intentionally called in his political debts, he did so with delicacy. During mid-September 1805 the editor wrote President Jefferson congratulating him on the "advantageous peace" with the Barbary pirates; before signing the note he appealed to Jefferson to show his brother-in-law, navy lieutenant Benjamin Franklin Read, "such civilities as your leisure will permit." Slightly more than a month later he wrote the president that his nephew Thomas ap Catesby had applied to the Navy Department for a midshipman's warrant. In that letter Meriwether admitted that he did not personally know Secretary of the Navy Robert Smith and asked Jefferson to intervene on his nephew's behalf. The president may also have been approached by his close friend Virginia congressman Dr. Walter Jones, who was also Thomas ap Catesby's great-uncle.[19]

If Jefferson spoke with Secretary Smith about Thomas ap Catesby's application, it was not immediately apparent. Near the end of October Smith had written Meriwether that there were no available midshipman warrants and that the young man's application would be considered when a vacancy occurred, although this did not appear to be likely as there were few vacancies. But only three weeks later, on 22 November 1805, Thomas ap Catesby Jones received from Smith a letter appointing him a midshipman in the U.S. Navy. The secretary also enclosed a copy of the navy's rules and regulations, a mariner's dictionary, and a blank oath for Jones to complete and sign. Secretary Smith concluded by telling the prospective midshipman that his pay would begin accruing from the date he signed the warrant. Jones wasted no time signing the document; it was notarized by the Richmond city magistrate only five days after Smith had drafted the original offer.[20]

The Jones family almost certainly used its political connections to provide for young Thomas ap Catesby. The Navy Department in the early nineteenth century was deluged with applicants for midshipman's warrants. In fact, one author has estimated that the department rejected three-fourths of those who applied and still had an overabundance of candidates. The Jefferson administration claimed to distribute appointments geographically, and this meant Virginia could not be guaranteed any preference. In fact, however, Thomas ap Catesby Jones was probably placed on the department's "private list" of preferential candidates, given that Uncle Meriwether was a political confidant of Jefferson and Great-Uncle Walter was a powerful Republican congressman and friend of the president. The presence of letters from two such prominent supporters in Jones's file virtually ensured the young man a quick appointment; he received a midshipman's warrant less than a month after being recommended.[21]

The U.S. Navy had but twenty-nine vessels and few active service vacancies in 1805, and many ambitious young men were forced to spend long periods onshore at half pay while awaiting an active assignment. Jones joined this group when he signed his warrant and accepted his appointment. Nor was Jones unique in his lack of sea experience, a deficiency shared by many of the midshipmen and even some of the lieutenants appointed to the service. This shortcoming did not discourage young men from applying for positions, or dissuade the secretary from appointing them. Always supportive, Secretary Smith suggested that all the young men try to improve themselves while they awaited an active appointment. Jones heeded the secretary's advice by remaining in Richmond to study geography, navigation, and surveying with the Rev. Hugh White.[22]

By the spring of 1806 Jones, believing his studies under Reverend White had prepared him for service, wrote Secretary Smith to request a commission aboard one of the nation's seagoing vessels. Jones believed that HMS *Leander*'s assault on an American trading vessel off New York harbor would prompt hostilities between the two countries and induce the government to increase the size of its naval establishment. But Jefferson, even at this juncture, did not want war, and Secretary Smith informed Jones that there were still no vacancies. Smith did tell Jones that he could join a merchant ship sailing either to Europe or the East or West Indies "for the purpose of improving yourself in your profession." But Jones was not able to heed the secretary's "friendly advice" because his uncle Meriwether was ailing from a wound that he had suffered in a duel. During the summer Jones accompanied his uncle to "partake the waters" at Warm Springs, Virginia, where later that season Meriwether died. Even though the family's affairs were settled by September, Jones still had to wait for his opportunity to go to sea.[23]

In early September 1806 Jones again requested an active commission aboard one of the country's frigates, adding that should the department not have an opening, he would "immediately sail in the merchant service to Europe." Secretary Smith granted Jones's furlough and instructed him to dress as a civilian while undertaking any such voyages. During the following winter and spring Jones traveled to Washington, D.C., and several seaport towns actively searching for an "advantageous situation in the merchant service." Given the country's deteriorating relations with Britain and France, it was no surprise that he could not find one.[24]

Jones's furlough finally ended in the summer of 1807 because of the *Chesapeake-Leopard* affair. On 22 June 1807 the USS *Chesapeake*, under the command of Capt. James Barron, departed Hampton Roads, Virginia, for the Mediterranean. On the orders of his station commander, Capt. S. P. Humphreys of the fifty-gun frigate HMS *Leopard* demanded the right to search the American frigate for English deserters. When Barron refused to muster his men, Humphreys ordered his ship to fire into the unprepared American vessel. Afterward a British officer boarded the *Chesapeake* and seized four men accused of desertion. The undamaged *Leopard* then rejoined the British squadron at anchor in American waters while the *Chesapeake*, with twenty-two holes in its hull, limped back to Norfolk with three dead and eighteen wounded.

The Navy Department responded to the incident by mobilizing the nation's gunboats for immediate action. Capt. Stephen Decatur, ordered to replace James Barron as commander of the damaged *Chesapeake*, assumed responsibility for the Norfolk flotilla. Eleven days after the affair Secretary Smith instructed Jones, who was then in Northumberland County, to report to Norfolk for duty. Although Jones was eager for service, family business prevented him from promptly responding to the orders; not until 25 July did he report that he would proceed immediately to Norfolk.[25]

By the time Jones arrived at the Gosport Navy Yard in Norfolk during the first week of August 1807, Captain Decatur had already bolstered the station's shamefully low morale and prepared its defenses. A flurry of activity pervaded the station as all prepared for the possibility of another British attack. Reinforcements from Baltimore, Philadelphia, and Washington poured into the city. Sailors drilled with weapons; workmen repaired and outfitted the Norfolk station's gunboats; and the Virginia militia mustered to meet the emergency. All the while, the damaged *Chesapeake*— a constant visual reminder of the British outrage—sat tied to a nearby wharf. The activity at the navy yard and the images of Norfolk that summer intensified Jones's sense of pride and made a vivid impression on him.[26]

Once in Norfolk Jones found himself assigned to gunboat *No. 10,* a small craft constructed during the spring and summer of 1804 at the Washington Navy Yard. Armed with two long 32-pound cannon and modified with a false keel, a longer rudder, and a yawl rig to improve its seaworthiness, the vessel had sailed to the Mediterranean to serve against the Barbary pirates. But *No. 10* never saw combat against the pirates; the conflict had ended by the time it arrived. Subsequently, the gunboat returned to Norfolk in August 1806 and was taken out of commission; it was reactivated only after the *Chesapeake* incident.[27]

Jones's first naval experience was uncomfortable at best. The small gunboat provided virtually no personal space; yet it carried armaments and ammunition, had working and sleeping berths, and supposedly had sufficient space for food and spirits to feed a crew of thirty or so seamen and officers. It was in these restricted quarters, under the immediate command of Lt. Arthur Sinclair, that Jones received his first taste of navy life.

Jones remained on the Norfolk station until January 1808. During his nearly five months on active duty his vessel served along with three other gunboats in Captain Decatur's third division patrolling Chesapeake Bay. Although British naval forces had evacuated the bay by the end of July 1807, before Jones began his service, the gunboat squadron nonetheless spent the remainder of the year watching for other British warships. During this initial tour Jones became accustomed to serving aboard a ship, learned the importance of discipline and duty during times of emergency, and gained insight into the attitudes and ethical values naval officers were expected to possess. That service provided invaluable lessons that Jones did not forget; he later recalled with fondness his tour of duty under Capt. Stephen Decatur.[28]

By the end of the year the crisis with Britain had abated and the increased military force at Norfolk could be reduced. Jones, having received a taste of naval service, awaited new challenges. In late December 1807 Secretary Smith ordered gunboat *No. 10* to the Washington Navy Yard, where Jones remained for a little more than a month before receiving new orders. In late January 1808 Jones said good-bye to family and friends, collected his travel advance and orders, and set sail aboard the schooner *Two Brothers* for the strange new environment of New Orleans and the Gulf coast. Jones did not know it at the time, but New Orleans was a station that ambitious officers tried to avoid.[29]

⤞ 2 ⤝

THIS INACTIVE, FORLORN STATION

Gunboats and the Battle of New Orleans, 1808–1815

On 1 May 1808 the schooner *Two Brothers,* laden with guns and naval stores, completed its two-month journey to New Orleans. After the vessel anchored off the Canal Street wharf, Thomas ap Catesby Jones gathered his belongings and stepped out into the stifling, humid New Orleans air. He must have looked at his surroundings with amazement, for they were completely different from anything he had ever seen. New Orleans was an exotic mixture of Spanish, French, and American culture and architecture, and proud of each element. The inhabitants were as varied as those of any city in North America, and maybe in the world.[1]

New Orleans was one of the most arduous posts on which a U.S. Navy officer could then be ordered to serve. An isolated outpost far removed from government authority, the station provided few chances for professional advancement and only limited opportunities for an officer to distinguish himself. Rarely visited by major warships, the station's complement of craft consisted entirely of gunboats and similar shallow-draft vessels. The type of duty associated with this station was onerous and unrewarding; curtailing smuggling, privateering, piracy, and slave trading meant expanding governmental authority along this lawless frontier rather than confronting the enemy on the open seas. Furthermore, the Louisiana Gulf coast had an inhospitable climate swarming with pestilence and disease. Most officers rightly believed that these conditions offered only two alternatives: exposure to a fatal disease or, equally bad, a professional death of obscurity. But New Orleans was a duty assignment, and there were few of these in the navy. Even so, it certainly was not an appointment coveted by energetic, aggressive, career-minded officers seeking advancement.

Jones had been instructed to report to Capt. David Porter, the newly appointed commander at New Orleans. On his arrival Porter had discovered that most of the station's gunboats were in various states of disrepair. In addition, Porter was not permitted to spend money on repairs without prior approval from the secretary of the navy and he had significantly fewer than the four hundred sailors needed to maintain and man the gunboats. With shortages of both manpower and vessels, Porter faced the daunting task of enforcing the nation's ban on the slave trade and ill-defined commercial laws on a station that was close to foreign territory and surrounded by an abundance of shallow waterways.[2]

After appraising his situation, Porter divided his fifteen-gunboat squadron into four divisions (Balize, Barataria, Lake, and River) and

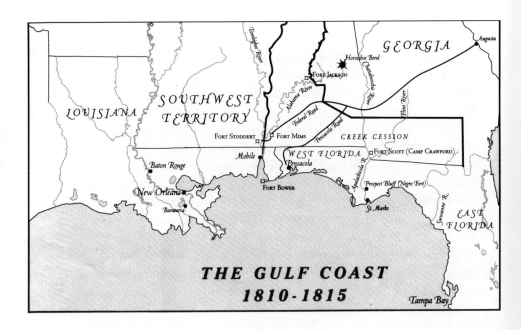

THE GULF COAST 1810-1815

positioned them along the Gulf of Mexico and Mississippi River to curtail illicit activities and establish a U.S. presence. He assigned Midshipman Jones as executive officer under Lt. John Owings aboard gunboat *No. 21* stationed north of New Orleans with the River Division near the Iberville River. Somewhat smaller than *No. 10*, on which Jones had served in Norfolk, the sloop-rigged gunboat was armed with two 24-pound cannon and was ideal for the shallow Gulf coast waters. Porter directed *No. 21* to seize "any negro, mulatto, or person of colour" who had been brought into the country contrary to the new January 1808 anti-slave-trade law. Jones and the crew were also instructed to detain merchant vessels while the registry of all "persons of colour" was determined. Porter informed Jones and his other officers that they should make every effort to intercept those involved in the widespread illicit trade.[3]

Jones soon received his first taste of the delicate nature of international border relations. In late July Lieutenant Owings landed a contingent of troops ashore at a Spanish West Florida plantation and apprehended a deserter from the naval station. A diplomatic crisis erupted when the Spanish governor of the territory, Carlos de Grand Pré, protested to William C. C. Claiborne, the governor of Orleans Territory, and demanded the man's return. In an attempt to muffle this "outrage on the territorial jurisdiction of a friendly nation," Porter immediately returned the deserter and suspended Owings, later sending him back to Washington. The consequence of Owings's rashness left a memorable imprint on Jones; it was one thing to enforce U.S. law in American territory and another to violate the sovereignty of a foreign country.[4]

Jones served aboard *No. 21* only until September, when he returned to New Orleans with several prizes the River Division had captured. The departure of Owings combined with Jones's timely return to the Crescent City provided the opportunity for an independent command. In October Lt. Michael Carroll, commanding the station in Porter's absence, offered Jones an acting lieutenant's commission and assigned him temporary command of gunboat *No. 17* in the River Division with instructions to cruise between Fort Adams and the Iberville River while enforcing the embargo and slave-trade laws. The eighteen-year-old Jones quickly learned that the proximity of Spanish West Florida and Spanish-held lands west of New Orleans provided many avenues for those trying to subvert U.S. law.[5]

Jones did not seize any vessels violating U.S. laws, nor did he infringe on the national sovereignty of Spain; nevertheless, he became embroiled in a controversial affair that brought him before his first naval court of inquiry. On 12 October 1808 Jones's gunboat was slowly moving north up the Mississippi. While his vessel struggled against the current, Jones walked along the riverbank carrying a fowling rifle. A pirogue approached the gunboat and was hailed by the marine guard, but the vessel's owner refused to stop and present his papers. The marine fired a warning shot over the boat, but the owner still refused to halt. Jones, watching the entire episode from shore, hailed the boat's owner before he himself fired into the air. Apparently this rapid succession of shots frightened the slaves who were navigating the pirogue, and they jumped overboard and swam to shore. Several of Jones's sailors in one of *No. 17*'s small boats then boarded the pirogue. Jones detained the owner until he could be identified as a Mr. Picou, a prominent resident of the area. Picou subsequently filed a written complaint against Jones, who was forced temporarily to relinquish command of his craft to go to New Orleans and face a court of inquiry, which exonerated him. The court ultimately found that the young commander had acted with a firm but courteous attitude and had properly executed his orders. In his first independent command decision Jones had strictly followed his orders and had helped to establish an American presence where one had not previously existed.[6]

While Jones awaited another active assignment, Captain Porter asked him to serve as the station's flag lieutenant charged with overseeing daily operations. During this assignment he gained a close attachment and fondness for his commander, and later in life he would boast that he had served under Porter's command. In late March 1809 Porter appointed Jones commander of gunboat *No. 25*, and for the next two and a half months he cruised the Gulf coast between the Sabine River—the border between Louisiana and Spanish Texas—and Ship Island, off Biloxi, Mississippi, attempting to apprehend smugglers, privateers, and slavers. Those months were particularly troublesome for Porter, Jones, and the squadron as they faced increased smuggling from Spanish Baton Rouge. Fortunately, on 25 March 1809 Congress repealed the embargo and replaced it with the Non-Intercourse Act, opening trade with all nations except Britain and France, and thereby legalizing trade with Spanish West Florida.[7]

Jones had been aboard *No. 25* only a short time before the gunboat had to be docked for extensive repairs; during the early fall the vessel was scraped, caulked, painted, and refitted for service. When Jones resumed command, he and Lt. B. F. Read, a distant relative by marriage who commanded the bomb ketch *Vesuvius*, returned to the Gulf coast, cruising from the Southwest Pass to the Sabine River to curtail illegal commerce. In mid-December Jones had to anchor in the swamps around the Tchifoncti River when his crew succumbed to yellow fever. Over the next few weeks Jones acted as cook, nurse, and physician (after the doctor's death) for fifty-six officers and men. For several days Jones was the only one fit for duty, and he even performed the last rites over the graves of thirteen men he buried in the Tchifoncti swamp. It was not until late January 1810 that the crewmen of *No. 25* were fit enough for the gunboat to return to New Orleans.[8]

Later in his life, Capt. Thomas ap Catesby Jones admitted that he did not capture many vessels while sailing along the lawless Gulf coast, but he claimed his presence near Grand Terre did much to discourage illegal activities and expand the authority of the federal government. In fact, Jones asserted that he served so diligently that the famed privateer/pirate Jean Lafitte offered him a ten-thousand-dollar-a-year bribe if he would retire with his gunboat to another area of the coast. Jones may have exaggerated, but the story may not have been entirely false. By 1810 the Lafitte brothers commanded a squadron of vessels and operated a large warehouse at the Temple, just south of New Orleans, and another at Donaldsonville, twenty-five miles south of Baton Rouge, that became their distribution centers for both legal and illegal goods. Moreover, the brothers had no qualms about bribing public officials in the attempt to maintain their operation.[9]

In the fall of 1810 Jones's *No. 25* cruised the Mississippi River north of Baton Rouge. He spent some time in the rough-and-tumble Natchez riverfront district before being sent, as a result of what became known as "the West Florida revolution," to the vicinity of Fort Adams near Baton Rouge. The revolution began on Sunday morning, 23 September 1810, when eighty armed Americans led by Philemon Thomas stormed and seized the dilapidated Spanish fort at Baton Rouge. The invaders streamed through the undefended gate and gaps in the stockade, ran past the unloaded cannon, and captured Don Louis Antonio de Grand-Pré, commander of the fort, and Governor Carlos de Lassus. Afterward the Americans called a convention of delegates representing the region and issued a Declaration of Independence for West Florida. The convention then requested annexation to the United States and protection against Spanish retribution.[10]

The convention's request for aid prompted the New Orleans station's temporary commander, P. C. Wederstrandt, to station Jones and the other gunboats at Fort Adams on the Mississippi. Secretary of the Navy Paul Hamilton had ordered *Nos. 156, 162,* and *163* to come up from St. Mary's, Georgia, to augment the New Orleans force, but these gunboats did not arrive in time to be of assistance. Nonetheless, in early December Jones sailed *No. 25* downriver to the vicinity of the fort at Baton Rouge and anchored with loaded cannon while Governor Claiborne and soldiers marched unopposed into the former Spanish position; and Baton Rouge was formally incorporated into the United States. Wederstrandt then sent Jones to Lake Pontchartrain and the Rigolets, along with four other gunboats, to prevent a Spanish counterattack.[11]

Tensions between Spanish forces and Americans in the region heightened considerably in the following months. In late December 1810 Jones accompanied a troop transport under the command of Lt. Daniel Dexter to Fort Stoddert on the Mobile River. Apparently the West Florida revolutionaries involved with the seizure of Baton Rouge had threatened to conquer Mobile as well, and Fort Stoddert needed additional troops to prevent an unwanted revolt. Unfortunately, Spanish forces controlled the mouth of the Mobile River, thereby making the American fort virtually inaccessible.

In early January 1811, gunboat *No. 25,* along with other vessels laden with troops and supplies, anchored near the Spanish fort at Mobile. Almost a month passed before Francisco Collell, commander of the Spanish bastion, allowed the troops to land and march overland to Fort Stoddert. Before the affair had been settled an unsubstantiated rumor circulated that four frigates had landed troops in Pensacola to regain the lands that Spain had lost. Fortunately for American forces at Fort Stoddert, the rumor proved false and the two nations avoided war.[12]

Later that summer, in June 1811, *No. 25* joined a thirteen-vessel expedition (eleven gunboats, the brig *Viper,* and a storeship) commanded by Lt. Joseph Bainbridge to ensure safe passage of military supplies to Fort Stoddert. Relations between the United States and Spain along the Gulf coast had further worsened in early June as Collell once again refused to allow the passage of supplies north to Fort Stoddert. Capt. John Shaw, then commanding the New Orleans station, responded by sending Bainbridge's squadron to deliver the supplies forcibly if necessary.[13]

Jones arrived in Mobile Bay on 2 July 1811, and for a short time it appeared that Collell would not allow the American vessels to proceed upriver. As Bainbridge moved his force into position, he learned that his flagship, the *Viper*, had too deep a draft to cross the sandbar that commanded the harbor. Bainbridge then transferred his pennant from his flagship to Jones's *No. 25* and informed Collell that he intended to execute his orders and supply Fort Stoddert. Three days later Bainbridge ordered six of his gunboats to anchor about five hundred yards off the Spanish fort with their guns ready for action. Meanwhile he and Jones proceeded up the river in *No. 25*, followed by the *Alligator (No. 166)* towing a storeship. In the end, Collell did not order the Spanish guns to fire on the American boats. During the expedition Jones learned how to use patience and force to achieve his ends in the face of a foreign power.[14]

Jones experienced some success stopping illegal activity to the east of the Mississippi River. While cruising between Lake Barataria and the Perdido River he captured a small boat manned by Frenchmen armed with a 4-pound cannon, cutlasses, and muskets. After securing the vessel, Jones transported his thirty-eight prisoners to New Orleans, only to see them released. Jones was even more frustrated when he learned that the men belonged to a group who had earlier violated U.S. neutrality laws by signing aboard a French privateer. The Louisiana legal system hindered Jones and his colleagues rather than providing them with the power they needed to assert federal control.[15]

Jones soon received command of gunboat *No. 156*. Although it was most unusual for a midshipman to have had three commands, Jones still felt that he was being overlooked by the Navy Department. Both Porter and Shaw had entrusted him with command of a gunboat, yet after more than four years in the service, three of them on the lawless Gulf coast, he remained a mere midshipman. Jones believed he had failed to advance in grade because he had been stationed at New Orleans and because his service had been exclusively confined to gunboats. As he prepared to join the Barataria Division, Jones appealed to Navy Secretary Paul Hamilton for a lieutenant's commission or for reassignment to another station.[16]

It may have seemed to Jones that his service on the New Orleans station was hindering his career, but early in 1812 an encounter occurred that helped pave the way for promotion. As his gunboat, *No. 156*, approached Grand Terre Island, Jones spotted a schooner at anchor. When he ordered the U.S. colors hoisted, the privateer fled. Jones fired after it and then gave chase. Since the gunboat could not overtake the faster schooner, Jones fired several shots that damaged its rigging and hull. The shots crippled the privateer, allowing Jones's gunboat to close on it. But as Jones prepared to overtake the schooner, its seamen manned pumps and threw overboard some of its guns to lighten the load, and the privateer escaped. On his return to Lake Barataria, Jones did capture a boat's crew and two officers from the *Marengo,* a French privateer outfitted the previous November in New York, but he was still smarting from the loss of the schooner.[17]

Shaw understood the problem Jones had experienced in attempting to catch the privateer. He reported to the Navy Department that the gunboats at New Orleans were "dull Sailors" and implied that the station's lack of success and inability to assert federal authority rested solely on the shortage of fast ships and had nothing to do with his officers. In fact, Shaw praised Jones, insisting that the midshipman was both an honorable and diligent young man who would be a benefit to any station and an officer who deserved promotion to lieutenant. Apparently Secretary Hamilton agreed, because he submitted a nomination for Jones's promotion which the Senate confirmed in early June 1812.[18]

During the spring of 1812 the small New Orleans station became increasingly busy because of the shortage of seamen and vessels. Jones's *No. 156* encountered two of Jean Lafitte's privateers off Bayou Lafouche with a Spanish armed prize but was unable to capture them. Later that spring rumors circulated throughout the region that the United States would soon be at war with Great Britain and Spain, and in fact, Shaw learned on 9 July 1812 that his country had declared war, but only on the British. Even so, he realized that the Gulf coast was greatly exposed, and he had only two brigs and eleven gunboats to protect it. Shaw complained to his superiors that this squadron was "by no means adequate to the defence of the extensive coast" in peacetime, much less in war. He needed more gunboats, copper-bottomed schooners, and men. Until such forces arrived, he would place New Orleans in the best state of defense he could manage. Shaw sent three gunboats to Mobile Bay, two to the Rigolets (the passage from New Orleans to the east by way of Lake Borgne), and five to the Balize—including Jones and *No. 156*—to patrol westward to Barataria. These forces covered the most obvious water approaches to New Orleans, but they could not provide any real protection for the city.[19]

Jones's first wartime test came in mid-August 1812. Shaw had ordered him to cruise west of the Mississippi Delta toward Veracruz and to inform Lt. Michael Carroll, commanding the U.S. brig *Syren,* of the declaration of war. After a month of searching, Jones discovered the sixteen-gun *Syren* being chased close to shore by the thirty two-gun English ship *Brazen*. Exposing his gunboat to the British, Jones diverted their attention long enough for the *Syren* to slip out to sea. For the next twenty hours the *Syren* and *No. 156* eluded the *Brazen* until they reached an American anchorage between Cat and Ship Islands.[20]

Shortly after this encounter, a series of storms, including a hurricane that blew in on 19 August, compounded the New Orleans station's troubles. The "dreadful" tempest, which "both in violence and duration exceeded any thing of the kind within the recollection of the Oldest inhabitants," grounded one of Shaw's brigs, damaged the other slightly, and drove four gunboats ashore. Jones and *No. 156* were off Cat Island when the storm struck, and according to some reports Jones's vessel was destroyed. His gunboat did sustain minor damage, but it was not "dashed to pieces" as some communications indicated. Nonetheless, it took Shaw months to overcome this setback, and in reality the New Orleans station never completely recovered from the losses.[21]

At the beginning of the war, U.S. naval officers stationed at New Orleans believed that service there would finally offer opportunities for transfers and promotions. Ships would be sent to sea to prevent the British from blockading the Atlantic coastline and harassing American trade. This was just the opportunity aspiring and energetic naval officers sought. Unaware that the Senate had already confirmed his promotion, Jones wrote again to the Navy Department expressing his "impatience for promotion" and claiming that his present duty assignment deprived him of opportunities for experience and advancement. Although Jones did not receive a transfer, by late January 1813 he had learned of his promotion to lieutenant; with it came new responsibilities for the twenty-two-year-old officer.[22]

Between the fall of 1812 and the summer of 1813, Jones's gunboat cruised between Pass Christian and Mobile Bay looking for British adversaries and violators of the law. Now his task entailed more than asserting U.S. authority along the Gulf; he also had to protect American sovereignty from British aggression—even if the inhabitants did not want such protection.

In the late spring of 1813 Jones joined Gen. James Wilkinson's expedition against Mobile; the general had orders to occupy all of Spanish West Florida between the Pearl and Perdido Rivers. Jones's *No. 156,* joined by four other gunboats on 11 April 1813, anchored two hundred yards off Spanish Fort Charlotte with guns primed. Jones watched as Wilkinson's four hundred men landed three miles below the fort and prepared for a landward assault. Although Jones waited anxiously for the order to fire, he did not get the chance; Spanish commander Cayetano Pérez, whose garrison numbered only eighty men, chose to give up. After the surrender Jones and the other gunboat commanders had the disagreeable duty of transporting Pérez and his men to Pensacola. Spain was not officially at war with the United States, but Jones nonetheless realized that "might makes right" when protecting American sovereignty and security; the Spaniards had to be removed to prevent the British from using the city as a base of operations against New Orleans.[23]

While cruising off Mobile Bay during the latter part of April, Jones learned of increased British activity in the Gulf. Apparently the twelve-gun British schooner *Shelburne* had anchored off Pensacola and was harassing American merchant ships. Jones quickly sailed for Pensacola, where he learned, after forcing his way past Fort Barrancas and into the Spanish harbor, that the British warship had already departed. Spanish authorities protested his aggression, but Jones insisted that he was only trying to ensure that Spain maintained its neutral obligations. While the American gunboat was still inside the harbor the eighteen-gun British brig *Anaconda* arrived offshore, and its commander sent a dispatch ashore boldly proclaiming that Jones's gunboat would never escape. Later that afternoon an influential merchant showed this message to Jones as he dined. After reading the note Jones declared that the British had given him the opportunity to "be a dead man before sunset or a post captain in thirty days." Every balcony and rooftop in town was soon crowded with spectators as Jones made his way out of port with the afternoon tide. But rather than readying for a fight, as its captain had insinuated, the *Anaconda* instead made for the open sea. Several days later Jones returned to Pensacola, and this time he was welcomed rather than admonished by Spanish authorities.[24]

In early June, Jones's gunboat, accompanied by *Nos. 65* and *163*, sailed west from Mobile to Balize, where they found the thirty-four-gun *Herald*. Although it was the only sizable British vessel operating along the Gulf coast, the *Herald* had caused considerable commotion by blockading Lt. Joseph Bainbridge's *Syren* and preventing it from going to sea. After a spirited ten-minute engagement the three gunboats drove the *Herald* from its position, giving their sister ship an opportunity to escape.

The captain of the British vessel declined to stay and fight the smaller gunboats even though the Americans had inferior firepower. After the *Herald*'s withdrawal the *Syren* resumed duty in the Gulf of Mexico, and Jones returned to Mobile Bay.[25]

Jones's service along the Gulf had provided far greater opportunities to learn his trade than Atlantic coast service had given most of his peers. Yet duty at New Orleans did not provide a chance to serve aboard cruising vessels, or the occasions for frigate engagements that brought the honor and wartime experience that opened avenues for promotion and advancement. Jones appealed to Navy Secretary William Jones during the spring of 1813 for reassignment, but no transfer was forthcoming.[26]

Jones learned firsthand one of the perils associated with command in November 1813 when Philip Philibert, a disgruntled midshipman whom Jones had recently disciplined, charged that Jones had committed sodomy with the cook aboard *No. 156*. The investigating officer, Lt. Louis Alexis, ordered Philibert to present witnesses, but each denied any knowledge of the event when questioned. Philibert was promptly placed under arrest. Master Commandant Daniel Patterson, who had replaced John Shaw as commander of the station in late 1813, did release him to participate in the Battle of New Orleans in January 1815, and he gained recognition from General Jackson and Patterson for his service. Unfortunately, Jones would hear more from Midshipman Philibert before his time in New Orleans was finished.

Master Commandant Patterson had inherited a precarious situation along the Gulf, with only five operable gunboats to protect an area that extended from the Sabine River in the west to the Perdido River near Mobile Bay in the east. The intensity of the war with Britain had increased, further compounding his problems. During the spring of 1814 Gen. Andrew Jackson marched into the heart of Creek Indian territory to confront Britain's Native American allies. As Jackson defeated the Creeks at the Battle of Horseshoe Bend, British attacks and privateering activities along the Gulf coast escalated, straining Patterson's already weak resources but providing great excitement and opportunity for Jones and other officers of the New Orleans station.

While the continued lawlessness and flaunting of U.S. commercial regulations had convinced Patterson by August 1814 that he should move against the Baratarians, British activities along the Gulf prevented an immediate attack. Moreover, in early August General Jackson, learning that the British planned to attack Mobile, diverted additional forces to reconstruct that city's fort. British naval forces subsequently arrived on 12 September 1814 and three days later unsuccessfully attacked Fort Bowyer. As events moved toward a crescendo at Mobile, the British sloop *Sophia* delivered an alliance proposal to Jean Lafitte and the Baratarians. For two days in early September Capt. Nicholas Lockyer and Jean Lafitte discussed the prospects of an alliance before the Baratarian leader rejected the British offer. Ironically, Lafitte chose to join the American cause just as Patterson and Col. George T. Ross finalized plans for an attack against the privateer's stronghold at Grand Terre.[27]

Jones's gunboat served as the flagship of Patterson's flotilla, which had grown to include the fourteen-gun schooner *Carolina;* the dispatch boat *Sea Horse;* gunboats Nos. *5, 23, 65, 162,* and *163;* and an armed launch and three armed barges carrying seventy men of the Forty-fourth Infantry Regiment. Shortly after 8:00 A.M. on 16 September Jones arrived at the Baratarian stronghold at Grand Terre and found that the privateers had anchored within the harbor several armed vessels flying the colors of Cartagena—the revolutionary republic of South America.

Jones and the other officers formed their gunboats into a battle line near the harbor's entrance with cannons ready. Patterson ordered Jones to raise a white flag in the hope of talking with the privateers, but the Baratarians did not intend to talk. Neither, however, did they intend to fight. They instead set fire to two of their schooners and began retreating into the surrounding swamps. Patterson ordered Jones to hoist a large white flag emblazoned with the expression "Pardon to Deserters." The commander had heard that a number of army and navy deserters who had joined the privateers would return to service if they were offered pardons.

As they advanced, Jones's *No. 156* and gunboat *No. 23* ran aground on a sandbar, and Jones ordered his men to continue toward the enemy in the small ship's boat. But as Jones's boat was rowed within range he found that the Baratarians had deserted their vessels and that fire was about to consume several of them. Disregarding his own safety, Jones boarded the burning schooner *The Lady of the Gulf* as flames consumed the fore shrouds, foresail, and planks around the foremast. He found that a quantity of gunpowder had been left in an open cabin, apparently to hasten the schooner's destruction. In an act of unquestioned bravery, Jones removed the gunpowder and smothered the blaze only moments before the schooner would have exploded.

Meanwhile other army and naval forces ransacked the Baratarian stronghold, seizing six small and two large schooners, a felucca, and a brig, in addition to about $500,000 worth of contraband merchandise, including jewelry. The federal force also burned forty houses onshore, apprehended eighty prisoners, and captured twenty cannon and a quantity of powder and shot. No American serviceman suffered injury during the bloodless conquest.[28]

Jones received praise from both Commodore Patterson and Colonel Ross for his role in the operation. In fact, Patterson even suggested that the navy purchase the schooner Jones had saved and that the lieutenant be named its commander. Although the navy did use *The Lady of the Gulf* (renamed *Firebrand* in honor of the episode) for the remainder of the war, Jones never personally commanded it. Patterson did reward "that enterprising officer" by initially leaving Jones at Grand Terre in charge of a small squadron of three gunboats and the rechristened *Firebrand*.[29]

Shortly after the attack Patterson decided to send Jones's enlarged squadron—now bolstered by the *Sea Horse* and prize schooner *Peter* from New Orleans—to clear the lower Mississippi River. By mid-October Jones's six-ship force had captured several vessels, including a felucca and an abandoned schooner, and had apprehended two army deserters onshore. Jones's success as a squadron commander on the river won Patterson's confidence.[30]

In early October 1814 Secretary of State James Monroe had passed along information that a British fleet with twelve to fifteen thousand men had departed Ireland for an unknown destination along the Gulf coast. Andrew Jackson substantiated Monroe's account when he reported that the British had outfitted barges at Pensacola for an operation against Mobile; their September 1814 attack on Fort Bowyer had verified Jackson's views concerning the British objective. But even after the failed British attack Jackson still concentrated his resources on Mobile, assuming that enemy troops would land and secure that city, unite with rebellious Creek and Seminole Indians, endeavor to incite a slave insurrection, and then march against New Orleans.[31]

Jackson had requested that navy gunboats be stationed at Mobile off Fort Bowyer, but Daniel Patterson had steadfastly refused, maintaining that New Orleans was the primary British objective along the Gulf. To that end Patterson planned to use his gunboats to discourage a British invasion through Lake Borgne, the saltwater estuary east of New Orleans that he believed offered the most feasible route for a British attack. But Patterson realized that he did not have enough vessels to command the lake and would have to use those he had in conjunction with Fort Petites Coquilles at the Rigolets, which connected Lake Borgne to Lake Pontchartrain. The gunboats and fort together would allow the Americans to maintain control over that critical water approach.[32]

Patterson sent Jones to Lake Borgne in early December with gunboats *Nos. 5, 23, 156, 162,* and *163;* the schooner *Sea Horse,* and the tender *Alligator.* Jones's seven-vessel flotilla numbered in all just twenty-six guns and 204 men. Patterson also provided Jones with simple instructions: wait for the enemy outside the Rigolets between Ship and Cat Islands; confront British barges and small boats unless assaulted by a superior force; and, if attacked, withdraw to the Rigolets and the protection of the land batteries at Fort Petites Coquilles. The Rigolets were to be Jones's last line of defense, the point where he should "sink the enemy, or be sunk." In accordance with his orders, Jones sent gunboats *Nos. 23* and *163* to Dauphine Island while the others remained off St. Mary's Island anticipating the impending arrival of the British fleet.[33]

On 8 December, gunboats *Nos. 23* and *163* spied the British frigates *Armide* and *Seahorse* and the brig-sloop *Sophia* sailing westward along the chain of islands between Mobile and Lake Borgne. The gunboats followed until the British ships anchored at dusk, then proceeded to St. Mary's Island to inform Jones of their discovery. Over the next four days Jones observed "from 20 to 30 sails," including four British ships of the line, several brigs, schooners, sloops, and barges, concentrating in the channel between Cat Island and Ship Island. To Jones, this indicated that Lake Borgne was to be their approach and that it was "no longer safe or prudent" to remain in his position.[34]

The British had thoroughly studied the possible invasion routes and, as Patterson predicted, had concluded that Lake Borgne was the best route of attack because it offered three approaches to New Orleans. The first was through Lake Borgne's Rigolets Pass into Lake Pontchartrain. Although this route would have permitted the English to move by water to within two miles of the Crescent City, it could be used only by light, shallow-draft vessels, which the British had problems securing. Fort Petites Coquilles also guarded this passageway. The second alternative was through Lake Borgne to the Plain of Gentilly, across which troops could march along the Chef Menteur Road into the city. This avenue was also well defended by both men and artillery, and a pitched battle there would have allowed the Americans to fall back and construct other lines of defense well away from the city.[35]

The third and most viable approach called for using Bayou Bienvenu, which drained the area east of New Orleans and stretched from Lake Borgne to within a mile of the Mississippi River. From there British forces could proceed north nine miles along the river levee, a narrow strip of land through the region's sugar plantations, toward New Orleans. Although this approach appeared to be the path of least resistance, it too was fraught with obstacles. The route was shallower than the British had expected, thus prohibiting their ships from entering the estuary or providing gunfire support to cover their barges' advance. Furthermore, the distance from Cat Island at the mouth of Lake Borgne to Bayou Bienvenu was sixty-two miles—thirty-six hours of hard rowing. But the most serious obstacle, according to those who witnessed the events at Lake Borgne, was Jones's "insolent little flotilla" of "five American gunboats, of great strength" that commanded the shoal waters. Those craft had to be destroyed or they would create havoc for the British invasion force.[36]

On the morning of 13 December 1814 British Vice Adm. Alexander F. I. Cochrane ordered his barges to advance against the American gunboats. Jones responded by sending Sailing Master William Johnson and the *Sea Horse* to destroy channel markers and supplies at Bay St. Louis. By 2:00 P.M. the British barges had secured the Pass Christian as they slowly continued westward toward Jones's becalmed gunboats. A strong westerly wind blowing for several days before the assault had reduced the lake's depth, leaving Jones's *No. 156* and the other gunboats grounded; he could therefore only watch as the British inched closer. Finally, Jones ordered his men to throw overboard "all articles of weight that could be dispensed with," and at 3:30 P.M. the tide "commenced," permitting the gunboats to withdraw toward the Rigolets.[37]

As Jones retreated westward, he saw that the British had sent three barges against the *Sea Horse* as it destroyed the supplies at Bay St. Louis. William Johnson's schooner, armed with its one 6-pounder and supported by two 6-pounders mounted onshore, fought off the initial British assault, but four other British barges soon joined the attack. Johnson held off the seven barges for more than thirty minutes before realizing that his situation was hopeless. With no other options, Johnson burned the storehouse and supplies onshore, ignited the *Sea Horse* to prevent its capture, and retreated overland; he climbed a tree and watched from shore the ensuing engagement between the remainder of Jones's flotilla and the British barges.[38]

Jones retreated westward until about one o'clock on the morning of 14 December 1814, when the winds died, the tide changed, and the gunboats ran aground near the Malheureux Island passage. At dawn's light Jones saw that the British were steadily advancing; he estimated their distance as nine miles away, rowing hard and closing fast. A lack of wind combined with a strong eastward ebb tide forced Jones to anchor his craft. He placed them in a defensive position to "give the enemy as warm a reception as possible." Although Jones wanted to concentrate his craft, a strong current drove his flagship and *No. 163* about one hundred yards east of the other three gunboats, leaving them exposed in the center of the American line.[39]

At 9:30 A.M. British barges overwhelmed the *Alligator,* which had been forced to anchor some distance to the southeast of Jones's squadron. Thirty minutes later Capt. Nicholas Lockyer, who commanded the British assault, anchored his flotilla just beyond the range of Jones's guns and gave his men a much-needed rest and the opportunity for breakfast. After half an hour Lockyer resumed his advance toward Jones, who was unable to restore his defensive line because of the tide. Jones's *No. 156* became the first gunboat to face the British attack.

As the enemy approached, Jones counted three light gigs and forty-two barges armed with light carronades and estimated that the craft carried upward of 1,000 men and officers. In reality the British force numbered more than 1,200 men, whereas Jones had but 183 men, and only 36 in his gunboat. At 10:39 A.M. the British barges came within cannon range of the gunboats and Jones ordered his ships to fire. For more than ten minutes Jones's flotilla discharged their long guns with little effect on the approaching enemy. At 10:50 the smaller British guns, now within range, began firing, and Jones noted that the "action became general and destructive on both sides."[40]

Jones had instructed his sailors to mount their boarding nets, and shortly before noon the soldiers on three of the British barges tried to board. Jones's sailors fired their cannon and small arms at the British, killing or wounding nearly every enemy officer and sinking two enemy barges. The "unfortunate enemy" barely escaped drowning by clinging to the capsized barges until other vessels came to their aid. Soon four more British barges came forward, and after a spirited fight they, too, were driven back. During this second assault Jones used his pistol to shoot a soldier trying to board his gunboat and then also mortally wounded Lt. George Pratt, the officer who reportedly defaced the naval monument at the Capitol during the British occupation of Washington, D.C., in August 1814. But as Pratt fell backward into his barge, a soldier behind him fired his musket. The musket ball penetrated Jones's left shoulder, and as he fell to the deck several others passed through his clothes and cap. Jones continued to scream orders as he lay on the deck of his gunboat covered with blood. A few minutes later he fainted and Master's Mate George Parker assumed command until he, too, was wounded. Once the smoke of the battle had cleared some minutes later and the British were in control, the victors counted eighteen killed or wounded Americans aboard *No. 156*, including Jones and Parker.[41]

After capturing Jones's vessel, the British turned the gunboat's cannon on the other American gunboats, and, one by one, they too succumbed to the numerically superior force. The British victory over *No. 156* had been the turning point of the battle. The British secured Lake Borgne, yet not without great loss to their own forces. When Jones wrote his report some months later, he claimed that British losses had been staggering, whereas the British reported losses of only seventeen killed and seventy-seven wounded. American casualties for the entire squadron amounted to only six killed, thirty-five wounded, and the remainder captured. The Battle of Lake Borgne was a costly defeat for the United States because it allowed the British to choose their point of attack against Jackson at New Orleans.[42]

Jones cannot be faulted for his actions at Lake Borgne. He followed Patterson's orders explicitly. He had harassed the British, withdrawn against a superior force, and, once his vessels were becalmed, had tried to give the British a "warm reception." Jones's sacrifice provided valuable time for Jackson and also demonstrated his unquestioned bravery; the engagement proved the gunboats' true value in waters that larger ships could not navigate. Jones always believed thereafter that the battle was the crowning point in his long career, and Commodore Patterson later boasted that Jones's "action will be classed among the most brilliant of our Navy."[43]

Once the battle was over, the British sailors and soldiers plundered everything belonging to Jones and his fellow Americans; someone even took the bed on which he laid wounded and the blanket that covered him. Jones and his companions were transported by barge back to the British squadron anchored near Ship Island. The trip took twenty-eight hours, and the wounded Americans were exposed to the elements and without food the whole way. After reaching the anchorage, the British placed Jones and the other wounded prisoners aboard the storeship *Gorgon,* which had been converted to a hospital vessel, and distributed the healthy prisoners among the fleet.[44]

Only after boarding HMS *Gorgon* did Jones receive medical attention as well as the normal courtesies extended to a commanding officer. During his confinement and interrogation Jones fed his British captors misleading information about the location and strength of Jackson's force. Several days later, Dr. Robert Morrell and Purser Thomas Shields of the U.S. Navy arrived under a flag of truce to care for and to seek the release of the wounded. Believing the two had been sent to obtain information, Admiral Cochrane questioned them, and during the interrogation noticed that Shields was virtually deaf. So before Morrell and Shields met with the wounded prisoners, Cochrane had the two locked in a cabin where their conversations could be overheard. The two loudly discussed American plans, and their descriptions confirmed what Jones had previously revealed. These separate incidents convinced Cochrane that the British army needed additional troops before it could proceed against New Orleans. The time required to transport those troops into position ultimately provided Jackson with the chance he needed to complete the city's defenses. Shields and Morrell, as well as Jones and the others captured at Lake Borgne, remained prisoners aboard British ships during the subsequent Battle of New Orleans. The British released Shields and Morrell on 12 January 1815, four days after their devastating land defeat, but Jones remained in custody much longer.[45]

In late January 1815 the British began evacuating Lake Borgne, transporting their healthy prisoners to Havana via HMS *Ramillies.* Five of those prisoners, including Jones, proceeded on to Bermuda to appear before a British Vice Admiralty court investigating the engagement on Lake Borgne. Jones apparently remained at Bermuda until March; he finally returned to New Orleans in mid-April.[46]

The wound Jones suffered in his left shoulder completely incapacitated him for several months. The British musket ball remained in Jones's shoulder for the rest of his life, leaving him unable to lift his left arm above his shoulder. The constant and painful reminder of that wound ultimately produced a bitter hatred of the British that Jones carried with him to his grave. After returning to New Orleans he recuperated at Antoine and Charlotte LaBarre Bienvenu's plantation home under the care of Mrs. Daniel Patterson. His stay at the two-story brick house south of the city must have been very therapeutic because some years later Jones named a portion of his own plantation "Bienvenue." He also named his oldest son Meriwether Patterson, after his favorite uncle and his commanding officer on the New Orleans station.[47]

Even before he had fully recovered, Jones had to appear again in court to explain his actions in several nonrelated incidents. In late April, Alexandre St. Helme sued Jones for the return of gold doubloons, banknotes, and other possessions taken by the lieutenant during the September 1814 raid on Barataria. The court ruled that Jones had to return the items, and he delivered the pocketbook containing them to Daniel Patterson, who was also on trial in the district court on another charge.[48] Less than a month later Jones again had to face the slanderous charges of Midshipman Philibert as well as a court of inquiry concerning the loss of his gunboats during the Battle of Lake Borgne.

In mid-April 1815 Philibert renewed his charge of homosexuality, this time with sworn depositions from four enlisted men: James Rowlée, Charles Fordham, James Nowlan, and Henry Jackson. Rowlée offered a detailed testimonial, including descriptions of his own experiences with Jones. According to his testimony, Jones had pursued Rowlée above and below decks trying to unbutton his pants. When unsuccessful, Jones supposedly threatened the enlisted man with lashes unless he masturbated him. Although Rowlée indicated that he did not want to participate, he "was obliged to comply and became an unwilling instrument of gratifying [Jones's] unnatural propensities." James Nowlan further charged that Jones had forced him at gunpoint to commit fellatio while at Ship Island in September 1814, and other times without the threat of violence.

Patterson forwarded the evidence and testimony to Secretary of the Navy Benjamin Crowninshield, who concluded that the charges were malicious and without foundation and that Acting Midshipman Philibert should be dismissed from the navy. Philibert had already left New Orleans and never returned to the service. Apparently, the Navy Department had chosen not to tarnish the reputation of a badly wounded warrior who had been instrumental in helping Andrew Jackson secure the great American victory at New Orleans.[49]

Although Jones was found innocent, Philibert's accusation raises an interesting question about the naval officer corps in the early nineteenth century. To what degree was homosexual activity present in the navy? One historian who explored this topic extensively discovered only one U.S. naval officer dismissed from the service for sodomy. Moreover, the Jones case was the only explicit reference to homosexual activity by an officer. Were such episodes the exception or the rule? Another historian argued that homosexual activity was widely prevalent among naval officers, but the practice was kept quiet by a strict code of silence. The troublesome Philibert, whom Jones had disciplined, had a strong revenge motive. If he could successfully bring such a heinous charge, the proceedings would stain Jones's reputation; and if he were found guilty Jones would be dismissed from the service. The desire for revenge may explain Philibert's accusations. Whether or not there was any truth in them is impossible to determine.

The court of inquiry, headed by Lt. Louis Alexis, found after a five-day (May 15–19) proceeding that Jones and his men had "performed their duties on this occasion in the most able and gallant manner and that the action has added another and distinguished honor to the naval character of the country." Patterson approved the board's decision and concluded "that the national and naval character has been nobly sustained."[50]

In the summer of 1815 the Navy Department ordered Jones back to Washington, D.C. After arriving in Baltimore in mid-July he was granted a three-month leave of absence to regain his health. This represented Jones's first leave in eight years as well as his first opportunity to escape the hostile climate of the Gulf coast. When he had arrived in New Orleans in 1808, he and other officers saw only the disadvantages of the appointment. But his service on that "inactive, forlorn station" provided Jones the chance of a lifetime. Never again would he encounter the constant excitement, the variety and number of enemies, or the freedom of command that he experienced along that isolated frontier. He had helped show the American flag along a lawless frontier, and in doing so had asserted federal authority for an expanding nation. And although Jones had not commanded a seagoing vessel, he profited greatly from his experience in the Gulf and won for himself a name among the naval community as a brave, energetic, and ambitious young officer. In fact, it has been hinted that Jones would have gained a place among the pantheon of American naval heroes had he died at the Battle of Lake Borgne defending the American flag against overwhelming odds. He went on, however, to live a long life of adventure and controversy, and ultimately disgrace.[51]

~3~

AWAITING AN
ARDUOUS DUTY

Career, Home, and Family, 1815–1825

*T*wenty-five-year-old Lieutenant Jones returned to Washington in the fall of 1815 hoping for a new assignment. Because he had not yet fully recovered from the wound he had suffered at the Battle of Lake Borgne, Jones received a leave of absence until the end of the year. Those three months allowed him to become reacquainted with his family. His sister Elizabeth Lee (Betty) Jones lived on the maternal family lands called Prospect Hill in nearby Fairfax County. His brother Roger, who had served gallantly at the Battles of Chippewa and Lundy's Lane on the Niagara frontier and recently had been appointed aide-de-camp to Gen. Jacob Brown, was also temporarily stationed at Washington.[1]

During that fall the Joneses attended the weekly church services of Rev. William Maffitt, a Presbyterian minister who lived and preached at his nearby Fairfax County home, Salona. Interestingly, Maffitt's home had served as a refuge for President James Madison in August 1814 when the British captured and burned the capital city. Maffitt, a well-respected educator and minister, had married Ann Beale Carter, the widow of Charles B. Carter of Richmond Hill, and had assumed responsibility for her daughter, Mary Walker Carter. Betty Jones and Mary Walker Carter had become well acquainted during the previous months, and it was probably Betty who introduced her younger brother Thomas to the attractive young lady. During the next few months Thomas and Mary developed a relationship that some eight years later would result in marriage.[2]

By the end of 1815 Lieutenant Jones had recovered sufficiently to seek a new assignment. He was among the top quarter on the list of lieutenants awaiting promotion to master commandant, yet Jones had never served anywhere other than on the New Orleans station, and never aboard a large seagoing vessel. Throughout the fall he petitioned the Navy Department for an assignment that would afford him the experience he needed in bluewater navigation and seamanship. In mid-December navy commissioner Capt. David Porter wrote an unsolicited recommendation to the department supporting Jones's request for sea duty. This apparently influenced Secretary Benjamin Crowninshield, for only ten days later Jones and a number of midshipmen, including David G. Farragut, received orders to report to Capt. William Bainbridge, commander of the Boston Naval Station. The young men were going to the Mediterranean aboard the seventy-four-gun ship of the line *Washington* for a three-year tour of duty.[3]

The *Washington* was one of the navy's largest and newest warships. Launched in the spring of 1816, it was to serve as the flagship of Commo. Isaac Chauncey's Mediterranean Squadron and would provide Jones with invaluable experience. Crowninshield had instructed Chauncey either to find Jones a position aboard the *Washington* or to transfer the "deserving officer" to another vessel in the squadron. He explained that Jones had "claims to service in preference to many others" and that his previous experience at New Orleans had not given him the chance to learn the nautical maneuvers of larger ships. Moreover, Jones had been "severely wounded in defending most gallantly the U.S. gunboats near New Orleans" and thus deserved such an opportunity.[4]

The *Washington*'s flag captain, John Orde Creighton, must have been pleased to have such a distinguished junior officer at his disposal. Creighton, who had the reputation of being the "greatest martinet in the navy," tried to instill in Jones and his other officers the importance of appearance and drill. He constantly challenged his men to improve their condition; he insisted that his ship appear in perfect order at all times; and he demanded that his officers and crew be ready for any occasion. "All of this was accomplished at the sacrifice of the comfort of every one on board," remarked Farragut, one of the young officers Creighton was determined to mold. While his ship did indeed seem trim, Creighton's junior officers and crew chafed and grumbled under his overbearing command. It was while serving under Creighton in the Mediterranean that Jones acquired his own insistence on discipline, efficiency, and attention to authority. This duty also offered him experience with personnel problems through which he came to understand the fine line between discipline and tyranny.[5]

When Jones arrived in Boston in mid-March 1816, he found the *Washington* still unready for sea. The ship had not yet been outfitted, and the recruiting officer had not signed aboard the full complement of crew. Finally, after six more weeks of preparation, the ship departed Boston on 8 May, and eight days later anchored off Annapolis, Maryland, where it remained for three weeks awaiting the arrival of William Pinckney, the newly appointed American minister to Russia. The appearance of a ship of the line off Annapolis was an unusual sight and brought a constant stream of visitors. Four days after its arrival, Board of Navy Commissioners John Rodgers and David Porter inspected the ship. The following day President James Madison and his wife, Dolly, accompanied by Secretary of War William H. Crawford and Secretary of the Navy Crowninshield, toured the vessel. On 29 May, Maryland governor Levin Winder came aboard. During those gala occasions the officers and crew paraded in dress uniforms, the ship's cannon fired salutes to the dignitaries, and the men offered cheers of affection and support. This was Jones's first experience with the navy's grand formalities, and it made a vivid impression on him.[6]

While at Annapolis Jones wrote the Navy Department to remind Crowninshield that he had served as a commander of a vessel, albeit a small gunboat, during the war and was thus entitled to the pay awarded to lieutenant commandants. Second, he requested written permission to be assisted by a servant who would be paid from public money. Although he acknowledged that the department normally did not provide additional pay for servants, Jones reminded Crowninshield that he did not have full use of his arm because of the wound he had received during the war. Moreover, the British had taken all of his personal effects while he was a prisoner, leaving him almost destitute. Jones believed that the department should make an exception in this instance, and it did, to a degree; Crowninshield gave Jones permission for the servant but never compensated him for his losses.[7]

William Pinckney and his family arrived in Annapolis on 6 June, and that evening the *Washington* sailed down the Chesapeake. After an uneventful twenty-six-day voyage the warship joined the rest of the Mediterranean Squadron off Gibraltar. The fleet, consisting of the flagship *Washington*; frigates *Constellation, Java,* and *United States*; and the sloops *Erie, Ontario,* and *Peacock,* was an impressive force intended to demonstrate America's resolve to the North African Barbary States. This show of force had become essential because Algiers had resumed its attacks on American commerce during the War of 1812. Commodores Decatur and Bainbridge had forced the Algerians to stop their attacks soon thereafter, but there were no assurances that pirate activities would not resume. With such a threat looming the U.S. government decided to maintain a continued naval presence in the region. Chauncey's orders instructed him to beware of possible depredations, to keep his squadron in a constant state of readiness, and to maintain communications with all American consuls in the area. Crowninshield also suggested that Chauncey establish friendly relations with other nations in the region and that he should frequently visit Sardinia, as that island nation had consistently shown friendship toward the United States.[8]

The Mediterranean station offered Jones a wonderful opportunity for both education and excitement. Although listed as a supernumerary aboard the flagship, he learned the duties and routine of life aboard a seagoing vessel. Creighton ran a "smart ship" and constantly had his men scrubbing the decks and dressing the rigging for parade. Jones also experienced the grandeur of civilizations past as he saw ancient temples and tombs, the sites of classic naval engagements, and the great cities of antiquity.[9]

The *Washington* remained at Gibraltar for only a few days before sailing east for Naples. After stopping for a day at Sardinia, the American flotilla anchored in the Bay of Naples on 14 July 1816 and remained there until the end of August. Although the people of Naples were friendly, the climate hospitable, and the scenery impressive—Mount Vesuvius overlooked the ships to the southeast—the men of the squadron soon became bored with the constant scrubbing and parading aboard the flagship. Morale and discipline deteriorated, and an epidemic of courts-martial spread throughout the squadron.

One noteworthy court-martial involved Captain Creighton and Midn. John Marston. In early July, as the *Washington* left Gibraltar, the captain was running back and forth on the deck, barking out orders and demonstrating the proper way to handle a ship, all the while scrutinized by naval officers from other nations. Midshipman Marston collided with the captain during this show, and Creighton supposedly struck him with his speaking trumpet for his indiscretion. This public humiliation prompted Marston to file charges. But according to regulations, such a complaint had to be forwarded to Commodore Chauncey through the captain of the ship—Creighton. Hoping to avoid an incident, Creighton offered the midshipman a private apology, but Marston refused it and pressed charges. During the three-day court-martial that followed in late August Creighton denied ever having struck Marston. The board of senior officers who presided over the case acquitted Creighton and chastised Marston for his "frivolous and malicious charges." This provided an unforgettable lesson for junior officers such as Jones, proving conclusively that rank had its privileges.[10]

Probably the most serious court-martial of the cruise occurred because of the ongoing conflict between navy captain Oliver Hazard Perry and marine captain John Heath. The two had argued on several occasions, and during one heated exchange in mid-September Perry had knocked Heath to the deck. The two later fought a duel in which neither suffered injury. During the subsequent court-martial Perry pleaded guilty to striking Heath but received only a private reprimand from Commodore Chauncey. The board of officers found Heath guilty of gross inefficiency and gave him a long suspension from duty without pay.[11]

These episodes demonstrated an alarming fact to junior officers such as Jones: captains could act as despots and not have to suffer the consequences; junior officers who protested were the ones who suffered. Even in a military environment Jones found these actions unjust and threatening. A group of forty-one junior officers, with Jones's name heading the list, reacted by sending Congress a spirited memorial in which they demanded that the Senate investigate the two courts-martial. The officers said that their faith in the tribunals, which had been created by Congress to protect their rights, had been greatly impaired. In conclusion, they maintained that they had "no guarantee for the safety of their persons" but through force of arms and personal strength.[12]

A group of nine marine officers and fifty-four midshipmen forwarded similar petitions, forcing the ships' captains and Commodore Chauncey to respond formally to the charges. The captains then forwarded a demand to the Senate that the individuals who had signed the petitions be recalled as soon as possible because they undermined discipline and

threatened order. Commodore Chauncey also submitted a lengthy statement on the uselessness of lieutenants, which was endorsed by the captains of the squadron. Ultimately the Senate Committee on Naval Affairs
determined that the problem lay not with the laws but rather with the
way they had been executed. Thus, the affair quietly ended. Even so,
Jones had taken a public stance—one that threatened his naval career—
demonstrating an intense conviction to the cause of justice. Ironically,
his later actions as a commodore would be challenged by a group of
young lieutenants who felt they had been unjustly treated by a dogmatic
commander.[13]

During the fall of 1816 Jones witnessed firsthand the intricacies of
naval diplomacy as the flagship cruised the Mediterranean, touching at
several ports. Relations between the United States and Algiers had worsened, and Chauncey was determined to prevent the North African state
from seizing American ships. At the end of September the squadron
appeared off Tripoli and the bashaw (pasha) sent fruit, vegetables, and
bread as tokens of friendship. Continuing westward the fleet anchored
in the harbor of Algiers in mid-October. Chauncey and Consul William
Shaler immediately presented the dey with a demand that he renew the
peace treaty between Algiers and the United States. After several attempts
to evade the commitment, the dey finally agreed to sign the treaty and as
proof of his continued friendship presented the flagship with food and
presents. A month later, in late October, the squadron dropped anchor
off Gibraltar.[14]

Some two months earlier, in early September 1816, the *Constellation*'s
captain, Charles Gordon, had died, and shortly thereafter his first lieutenant, Joseph Smith, requested permission to return to the United States.
In October Capt. William M. Crane took command of the *Constellation,*
and a month later Jones became the ship's first lieutenant. The position
did not entail as much personal responsibility as commanding a gunboat, but it certainly marked a promotion for Jones, placing him a step
closer to receiving his own sea command.

During the summer the *Constellation* paid important diplomatic calls
to Cavita Veechia, Naples, Palermo, Messina, Syracuse, Tripoli, Tunis, and
Algiers. That summer cruise provided Jones with his first taste of real
responsibility aboard a seagoing ship. He learned firsthand the importance of ceremony and how to entertain dignitaries when on several
occasions European royalty visited the ship. He supervised daily opera-

tions, including the assignment of tasks and the constant repair and painting of the frigate; and he called a series of courts-martial, after which discipline improved greatly aboard the frigate.[15]

On 21 October 1817, two weeks after the squadron anchored below the British fortress at Gibraltar, Captain Crane and Lieutenant Jones transferred to the frigate *United States* and sailed to Port Mahon for the winter. As Jones adjusted to his new ship, an incident occurred that unfortunately reflected the attitudes of many of his fellow naval officers. In early February 1818, while off Syracuse, the *United States* received a complement of new lieutenants, including one Uriah Phillips Levy, a Jew. When Levy reported to the frigate, Captain Crane told him that the ship needed no additional officers and ordered him to return to the *Franklin*. Levy was humiliated by the rebuff, especially when Crane ordered a marine guard to escort him back to his previous ship. Commodore Chauncey's replacement, Charles Stewart, considered Crane's rejection to be an act of insubordination and ordered Levy to report again to Crane. It took this threat by a superior officer to force Crane to allow Levy onboard the *United States*.[16]

In the face of the captain's hostility, Levy sought out First Lieutenant Jones for advice. Jones, as the executive officer, could ease Levy's transition aboard the ship and would be the key to his acceptance. In a private meeting Jones listened to Levy's problem and offered simple advice: "Do your duty as an officer and a gentleman, be civil to all, and the first man who pursues a different course to you, call him to a strict and proper account." Jones then set an example for the other junior officers aboard the ship by accepting Levy as a brother officer. For the next several months Levy acted in a professional manner, as Jones later recounted, and "those who opposed his joining our mess not only relented, but deeply regretted the false step they had incautiously taken." Jones demonstrated an uncommon open-mindedness and sense of fairness based on ability and not ethnic or religious identity. He would show the same respect for Pacific island peoples during a later cruise.[17]

Shortly after his arrival, Levy witnessed the flogging of a middle-aged gunner's mate charged with drunkenness, profanity, and insolence to an officer. Lieutenant Jones assembled the crew for the punishment, and after thirty-six lashes, which cut deep into the back of the mate and covered him with blood, the sailor was taken below to the surgeon. This barbaric display of punishment sickened Levy and prompted a prolonged discussion with Jones. Both agreed that there must be other effective but less harsh methods of discipline. They knew that Adm. Lord Horatio Nelson and Capt. Cuthbert Collingwood of the British navy had not relied on the lash to maintain discipline, and both had run efficient ships. Yet neither Jones nor Levy could explain the reason for the success of those officers; nor could they agree on a solution to the discipline problems for the American navy.[18]

During the winter of 1818 Jones asked to return to the United States, even though he had completed only two years of a three-year tour. Since the squadron had an excess of lieutenants, Stewart granted his request. On 16 April 1818 Jones reboarded the homeward bound *Washington* as a supernumerary. The ship arrived in New York on 7 July, and a few days later Jones left for Washington, D.C., to pick up his back pay from the Navy Department.[19]

Jones's thirty-month tour of duty in the Mediterranean had been very beneficial. He had gained experience with capital ships and squadron maneuvers, and he had learned the duties associated with command. He had acquired experience with personnel problems and had learned that discipline and tyranny were on opposite sides of a very fine line. It was a line that Jones would learn to straddle, making him popular with the men under his command but constantly incurring the rancor of his junior officers. Jones also discovered the intricacies of naval diplomacy, information he would remember for the remainder of his life.

After receiving his pay Jones took a short leave of absence, which he spent at Sharon, the small house built by his sister Betty near Prospect Hill in Fairfax County. When he arrived home, Jones learned that there was considerable family business that needed his attention. In 1816 his siblings had filed a lawsuit against two of his paternal uncles to secure maternal lands in Fairfax County. The judge ruled in November 1817 that the acreage in question should be divided between Jones and his five co-plaintiffs. The decision provided Jones with the land he needed to become a gentleman farmer, but it did not bring an end to his financial instability.[20]

He had not yet settled in at Sharon when he received orders in late July to report immediately to Capt. Edmund P. Kennedy at Norfolk. Jones sought to delay another long absence from home by asking that the orders be delayed or that he be assigned to Washington or Baltimore. He had just returned from a long cruise, he explained, and family affairs required his immediate attention. Although the department did not grant his request, his tour of duty at Norfolk proved to be brief. At the end of January 1819 Jones was transferred to the Washington Navy Yard and thus began a six-year assignment at the capital that gave him the opportunity to start a domestic life at Sharon. Living in Fairfax County, only nine miles up the Potomac River from the capital, opposite Georgetown, allowed Jones to begin a second career as a farmer. He enjoyed his Washington assignment in part because it allowed him each day to ride his horse south along the Georgetown Pike, across the "Chain Bridge" over the Potomac, to his post at the navy yard. Jones may have been the first daily commuter into the capital city.[21]

It was an unfortunate time to begin a farming venture. Almost immediately a financial panic rocked the nation's economic infrastructure, and Virginia was hit particularly hard. Old, exhausted tobacco lands could no longer provide financial returns; land values dropped precipitously; the prices for consumer goods greatly increased; and loans became virtually impossible for farmers to obtain. Many faced ruin and lost family lands while others barely survived. Jones, just starting out, was faced with this depressing downward spiral. The situation appeared bleak, and as Jones later recalled, "no agriculturist, . . . had ever embarked on a more forlorn hope." Of the 140 acres of land he inherited from his mother's estate, half was virgin woodland and half was worn-out tobacco and corn lands. The farmlands appeared worthless, and the property also had almost no material improvements; there were no fences, no barn, no slave quarters, and only a small dwelling.[22]

By selling forty acres of his woodlands, Jones made enough money to improve the rest of his holdings. With a salary of but seven hundred dollars per year, hardly enough to renovate his farm and make it worthy of his aspirations, he nevertheless started planting a variety of soil-replenishing crops aimed at restoring the land's fertility. He set out fruit trees and built a barn with a loft capable of holding thirty-five to forty tons of hay. Years later Jones remembered that his neighbors thought he was crazy for building a barn of such enormous dimensions. Other farmers and visitors thought that all of Fairfax County would not produce enough hay to fill it. Jones soon proved the skeptics wrong. Within three years his industry and experimentation with crop rotation started paying dividends. He harvested quantities of clover hay, and by planting timothy he reclaimed an acre of former swampland. Although it was only a minor success, it was nonetheless a victory and the beginning of his plantation.[23]

Being stationed in Washington gave Jones easy access to his superiors in the Navy Department as well as to his farm. His new appointment made his name instantly recognizable to the ranking officers of the navy, the secretary of the navy, and the Board of Navy Commissioners. In late March 1820 Jones learned of his promotion to master commandant, and he immediately requested "the most active *sea* service" that the department could offer. He was now eligible to command seagoing vessels, but at the moment the department had no commands open for him because there were many more senior officers. Over the next two years Jones applied on several occasions to the department seeking a sea command. Denied such a position, he worked instead to master the art and science of naval ordnance.[24]

In the aftermath of the War of 1812, the newly created Board of Navy Commissioners became increasingly concerned with improving gunpowder and ordnance. The board signed a contract with the Du Pont de Nemours company to provide powder and authorized Andrew Oehlers to conduct experiments with shells at the Washington Navy Yard, where it established the navy's first ordnance laboratory in 1820. The commissioners also awarded gun contracts to three foundries: the West Point Foundry Association of West Point, New York; John Mason's Columbian Foundry in Georgetown, District of Columbia; and the Bellona Foundry of Richmond, Virginia. With this increased emphasis on the efficiency of naval weapons the Board of Navy Commissioners also appointed a naval officer, initially Stephen Cassin, to visit foundries, inspect castings, and test the guns. On 8 April 1822, Commo. John Rodgers recommended Jones, "an intelligent officer," to the secretary of the navy to be the second person to undertake those duties. Without an immediate sea command available, Jones gladly accepted the position as inspector and superintendent of ordnance for the Washington Navy Yard; in 1824 he became the first inspector of ordnance for the entire navy.[25]

Although he was assigned to the Washington Navy Yard, his post called for Jones to travel to New York, Richmond, and nearby Georgetown. The board gave Jones strict instructions regarding his new position: "Every gun must be searched with a searcher; and any gun found to have a defect or to be honeycombed one-tenth of an inch inside or two-tenths of an inch on the exterior is not to be received without being proved four times." Powder also had to be tested for its power to project shot. During the fall of 1822 Jones traveled to New York to inspect cannon, shot, and powder at the West Point Foundry. When he compared powder from the Washington and New York navy yards with that produced at West Point, he discovered that the West Point Foundry Association produced a higher-quality product. In December he reported that the shot produced at John Mason's Georgetown Iron Works had a minor flaw, one he called "more optical than absolute," but "in every other respect was perfect, and [had] castings of good quality." Jones quickly became the Navy Department's expert on ordnance, and even the commissioners deferred to his judgment. Jones did not appreciate it at the time, but he had found a unique niche that brought him a degree of recognition and independence within the service.[26]

As Jones's career rapidly changed after he accepted his new position, so did his domestic life. In the spring of 1822 his sister Betty died, naming him one of her estate's executors and assigning him the responsibility of paying off her debts. Jones also inherited the small house Sharon and 140 acres of land that adjoined his to the north, though he did not gain clear title to it until some years later when all Betty's debts had been completely settled. Betty also bequeathed him several slaves, detailing what care he should provide for each. For her slaves Amy and Nancy, he was "to continue . . . the Asylum they now enjoy of the house and garden on the land devised to him as . . . long as they may need it, as a place of Shelter." Nancy's son David was to be freed and educated as a missionary, which he was. With the property Jones acquired from his sister's estate, he now owned nine slaves, four horses and mules, and more than 250 acres. By the end of the year he purchased an additional 76 acres of Betty's former estate from his brother Lucius Jones, bringing his landholdings to slightly more than 300 acres.[27]

The additional lands also increased Jones's taxable personal property. Moreover, during the spring of 1822 the Fairfax County Superior Court had ruled—in a case originating in 1819—that Jones owed Elizabeth and Margaret Williams $339.02 plus interest. These additional expenses forced Jones to become a more aggressive farmer. He started using lime and locally produced manure, and he sowed timothy and clover to resurrect his soil. Jones acquired a subsoil plow to turn up the fertile ground below the exhausted topsoil. He also contracted to purchase cherry, pear, apple, plum, and other "ornamental" trees. True, Jones incurred greater debt through these activities, but his purchases allowed him to develop "a pattern farm of the entire region."[28]

By 1823 Jones had made a name for himself in the community as a successful young farmer, and in the U.S. Navy as an aspiring naval commander. Yet he felt a need for the stability of a wife to oversee his investments once he returned to sea. He first met Mary Walker Carter during the fall of 1815. They probably became reacquainted at his sister's funeral in 1822. In any case, the twenty-year-old, brown-eyed, buxom brunette, a descendant of the Lees of Virginia and of "King" Robert Carter of Carter's Grove on the James River, possessed the family lineage that a gentleman would have thought important. She was also attractive and educated, and she possessed an independent spirit that was well suited for the wife of a naval commander frequently at sea. After his sister's death, Jones began to court the young woman and within a short time had persuaded her to marry him.

On 1 July 1823 Thomas ap Catesby and Mary were wed at Salona, the home of her stepfather, the Reverend William Maffitt. As they awaited the arrival of Mary's brother-in-law, the Reverend Thomas Bloomer Balch of Washington, D.C., who was going to perform the ceremony, Jones paced nervously about the house and Mary began to cry. But Balch never arrived, and Maffitt performed the ceremony instead. For some unknown reason, perhaps he was distracted in the confusion of the moment, Maffitt failed to file a minister's return, and the marriage was not legally registered until July 1825. Nonetheless, the young couple believed they were married in the eyes of God, family, and friends, and they began their life together at nearby Sharon.[29]

Mary brought a woman's touch and an air of dignity to the small estate. The white masonry, two-story, stuccoed home with its white-columned porch was surrounded by shrubbery, orchards, gardens, and meadows. The parlor, although sparsely furnished at this time, would soon contain several fine tables and chairs, formal portraits of the young couple, a model of a frigate under sail, a red-and-blue parrot, and a plethora of books on topics ranging from Captain Cook's voyages to literature and theology. The couple's master bathroom had a shower and running water supplied by lead pipes from a nearby springhouse. It was a charming, comfortable home for the young couple, and it would be their home for the remainder of Jones's life. Sharon would also be the home for the next generation of Joneses, for Mary gave birth on 23 August 1824 to a baby boy, whom the couple named Meriwether Patterson Jones in honor of Thomas's uncle Meriwether Jones and his former commander Daniel Todd Patterson.[30]

Though taxing, Jones's position as inspector of ordnance was financially remunerative and allowed him to increase his family's holdings, for he earned more than his regular salary. He also received an allotment for the servant who took care of his personal needs and could pocket any funds not expended on him. Furthermore, he received a per diem allowance for food and lodging during his time away from Washington plus fifteen cents per mile for travel. Jones soon learned that if he managed money wisely, his assignment could be extremely profitable. His estate grew from about one hundred acres, six slaves, and four horses in 1821 to more than three hundred acres, thirteen slaves, and seven horses by 1824. Inheritance explains some of his financial improvement, but certainly not all.[31]

In addition to his economic prosperity, Jones flourished in Washington society, where his family connections were well established. President James Monroe was a distant cousin, and a paternal cousin, army general Walter Jones, was stationed in the capital city. Brother Roger, now the army's adjutant general, worked closely with Secretary of War John C. Calhoun. Jones also knew well the officers of the Board of Navy Commissioners and Secretary of the Navy Samuel Southard. He apparently became acquainted with Secretary of State John Quincy Adams and a number of influential congressmen as well.[32]

Jones continued proving ordnance throughout 1824. In a late-November trip to the Columbian Foundry in Georgetown, he examined more than 2,200 42-pounder shot and found 22 too large, 11 underweight, and 8 more defective in other ways. Jones "suspended a final decision" on 875 others until he could discuss their problems with the board. Apparently the shot passed the weight and measurement specifications but had holes, varying from one to two inches in depth, and he wanted approval from the board before the department accepted them. It was meticulous work because each shot had to be weighed, measured, visually inspected, and recorded to determine if it met specifications. It took a great deal of time to handle each piece and record the findings. Only a patient, fastidious, disciplined person would be successful at such an undertaking, and the board considered Jones an excellent inspector.[33]

Before the end of the year Jones made another trip to examine shot produced at the West Point Foundry, and in early 1825 he again traveled to Richmond. During his inspection of the guns cast there by John Clarke's Bellona Foundry, Jones found that the cannon were "beautifully cast & I think the most handsomest guns I have ever inspected." Even so, many did not pass inspection. Regardless, the foundry received another Navy Department contract the following May.[34]

At the beginning of 1825 Jones was in the top half of master commandants on the Naval Register, but he was still awaiting "an arduous duty" at sea. He knew that if he did not receive one, he would not qualify for another promotion. In January and February Jones aggressively petitioned Secretary Southard for a sea command. He had heard that the sloop-of-war *Peacock,* stationed with the Pacific Squadron, needed a commander and asked Southard for that position. Eventually Southard agreed. He instructed Jones to go to Norfolk, board the *John Adams,* and proceed to the Pacific to assume command of the *Peacock;* Jones finally had an independent ship command, and he was determined to make the most of it.[35]

❧ 4 ❧

THE KIND-EYED CHIEF
The *Peacock*, 1826–1827

A s a young boy in Richmond, Jones had read voraciously of the adventures of Capt. James Cook in the Pacific Ocean and had dreamed of seeing the same exotic sites that Cook had described a half century earlier. The command of the *Peacock* in the Pacific in 1825 was the fulfillment of a childhood and adult dream; he would finally command a ship, and it would sail in the Pacific.

Before his departure Jones met with Southard to review his orders, and the secretary provided him with explicit instructions. Peru was struggling to win its independence from Spain, and the patriot government had proclaimed a blockade of the entire coast still under Spanish control; Britain's Royal Navy recognized the blockade in order to curry favor with the new nation. The United States did not. Southard also told Jones that Peruvian patriot Vice Adm. Martin George Guise, a former commander in the British navy, had been illegally detaining American merchant ships and that the blockade infringed on U.S. commercial interests. He ordered Jones to protect American ships' right to trade with any port in the region.[1]

During their discussion Southard reassured Jones that because of his debilitating wound a slave would be allowed to accompany him as a body servant; the slave could be listed on the ship's payroll, and all his provisions

and transportation costs charged to the federal government. Shortly
before Jones departed Southard also provided him with a packet of dispatches to be delivered to Commo. Isaac Hull, commander of the Pacific
Squadron. Those sensitive letters discussed U.S. commercial interests
in the Pacific and repeated much of what the secretary had discussed
with Jones.[2]

Arriving in Norfolk in mid-April 1825, Jones boarded the sloop *John
Adams* and, along with Lt. William Ramsay, traveled as far as Panama.
After disembarking at Chagres on 4 May, Jones and Ramsay made a
three-day trek along jungle paths across the Panamanian isthmus. By the
time they reached the Pacific it was the season of the southern winds
and virtually all southbound traffic had stopped. It took sixty days for a
ship to sail south against the winds to Valparaiso and only half that time
to return. These conditions forced the officers to wait almost a month,
until 4 June, before they could find a small brig to convey them to Peru.
Even then, Jones and Ramsay had to share with an Englishman the
eight-hundred-dollar expense to charter the vessel. Jones did not arrive
in the harbor of Chorillos (off Lima, Peru) and board the *Peacock* until
mid-September.

His experiences on this time-consuming and harrowing journey provoked Jones to write a thoughtful letter to the secretary of the navy that
emphasized the importance of the Panamanian isthmus to naval communications. Jones suggested that the Navy Department station small
ships on each side of the isthmus; two would sail the Pacific between
Panama City and Lima, while two more would maintain communications in the Gulf and Atlantic between Chagres and the United States.
The four ships would provide timely information on events in the Pacific
and Gulf of Mexico and reduce the burden placed on far-removed commanders. The improved communication would allow the navy to provide
better protection and assistance for merchants and whalers. Although it
was a good suggestion, the department did not act on his advice; the
same communications problem existed when Jones rejoined the Pacific
Squadron in 1842.[3]

Lt. Beverly Kennon mustered the crew of the *Peacock* and fired a
thirteen-gun salute on 15 September when Jones, an old friend from the
Mediterranean, boarded the ship accompanied by his slave, Lieutenant
Ramsay, Steward James Conway, and Clerk John Norfleet. During his
temporary command of the *Peacock* Kennon had transformed the crew

into a highly disciplined unit. Kennon probably greeted Jones with mixed feelings, his pleasure at seeing an old friend offset by the loss of command and by his reappointment as the *Peacock's* first lieutenant. The sight of Ramsay most likely provoked strong emotions for Kennon as well. Ramsay had been serving in the *Peacock* when Commodore Hull appointed Kennon to command the sloop. The commodore had wanted to give Kennon a more experienced first lieutenant, so he replaced Ramsay with someone more senior. Ramsay took the transfer as a personal slight and vehemently protested, whereupon Hull relieved him from duty and ordered him to report to Washington. Almost as soon as Ramsay had arrived at the capital, Secretary Southard had ordered him back to the Pacific. Ramsay considered this a vindication and viewed his return as a personal victory over Hull.[4]

Alas, Ramsay did not know when to leave well enough alone. Even before he arrived on the station he wrote a condescending note to Hull telling the commodore that Southard had made the correct choice by returning him to the Pacific. Hull, angered by Ramsay's impertinence, forwarded the note to Southard. Jones almost certainly knew about Ramsay's disdain for Hull and the insolent note. By the time Jones and Ramsay boarded the *Peacock* they had spent almost five months together, and Ramsay's arrogance must have disturbed Jones. Disregard for discipline and authority did not sit well with Jones, who intended to run a smart ship. Certainly he was not going to allow Ramsay to prevent him from doing so. After only a few months aboard the *Peacock* Ramsay began to exhibit the same disrespect for Jones he had shown toward Hull. But the event that finally provoked Jones to act was Ramsay's punishment of a seaman, a prerogative always reserved to a ship's commanding officer. When Jones confronted Ramsay about his indiscretion the lieutenant obstinately retorted that he would punish anyone he pleased. Jones promptly had Ramsay arrested and confined to quarters.

After the arrest Jones informed Hull that Ramsay was "a young officer not without fair pretensions in many respects, but like all mankind [with] his faults." He predicted that with time and reflection Ramsay would recognize his shortcomings and arrogance. But with the *Peacock* preparing for a prolonged cruise, Jones did not have enough time to bring the lieutenant to see the error of his ways. Nor did he want to keep him confined during the voyage. Such an extended confinement would be both "excessively unpleasant" for Ramsay and embarrassing for his family; it might also undermine discipline among the officers and crew. Jones concluded that the lieutenant should be sent to Washington so the secretary of the navy could review the charges against him.[5]

Hull decided against sending Ramsay to Washington and instead ordered him tried on the station with Jones serving as a member of the court. This decision produced new protests from an already remonstrating Ramsay, who said that Jones should not preside over the court-martial because he had initiated the charges. Hull was forced to agree, but instead of allowing Ramsay to return immediately to Washington, Hull ordered him to remain at Lima until the *Peacock* was ready to return home.[6]

During the winter of 1826 the *Peacock,* often in company with Hull's flagship, the *United States,* cruised the western coast of South America. In January Jones entertained the English consul general, William Newgen, and Consul Wheelwright. In February Spanish general Don José Ramón Rodil, who had recently surrendered the city of Callao to the Peruvian patriots, and the Dutch consul called on the sloop. Jones's convivial treatment of dignitaries underscored the diplomatic importance of this newly independent region as well as the necessity for the United States to maintain good relations with the emerging nations.[7]

Jones enjoyed entertaining foreign officials, but he also found that discipline among his crew generally declined whenever he and his officers hosted parties. On the morning following a party late in October he learned that four men had deserted and several others were tardy returning from shore leave. Two weeks later, after another festive occasion, sailor Henry Elliot was found drunk. The lapses in discipline prompted Jones to issue a new code of internal rules for the ship, but even these did not completely curtail the problems. In late April Seaman H. R. Poole received twelve lashes for disrespectful conduct, and a few days later Seaman John Williams was punished for stealing a boy's money. In late May 1826 Teremias Barnes was given twenty-five lashes for disrespectful conduct, and Seaman Daniel Mager was flogged for drunkenness. Jones showed no qualms about using corporal punishment to restore order, and after a gala event in late June, Midn. Thomas J. Harris reported that not a single man deserted or broke liberty.

One of the most serious disciplinary episodes Jones had to face occurred on the evening of 27 April 1826. En route from Chorillos toward Callao, the *Peacock* passed the merchant ship *Georgia Packet* traveling in the same direction. When Jones went below that evening he warned the deck officer, Lt. James M. Williams, to keep a sharp lookout for the merchant ship as it would probably return to calmer, deeper waters after encountering the stormy surf along the coast. At about ten o'clock Jones heard the deck officer shouting orders followed by the frightening sound of splintering wood. Jones quickly dressed and hurried on deck to find that the *Peacock* had collided with the *Georgia Packet* on a calm, clear, starlit night. There was no apparent reason for the accident. The merchant ship suffered damage to its bowsprit and spars and had to put into port for repairs, but the *Peacock* was not seriously injured in the accident. Even so, Jones was livid because he had personally warned Williams to be alert. At the court of inquiry held aboard the sloop four days later witnesses declared that the ship had been visible for ten to twelve minutes before the crash, but Williams had hesitated until the last moment to give the orders that would have prevented the accident. Jones suspended Williams from duty and transferred him to Hull's flagship until the secretary of the navy could review the case.[8]

Secretary Southard had ordered Commodore Hull to keep most of his squadron on patrol along the coast of South America. But when a convenient time arose Hull was to sail to the Pacific islands to chart the principal reefs, negotiate with the local rulers, and protect the growing American commercial interests in the region from mutinous sailors and British incursions. Although Hull understood the growing importance of the Pacific, he believed that events on the coast of South America required his presence. Thus, he decided to send Jones—a senior master commandant— to visit the islands in his stead. Hull was confident that Jones would carry out the letter as well as the spirit of Secretary Southard's orders, and Hull probably shared with Jones a private letter from Southard suggesting cooperation with the missionaries in the Pacific.[9]

The South Pacific had become increasingly important for American merchants and was a fresh hunting ground for New England whalers. Yet Americans there felt a growing uneasiness at the lawlessness of the region, and forty-four Nantucket merchants submitted a petition to President John Quincy Adams requesting the establishment of a "naval force in those [Pacific] seas, where so much property and so many lives are exposed." Specifically, the merchants complained of the lack of discipline, as evidenced by the recent mutiny aboard the whaling ship *Globe*. In January 1824 seamen recently recruited in the Sandwich (Hawaiian) Islands had seized the *Globe,* brutally killed sailing master Thomas Worth and his officers, and then sailed the ship to the Mulgrave (Marshall) Islands. After intimidating the natives there and then being imprisoned, six of the seamen escaped, reboarded the *Globe,* and sailed to Valparaiso. The New England merchants believed the mutiny set a dangerous precedent, and should order and stability not be restored, most particularly to the Hawaiian Islands, the region would "become a nest of pirates and murderers."[10]

A petition from several New Bedford merchants evoked the same image of lawlessness and violence caused by rogues in the islands while also trying to arouse national pride. The fear of bedlam was evident in their petition, but the merchants chose to emphasize the fact that the islanders believed Britain to be a superior maritime nation because of its warships. As of April 1825 the Americans had never sent a warship to the region, so the islanders believed the United States had only whalers and merchant ships. If that belief were not corrected, the petitioners warned, American property would be at risk. The merchants believed that the only remedy was to send a warship to the Hawaiian Islands to restore order and protect U.S. commercial interests.[11]

In late May 1826 Hull instructed Jones to proceed with the *Peacock* on an extended voyage to the South Pacific. Jones spent the last two weeks of June supplying his ship with wood, vegetables, sugar, and fresh water. Aware that his crew's enlistments would soon expire, Jones asked the sailors to renew their contracts until 31 March 1827. He promised an extra month's pay and additional shore leave in Guayaquil (at that time in Gran Colombia) for each man who accepted. Jones proudly reported that "this proposition took much beyond [his] expectation" as all but seven of the men signed new contracts.[12]

The primary object of Jones's mission was to visit the Marquesas, Society, and Hawaiian Islands, and, if time permitted, to return via California and Mexico. Jones and the *Peacock* were to remain at each location as long as was necessary to protect American citizens and commerce. Moreover, Hull reminded Jones that this "part of the Pacific [was] little known, and [its] islands imperfectly surveyed." Last, Jones was to secure information about, and if necessary assist, the schooner *Dolphin* commanded by Lt. John "Mad Jack" Percival, which Hull had sent in August 1825 to the Mulgrave Islands in search of the *Globe.*[13]

Percival had been making quite a name for himself in the South Pacific. When he arrived in the Mulgraves Percival found that only two of the *Globe*'s mutineers had survived; the others apparently had been killed by the natives they had tried to intimidate. From the Mulgraves the *Dolphin* had sailed north to the Hawaiian Islands, where the "mischief-making man-of-war," as the Hawaiians called the ship, remained for several months. During his stay "Mad Jack" alienated the local chiefs, bickered with the missionaries, and gave his men free rein over the island. When missionaries forbade young half-naked Hawaiian girls to visit the ships in Honolulu harbor, Percival looked the other way as his seamen ransacked a missionary house and assaulted clerical leader Hiram Bingham. "Mad Jack" showed such disrespect to Queen Regent Elisabeta Kaahumanu that the ruler asked Rev. William Richards whether Percival was a naval officer or a pirate. The missionaries rejoiced when Percival and the *Dolphin* departed in May 1826, but merchants and whalers lamented for they had benefited greatly from the ribald order the warship had brought.[14]

During his thirteen-day stay at Guayaquil before leaving for the South Pacific, Jones spoke with the American consul on several occasions, trying to learn more about the diplomatic situation in the Pacific and to gain more insight into the art of diplomacy. Apparently he felt great concern over the nature and probable outcome of his mission and predicted that the government would likely be disappointed with the results. He told Hull that the government had been "thoughtless" in not providing suitable presents for the island chiefs. Without them, he doubted his ability to win the friendship and admiration of the islanders. Jones had learned that Lord Byron had recently visited the islands with the British frigate *Blonde* and had lavished presents on the islanders. He asked Hull what impression the United States would make when he arrived with "empty hands."[15]

Jones decided that, lacking gifts, he would have to pursue another course. He planned to use the missionaries to provide the natives with "some idea of our form of government, its republican simplicity, and our utter disregard and contempt for vain pomp and show." Jones thought this would allow him to show the advantages of a friendly relationship with the United States based on the "principles of just reciprocity." He told Hull that he intended to return to their native island two "deluded females" who had been lured from Wauhoo and abandoned at Payta by unscrupulous ship captains. He had also rescued a male islander from an American brig at Payta and planned to return him to his home as well. Jones hoped that these benevolent acts would strengthen the position of the United States in the region.[16]

Departing Guayaquil on 27 June 1826, the *Peacock* anchored in the Galápagos at Charles Island on 4 July. Here Jones and his crew found a freshwater spring from which they replenished their drinking casks. On the west side of the island they discovered a large colony of terrapins, and Jones instructed his crew to bring 250 aboard for a fresh meat supply. It was probably in the Galápagos that Jones first learned of guano, bird manure that could be used as a natural fertilizer. The mounds of guano on the island, some as large as small mountains, made an impression on the farmer who hoped to rejuvenate his depleted lands. With the help of the guano, his barren land in northern Virginia might be reclaimed and made productive. Jones would later be credited as the first Virginian to import the product, and by the 1850s he had performed many experiments with the rich natural fertilizer.[17]

On the afternoon of 9 July the *Peacock* departed for Nuku Hiva in the Marquesas Islands; fifteen days later the ship's lookout reported "valleys covered with trees" and a small settlement overlooking Massachusetts Bay. It was late in the evening when land was sighted, so Jones waited until the morning of 24 July before entering the harbor. Almost as soon as the sloop arrived, natives appeared to watch the Americans' every move, but no one ventured near the ship until late afternoon, when several "native girls 14 to 16 years old swam naked" around the ship. Afterward a delegation consisting of the king's interpreter and three chiefs approached in a canoe and informed Jones and his officers that the king would visit the next day.[18]

Shortly before noon on 25 July, King Havatoo and two of his sons arrived and offered Jones and his crew fruit, water, and wood. Havatoo was pleased when he learned that Jones had come in peace. According to his interpreter, the king had expected a "deadly enemy." Once he learned that Jones and his companions were Americans, Havatoo eagerly inquired about Capt. David Porter, who had refitted his small squadron there (claiming it for the United States) in October 1813. Apparently the king had been favorably impressed with Porter and wanted him to come again. Jones, conversing through the *Peacock*'s cooper, who spoke a Hawaiian-related language, told the king that Porter was not a part of this mission, but he would pass along the king's regards. In the meantime, Jones suggested that the islanders should treat all crews with the same hospitality. After the translation Havatoo and his delegation reported that in many instances ships refitting at the island took sandalwood, fruit, and water without paying. There had been times when chiefs requested payment for the goods and ship masters had them bound and flogged for their supposed impertinence. Episodes such as these had left the natives understandably suspicious of white visitors.[19]

During his eight-day stay at Massachusetts Bay, Jones realized that he could cultivate good relations and thus strengthen the commercial position of the United States simply by treating the natives with courtesy and respect. Jones instructed his officers and crew to be on their best behavior. In a more determined attempt to win the islanders' trust, Jones allowed them to visit the ship on chosen days, and he reported that there were "frequently several hundred on board." Jones instructed crewmen to lock away "all small iron and other articles" during the visits so the islanders would not be tempted to steal. Perhaps because of the precautions there was but one episode of theft. An old woman somehow stole a ten-pound iron gun bar, which the king later recovered and returned to the ship.[20]

Although Jones was trying to win the natives' friendship and admiration, he was not beyond flexing his country's military muscle to show that the "balance of power was all on our side." In the early afternoon of 28 July, Jones had two of the *Peacock*'s guns fired to impress King Havatoo with the strength of his warship. Two mornings later Jones sent Lt. Joseph Smoot and eighty marines ashore for a military parade. Jones and Havatoo watched together as the marines demonstrated their prowess and precision with small arms in the exotic setting. The display favorably impressed the spectators, who treated the Americans to a magnificent feast that lasted until the early evening.[21]

On the morning of 1 August Jones met with Havatoo and his advisers for the last time. He impressed on the islanders the importance of friendship and gave the king an official memo to be taken aboard every American ship that anchored in the harbor. If they treated Americans with courtesy and showed the certificate from the *Peacock*, Jones promised, the abuses would stop. The pledge made such a strong impression on those present that Prince Happü—the heir to the throne—asked for and received duplicate certificates. Shortly after noon Jones ordered the sloop's anchor raised and the sails unfurled. King Havatoo, sad that his new American friend had to depart, remained aboard the ship until the last moment, and even then instructed two young men to travel with the ship until it returned.[22]

Two days out of port the *Peacock* arrived at Mwow (Morrow), a tiny uncharted island southwest of Noaheevah. The lookout reported men on the beach waving a white flag. Jones and his officers, believing they had found a shipwrecked crew in desperate need of assistance, learned instead as they neared shore that the people waving the flag were islanders who wanted only to trade for rum. Jones refused to provide them with spirits, but he did chart the island before continuing the voyage.[23]

Late on the afternoon of 4 August the sloop arrived off the coast of Otaheiti (Tahiti) in the Society Islands. Choosing not to enter Matavia Bay without an experienced pilot, Jones waited until 9:00 A.M. on 6 August to enter the harbor. Jones and the *Peacock* were greeted by a delegation led by the island's governor and military commander, the Reverend Mr. Wilson, and Pawaü, the chief justice of the island. The delegation immediately asked Jones a series of probing questions. After hearing his responses Pawaü rhetorically asked how America could be such "a happy country . . . governed without a king."[24]

During his week in Matavia Bay Jones met on several occasions with the chiefs and missionaries. At one meeting Jones learned that the regent to the six-year-old monarch, Pomare IV, wanted the United States to send a consul to her island. One chief insisted that such an official would "increase our resources for obtaining political information." The chiefs also indicated that a political association with the United States was now very important because former Botany Bay convicts had been trying to gain political control over the island. Jones responded by offering "a few simple regulations," which he claimed were "designed to counteract the evil affects" of the criminals.[25]

The regulations resembled a formal treaty between the two nations. Drafted in two columns with English along the left-hand side and the English version of the Tahitian language along the right side, the agreement proclaimed:

1. Peace and friendship between the two parties;
2. That the United States would send to Tahiti a consul who would be protected and granted all benefits under most favored nation status;
3. American ships would be protected in Tahitian harbors during wartime;
4. Free trade, except for alcohol; and protection would be guaranteed by the Tahitians as long as American ships obeyed native laws;
5. Shipwrecked Americans were to be protected, and Tahitians would be assured one-third of the value of any salvaged goods;
6. Deserters would be apprehended by the Tahitian government and returned to their rightful ship; and

7. Tahitian tonnage duties could not exceed the rate charged to most favored nations, and trade with the United States would be conducted on the same basis.

After the resolutions had been translated by Jones's interpreters, Revs. Osmond and Williams, they were given to the regent and council, who immediately enacted them into law. Although the U.S. State Department and the Tahitians accepted the "treaty" as a binding agreement between the two nations, the U.S. Senate never approved the agreement, and therefore it never officially went into effect. Regardless, in the future the two countries continued to abide by the informal agreement signed by Jones, Pomare IV, and the queen's regent until France assumed a protectorate over the islands in 1843. Jones had offered his own interpretation of Hull's instructions, and his policies—which asserted American nationalism and a nascent Manifest Destiny that would later be reflected in his seizure of Monterey—established an important precedent for diplomacy in the South Pacific islands.[26]

On Monday, 14 August 1826, the *Peacock* made the six-mile journey to Papeete Bay, where Jones learned of a riot aboard the whaling ship *Fortune* out of Plymouth, Massachusetts. Apparently an "English Renegade" named Wells, who had signed on the ship in New Zealand, had led a group of six drunken mutineers in an attempt to seize the vessel. Capt. Charles Swain had come topside armed with loaded and cocked pistols when he first heard the trouble and held off the mutineers long enough to secure help from a nearby ship. When Jones learned of the unrest two days later, he sent marines to apprehend the accused aboard the *Fortune*. In a speedy trial held aboard the *Peacock* the six defendants were found guilty of mutiny. While Jones wondered whether he had the authority to administer punishment to civilians serving aboard commercial vessels, he knew that if he did nothing discipline aboard American ships in the South Pacific would suffer greatly. Perhaps morale aboard navy vessels would also deteriorate. After consulting with Swain, Jones decided that four of the six offenders should be flogged. At the last moment Jones pardoned two of those four because he considered them too young to suffer such harsh discipline. The episode demonstrated Jones's willingness to use the lash, but it also revealed that he could show leniency when the situation called for it. Two weeks later the *Fortune* departed Tahiti, according to Jones, "as an orderly ship."[27]

After returning to Matavia Bay, Jones gave his crew liberty and met with several English missionaries and Pomare IV. He also ordered the sloop's cannon to be fired and a feast to be held aboard the *Peacock*. The ceremony apparently impressed the young queen, for some three years later she wrote President Andrew Jackson that Jones had treated her people with great kindness. Jones wanted to restore a sense of order to the island and "nip in the bud those evils" such as mutiny, so he provided Pomare with a translated copy of the regulations that had been prepared previously at Tahiti and explained the provisions. On 7 September 1826, after surveying the harbor, Jones departed for the island of Raiatea.[28]

The voyage to Raiatea, some 130 miles west by northwest of Tahiti, took less than two days. After first attending a church service ashore, Jones met with King Tamatoa and his entourage, which included Revs. Williams and Pitman of the London Foreign Missionary Society. Tamatoa acknowledged the sovereignty of Pomare when Jones gave him a copy of the agreement drafted at Tahiti and informed him that the queen approved of the arrangement. But the king, apparently at the behest of the missionaries, refused to accept the treaty. Instead he asked Jones ten questions, which were later submitted in writing.[29]

Jones's written responses to the questions offer further evidence of his diplomatic sensibility and his desire to establish U.S. influence in the region. Believing that the United States was a British colony like Australia and New South Wales, Tamatoa asked if the British consul knew of the articles and, if so, what were his thoughts about them. Jones replied that the British consul's consent was not needed because the United States was a free and independent country. That answer astonished the king and forced him to reevaluate his position. Several of Tamatoa's other questions concerned the role a U.S. consul would play on the island. Jones tried to reassure the king that a consul would not interfere with domestic activities, nor would such an official bring the evils the king anticipated. A consul, Jones contended, would merely represent the United States on the island. In an attempt to alleviate Tamatoa's fears, Jones added a concluding nonentanglement article that he believed would win the king's immediate approval: the treaty would expire on 31 December 1830 unless voluntarily renewed by both parties.[30]

Over the next ten days Jones met with the king and his advisers on several occasions in an attempt to convince Tamatoa of his good faith. Before Jones departed on 18 September the king informed him that he wished to remain on friendly terms with the United States. Tamatoa offered free use of the port of Raiatea to American ships. He also promised support should the United States be at war with a foreign nation, unless that nation were Great Britain, in which case Raiatea would remain neutral. Jones had to be satisfied with the arrangement, but he believed that had he remained there longer he could have persuaded Tamatoa to sign a formal treaty of friendship and commerce.[31]

Jones intended to sail toward Bora Bora, but heavy winds, a strong current from the west, and squalls forced him north to Hawaii instead. After twenty-two days at sea, on 11 October, the *Peacock* anchored in spacious Honolulu harbor, which, according to Jones, had no equal in the Pacific. The city was the residence of the royal family as well as the center of trade and commerce for the island group. It boasted a population of "7 to 9,000 inhabitants and about 200 foreigners . . . with two very able, well-kept hotels, several billiard tables, ball alleys and tippling or dram shops never failing bane of good order and industry." Honolulu also had nearly two thousand "huge hay bricks," or thatch houses, and was protected by a "mud fort" containing forty guns and two hundred uniformed soldiers. The city encompassed the most cosmopolitan village Jones had seen since he began his mission.[32]

The Hawaiians were not pleased by the presence of another warship flying the Stars and Stripes. "Mad Jack" and the *Dolphin* had departed only five months earlier, and that officer's escapades remained fresh in the minds of the islanders. Although Jones was obviously not Percival, the Hawaiian leaders were unsure of his intentions. Two days after anchoring Jones went ashore to meet with Prime Minister Karaimoku, eleven-year-old King Kaikeoule, and Governor Boki of Oahu. Karaimoku, acting for the king in the absence of Queen Regent Elisabeta Kaahumanu, offered free provisions for the *Peacock*'s crew, which Jones politely refused. The prime minister also made available to Jones a two-story frame house on the harbor and a purebred saddle horse from the royal stables, which Jones accepted; he used both the house and the horse for the duration of his stay. Jones also talked with missionaries Hiram Bingham and Elisha Loomis to learn more about the islands. He conferred almost daily with the ministers and used Loomis, a printer by trade, to translate his letters into the Hawaiian language.[33]

Jones reported to the Navy Department that the Hawaiian Islands had been overrun by escaped—or perhaps even released—British convicts

from Botany Bay. These criminals, he insisted, were slowly and system-
atically taking control of all the islands in the South Pacific. Jones surmised that should any war begin between the United States and Great
Britain, the criminals would conduct "predatory warfare upon our
defenceless commerce and whale fisheries in the Pacific" and ultimately
assume economic control over the entire region. He concluded that the
growing influence of this "refuse of human species" [convicts] was part
of a British conspiracy. Jones tried to sway the islanders to the American
side, but he instead found them influenced by John Bull.³⁴

According to Jones, he had to suppress a mutiny or round up deserters in virtually every harbor he visited, which prompted him to conclude
that "there is no Law round Cape Horn." The power exercised by the
captains of whaling ships further compounded the problem of lawlessness in the Pacific. Generally the ships sailed from New England with
only a skeleton crew and recruited men for the hunt after they reached
the Hawaiian Islands. Seamen who signed on for a season's cruise, generally with an oral contract, were treated so harshly that many of them
deserted whenever their ships landed. They sacrificed their pay and their
share of the cargo while the captains and permanent skeleton crews
reaped significant benefits. It was an abusive relationship that left crewmen angry, hostile, and sometimes willing to risk their lives in mutiny.

Jones informed King Kaikeoule that the desertion problem was creating anarchy. If something was not done to restore order, the safety of
American merchants and traders could not be ensured, nor could continued trade between the United States and the islands be guaranteed.
The king responded to Jones's letter with a copy in English of the port
regulations, which included several provisions covering desertions. Jones
studied these and offered several suggestions. One stipulated that all
American seamen who had deserted while in the islands would be immediately removed by U.S. warships, regardless of the circumstances surrounding the event or how long ago the desertion occurred (this rule
would affect Herman Melville seventeen years later). Likewise, any
American without visible means of livelihood would be removed from
the islands. Last, Jones suggested that "all other foreigners who did not
support a good character" should also be deported.

On the morning of 1 November Jones met with Governor Boki, U.S.
commercial agent John Coffin Jones, and English consul Richard Charlton. Acting on Jones's order of the previous day, these men had directed

the apprehension of some thirty deserters. Jones and the others then
questioned the men to determine their status. Most of them had will-
ingly signed aboard whaling ships at anchor in port, but some agreed to
join the *Peacock* rather than face incarceration. Only "one or two . . . of
notorious bad character" were placed in a Hawaiian prison. In a matter
of days Jones, supported by the Hawaiian government, had settled one
of the most pressing problems on the islands and thereby won the
respect of the Hawaiian chiefs.[35]

Jones realized that the Hawaiians were "a cautious, grave deliberate
people, extremely jealous of their rights as a nation, and slow to enter
into any treaty or compact with foreigners by which the latter can gain
any foothold or claim to their soil." He learned from the missionaries
that in 1823 the Russians had feigned friendship with the Hawaiians
and afterward tried to erect a fort on the island of Kauai, but the
Hawaiians quickly "put a stop to the clandestine encroachment of their
false friends." From this episode Jones concluded that he would have to
be forthright with the islanders, and in order to demonstrate his good
intentions he had all of his correspondence translated into the native
language. He also learned never to press his point when the Hawaiians
seemed disinclined, even in the slightest sense. His understanding of
the islanders and his honesty brought diplomatic success, ultimately
allowing him to arbitrate some of the more serious disputes between
the government and merchants and between the merchants and the
clergy.[36]

One of the most pressing problems facing the islands concerned large
debts owed by the Hawaiian government. When Jones arrived, he was
approached by American merchant John C. Jones, who reported that
traders on the islands hoped the presence of the *Peacock* would persuade
the chiefs to pay their debts. The Hawaiians did not realize the extent of
what they owed. Since most did not read or write English, they knew
nothing of Western banking practices, including the concepts of principal and interest. And the debts owed were not theirs alone, for much had
been inherited from the extravagant King Liholiho and the late King
Kamehameha. Merchant creditors insisted that the government owed
almost $500,000. Jones did not readily accept the estimates of the mer-
chants, however. Instead he studied the situation and conducted extensive
interviews with the merchants, missionaries, and government officials
before he contacted the king.[37]

The merchants demanded immediate action on the debts and insisted that Jones use his influence to settle them. They impatiently visited him again in early December to press their point. By then Jones thought he understood the debt issue and urged the chiefs to settle. Yet on 14 December, when Jones finally met with the king and chiefs to discuss the matter, he found that they were not prepared to consider either their arrears or the draft of a proposed treaty that he had sent the king in mid-November. Although frustrated by the islanders' lack of action, Jones tried to avoid a dictatorial tone in his subsequent communications. Even so, he indicated that the United States had "the *will*, as well as the power to enforce [compliance] when other, and more pacifistic measures were disregarded." After this threatening suggestion, negotiations on both the debt question and the treaty moved forward quickly.

When Jones suggested that $200,000 was closer to the sum owed by the chiefs to the merchants, both parties surprisingly agreed. Although the islanders did not have such a large sum in specie, they did have access to the sandalwood that grew along the island's mountains, and the women produced high-quality mats and tapa cloth. On 27 December all parties agreed that the government would pay fifteen thousand piculs (each picul weighing 133.33 pounds) of sandalwood; the estimated value of the aromatic wood was between $120,000 and $160,000 depending on its quality and where it was marketed.[38]

Jones also suggested to the king and chiefs a taxation system that would produce the needed revenue. He proposed that before 1 September 1827, every Hawaiian man should either provide the government with one-half picul of sandalwood or pay four Spanish dollars. Every female aged thirteen and older would give the government one reed mat twelve feet long by six feet wide, tapa cloth of equal value, or one Spanish dollar. A unique incentive in Jones's proposal was that every man could harvest a maximum of one picul of sandalwood. After delivering one-half picul to the government he was "entitled to sell the other half, on his own account, to whomsoever he may think proper." This combined for the islanders a profit motive with their treaty obligations.[39]

Jones, trying to act as an unbiased "umpire between the parties," believed his solution was fair and equitable and not a burden for the islanders. Others did not agree. Years later he recalled that he would not have permitted himself "for a moment to think of laying so heavy a tax upon this generous people." But in fact Jones had inadvertently levied a heavy tax on the Hawaiian commoners, for they had to bear the burden of paying the debt. It was apparent that the treaty and questions of debt and property were imposed from a Western rather than Hawaiian perspective. Equally important, Jones had implied the use of force to settle the disagreement. The merchants accused him of "taking the side of the chiefs," while others accused him of siding with the merchants and claimed that "the Hawaiian people suffered an injustice through [his] actions." Critics charged that Jones took "advantage of a poor and ignorant people, on strictly *ex-parte* statements." More than fifty years later, Hawaiian nationalists maintained that Jones "bribed" the chiefs and regency with presents and entertainment; and had the islanders not agreed to his proposal, Jones had "behind him the guns of his ship to give force to his persuasions." Indeed, Jones had implied the use of force to settle the disagreement, but he did not think that his settlement was anything but fair. Unfortunately the agreement did hasten the destruction of the sandalwood forests, which thereafter left the islanders in a perpetual state of poverty until the popularity of tourism in the twentieth century brought new life to Hawaii's economy.[40]

While negotiations over the debt and the commercial treaty were going on, Jones learned of a growing conflict between the merchants and traders on the islands and a select group of missionaries that stemmed from the growing influence of the church. Apparently the merchants were angry because the missionaries encouraged constant religious worship and ceremonies rather than work or other commercial activities. One critic remarked that "nothing but the sound of the church going bell is heard from the rising to the setting sun," and claimed that the island's newfound orthodoxy brought nothing but distress, governmental ineffectiveness, a business slump, and even unusually rainy weather. Some traders even maintained that the missionaries had violated foreigners' rights on the pretense of saving souls.[41]

John C. Jones, English consul Charlton, and Governor Boki—the leaders of the antimissionary movement—joined with most foreign residents of the port to spread rumors that challenged the missionaries' motives and policies. The missionaries responded by appointing a committee, which announced that the church had not tried and would not try to influence politics on the island. But the missionaries also insisted they would continue to fight vice and inform the islanders of the laws of God and the laws adopted by Christian nations. The missionaries invited anyone who questioned their motives or their political or commercial influence to submit a written challenge.[42]

A group of merchants including John C. Jones and Charlton called on Jones to serve as an impartial judge in the dispute with the missionaries, unaware that Jones was a devout Presbyterian who supported the missionaries' work. Nor did they know that he had been given explicit instructions to support the missionaries when possible. On the morning of 8 December, the merchants and missionaries met with Jones at the home of Governor Boki. The missionaries had come prepared with an impressive array of documents supporting their case, including letters written on their behalf by the chiefs. The only documentary evidence produced by the merchants was a letter, signed by twelve Honolulu merchants, demanding an investigation of the mission. When the meeting began Consul Charlton attacked the chiefs, the mission schools, and even the missionaries themselves, charging that religion was being emphasized at the expense of all else. He claimed that farmlands were lying idle, work was not being completed, and people were starving.

Rev. Richard Williams retorted that the missionaries had neither violated the law nor ignored their Christian duty. He insisted that until the merchants presented specific charges against the missionaries, in writing, there would not "be anything for us to do, either offensive or defensive." Charlton, flushed and seething with anger, screamed that no chief would dare testify against any of the missionaries and it was therefore impossible to assemble any evidence against them. After a moment of silence Jones rose and proposed that the ministers' petition be read aloud so that all present would understand its intent. Afterward Jones commented that although "he did not appear as the advocate of the missionaries, . . . he thought their circular was full and fair." He then reprimanded the merchants for not corroborating their allegations. Jones concluded that the meeting should be adjourned unless anyone could prove, in writing, that the missionaries had acted immorally. When no one brought forth accusations or evidence, Jones dismissed the meeting.[43]

After the meeting Jones issued a circular giving his opinion of the entire affair. In it he said that he "trembled for the cause of Christianity and for the poor benighted islanders" when they were confronted by "the British Consul, backed by the most wealthy . . . and influential residents and shipmasters in formidable array." As the impartial judge he saw "half a dozen meek and humble servants of the Lord, . . . ready and anxious to be tried by their bitterest enemies, who on this occasion occupied the *quadruple station of judge, jury, witness, and prosecutor.*" Jones claimed that the meeting was more than a complaint against the missionaries; it was designed "to overthrow the mission, and uproot the seeds of civilization and Christianity." He would not allow all that the missionaries had worked for to be destroyed by merchants interested only in personal profit.

In one short meeting Jones earned the respect and friendship of the missionaries and, more important, the chiefs. His fair-handed management of the merchant-missionary dispute, moreover, paved the way for a decision concluding the debt question and for negotiating a commercial treaty between the United States and Hawaii. More important, Jones appeared as a champion of the missionaries, whose influence greatly strengthened the bonds of friendship between the Hawaiians and the United States.[44]

Monday, 22 December 1826, the day set for the official signing of the treaty between the Hawaiian Islands and the United States, was a solemn day for Jones and his seamen, who had just learned of the deaths of Thomas Jefferson and John Adams the previous Fourth of July. Jones ordered a full military procession of marines and sailors ashore to honor the former presidents. It was an especially sad day for Jones because Jefferson had signed the midshipman's warrant that had started his naval career. After the opening ceremony Jones, adorned in full military dress including sword and gold braids, met with the chiefs at the home of ailing Prime Minister Karaimoku. The chiefs were dressed in their best "dove-colored satin and brocaded silks," and the ministers appeared in formal black suits with white collars. At Karaimoku's request Rev. Bingham offered a prayer, and the formal "Articles of Arrangement" were presented for the chiefs to sign.[45]

Richard Charlton rose in protest before anyone could sign the documents. The consul argued that the islanders "were mere tenants at will, subjects of Great Britain," and could agree to no formal treaty without the approval of King George IV. The chiefs, confused and startled, looked to Jones for reassurance. He did not disappoint them.

Jones slowly rose and asked the Englishman what type of commission he held. Charlton responded that the British king had named him "Consul General to the Sandwich Islands" and that he had authority to appoint vice consuls for the other islands of the region. That was exactly what Jones wanted to hear. Jones then asked the consul to explain the duties and functions of a consul general. Charlton, annoyed by this seemingly pointless line of questioning, angrily retorted that his obligations were "in accordance with the acknowledged international understanding of the office." Again, that was the answer Jones anticipated. Jones continued by asking Charlton if a king ever sent a consul, a consul general, or even commercial agents to any port or place within his own dominions. The Englishman, trapped by his own words, could not answer without completely undermining his entire argument. According to Jones, Richard Charlton "was dum-founded."

Once the interchange had been translated to the chiefs the regent Kaahumanu came forward and signed her Christian name, Elisabeta, in big, bold letters. Prime Minister Karaimoku, Governor Boki, and several chiefs did likewise. Last, Thomas ap Catesby Jones signed as the lone American representative.[46]

In this one episode Jones virtually destroyed the credibility Richard Charlton had spent years trying to create. Jones had informed the islanders that they could govern themselves without instructions or directions from England. He had also taught them that the United States and Great Britain were equals. British influence in the islands would be greatly weakened after this and would further deteriorate as the missionaries converted the islanders to Christianity and surreptitiously moved them closer to the United States. Jones's diplomatic victory against the British must have brought him great satisfaction and perhaps even a morsel of revenge for the defeat he had suffered at the hands of British soldiers in the Battle of Lake Borgne.

The seven "Articles of Arrangement" was the first treaty signed by the Hawaiians. It gave the United States most favored nation status, protected American commerce, required Hawaiian officials to suppress desertion, and compelled the islanders to assist in the salvaging of shipwrecked American vessels. The agreement gave much to the United States and offered little to the Hawaiians in return. Despite its apparent advantages, however, the treaty was never formally approved by the Senate. Critics charged that Jones had overstepped his authority and had drafted an unsanctioned agreement. Regardless, both the State Department and the Hawaiian government considered the document "morally binding" and continued to respect its provisions. All subsequent agreements between the two parties would be based on Jones's 1826 "Articles of Arrangements."[47]

The *Peacock* remained at Honolulu until 6 January 1827. During eighty-seven days in port Jones had settled the desertion problem, the missionary-merchant dispute, and the debt question. He had overstepped Hull's orders, but he had successfully negotiated a commercial treaty; he had entertained lavishly, thereby winning allies in the islands; and, most important, he had raised the American flag in the South Pacific, demonstrating his understanding of the importance of nationalistic expansion. Although Jones always contended that his generosity won the friendship of the islanders, his implied use of force was undoubtedly more influential. Regardless of whether he had the carrot or the stick to thank for his success, Jones had spent far more money than had been authorized by the Navy Department, and he had to pay most of the expenses himself. Later he would feel that his efforts had not been appreciated, but as he departed Honolulu Jones was pleased with himself. He reported that he heard an "aloha" from every open door. Moreover, Queen Regent Kaahumanu, King Kaikeoule, Governor Boki, and even John C. Jones joined Jones onboard the *Peacock* for one last meal. After dining, all the guests departed except for the queen regent, who stayed with the ship until it sailed over the sandbar at the mouth of Honolulu harbor. When the sloop departed, the "mud fort" fired a twenty-one-gun salute. Afterward Kaahumanu and the harbor pilot returned to Honolulu.[48]

Jones did not have enough time to visit California before returning to South America. Instead the *Peacock* sailed to San Blas, Mexico, arriving there in only twenty-five days. It was a remarkably quick trip, especially since the sloop battled a full gale and tumultuous seas for two days. The rough trip took its toll. The *Peacock* began to leak profusely along its seams and desperately needed caulking. Once repairs began Jones learned that the outside boards were so rotten that they could not be mended. Crewmen had to caulk and recaulk the seams as well as to operate pumps continually in order to slow the rising water within the ship's hold.

While at San Blas Jones heard rumors that the disagreements between the United States and Great Britain over the Maine-Canadian boundary had escalated into war. Wanting confirmation before he took any hostile action, Jones remained at San Blas for a month awaiting news from the U.S. ambassador to Mexico, Joel R. Poinsett. Finally, on 7 March, Jones received a dispatch from Poinsett informing him that there was no war. Two days later the *Peacock* departed for Lima.[49]

During the voyage south the sloop took on ten to fifteen inches of water an hour. The rising water level spoiled food and contaminated the drinking water, ultimately forcing Jones to put his men on short rations. Another unexpected problem occurred on 22 March when a large sperm whale collided with the sloop, the second whale collision during the voyage. And although the first collision was not noteworthy, this one felt as if "the ship had struck a rock." Jones believed they were extremely fortunate because the whale had only glanced off the ship. Had there been a direct impact the sloop probably would have sunk. More bad luck resulted from a storm front near the Galápagos Islands that slowed the sloop and forced further reductions in the crew's rations.[50]

The 348-day South Pacific adventure did not end until the *Peacock* arrived at Callao on 14 May 1827. During the next six weeks Jones gave the crew much-needed liberty, secured food and water, and had the ship temporarily repaired. For nine days, caulkers from Commo. Jacob Jones's flagship, the *Brandywine,* worked on the sloop to stop the leaks. They were not entirely successful, but they did slow the rising water level to a rate of about two inches per hour. Finally, on 25 June, the *Peacock* set sail around Cape Horn, bound for the United States.

The homeward voyage was extremely difficult as the sloop encountered snow, ice, sleet, and high seas. Jones knew the dangers associated with the trip around the Horn. He demanded that his seamen maintain a constant vigil and measure the water and air temperatures hourly; a sudden drop in the water temperature would indicate the proximity of floating ice, perhaps an iceberg that could slice through the sloop's rotten wooden shell. This prudent attention to detail ensured a safe voyage, and on 11 August the *Peacock* anchored in Rio de Janeiro.[51]

While in Rio, Jones drafted a letter to the Navy Department recounting his deeds in the South Pacific. He also finished a long report to the navy secretary on U.S. commercial possibilities in the Pacific. The Pacific trade, Jones claimed, could be extremely profitable and should be exploited only by the United States. As this commerce increased, U.S. merchant vessels would begin to dominate trade between the Pacific coast of North and South America and the coast of China. Jones anticipated an increasingly important role for the navy in this maritime version of Manifest Destiny because merchant and whaling ships flying the Stars and Stripes would have to be protected. His comprehensive report soon became the primary source of information about commercial possibilities in the Pacific and offered a materialistic reason why the American flag should be flying in the Pacific.[52]

The voyage from Rio to New York took only two months, and the sloop arrived home in late October 1827. After the crew had been discharged and the ship's accounts settled, Jones returned to Sharon, where he relaxed near a feather cape given to him as a gesture of friendship by the Hawaiian government.[53] Jones was extremely proud of his accomplishments during his first independent command. He had shown the flag in the Pacific and had momentarily broken the British hegemony over the region. The United States did not replace Great Britain as the major power in the Pacific, especially in Tahiti and the Marquesas; nor did the country immediately exploit Jones's successes. The United States did, however, gain a foothold in the region that it would not relinquish. Jones had demonstrated that he thought in broad terms of strategy and national objectives; he wrote thoughtful reports on commerce, naval deployments, and communication and cooperation; he negotiated diplomatic agreements with several island governments; and he brought stability to a region previously devoid of law and order. In the end, Jones had ably performed his duty and would be fondly remembered by many in the Hawaiian Islands as *"the kind eyed chief."*[54]

~⭑5⭑~

THE DIE IS CAST
The Pacific Exploring Expedition, 1828–1837

*M*ary Walker Carter Jones and young Meriwether Jones were happy to see Thomas ap Catesby return to Sharon in early November 1827. He had been away for more than two years, and much had changed in his absence. Little Meriwether was now an energetic three-year-old toddler. Twenty-four-year-old Mary, who had been new to farm life, had ably maintained the family farm in her husband's absence; the crop yield had remained constant and the farm's number of slaves had increased by 14 percent.[1]

The squire of Sharon was on leave from active duty, but he still had to travel to Philadelphia, Washington, and Boston on navy business during the winter of 1827 and the spring of 1828. Such trips must have been an aggravation. Jones wanted to settle into his northern Virginia home and spend more time with his family, but duty and financial necessity always prompted him to fulfill the secretary of the navy's orders.[2]

Jones had spent far more money during his cruise in the Pacific than his official allowance, and he expected the Navy Department to repay him. When he learned in late January 1828 that the department would not reimburse him, he was very disappointed. Southard informed him that vessels such as the *Peacock* were "provided expressly for Master Commandants," and those who commanded them would not be paid as much as captains, regardless of the circumstances.[3]

In April Southard sent Jones to Boston to serve on a court of inquiry examining John "Mad Jack" Percival's actions in the Pacific. More than a year earlier Jones had written a detailed yet "calm [and] dispassionate narrative of facts" about Percival's mission and had concluded that the lieutenant left a "foul stain . . . upon the American Naval and National Character." The trip to Boston brought the accuser and defendant face-to-face. The trip also offered Jones the opportunity to recoup some of his lost money, especially if he spent his and his servant's per diem judiciously during the prolonged inquiry. While the board of officers found insufficient evidence to court-martial Percival for his conduct, the opportunity for remuneration made it a satisfactory service for Jones.[4]

By the summer of 1828 Jones was back in Fairfax County overseeing his growing farm operations. During the nine years that he had owned Sharon, Jones had reclaimed exhausted farmlands; planted ornamental and fruit orchards; and constructed a beautiful stone home, a small stone overseer's house, dwellings for his slaves, two barns, and a tavern at the corner of his estate. Financing these improvements severely cut into his meager salary, even with the eight hundred dollars a year in rent he received from the tavern.[5]

Jones, a classic Virginia gentleman farmer from a patrician background, wanted to emulate the affluent lifestyle of his ancestors. Yet he almost always spent more than his salary in pursuit of a comfortable existence, and this left him perpetually in debt and scrambling for additional money. Moreover, his wealth was in land and slaves, and while both were considerable, neither could be liquidated at a moment's notice to cover unexpected expenses. By the end of 1828 Jones's financial problems had not improved. He had to sell two slaves in addition to several head of livestock just to meet his obligations. His money problems would be momentarily forgotten, however, when in mid-November 1828 Secretary of the Navy Samuel Southard named him commander of the South Pacific Exploring Expedition.[6]

In the 1820s the United States was experiencing a cultural revolution that promoted, among other things, science and exploration. In 1822 Congress had received several memorials requesting that the government outfit a scientific expedition to explore the Arctic. Congress took no action on those memorials until Jeremiah Reynolds, the editor of the *Wilmington (Ohio) Spectator*, conducted a newspaper campaign and lecture tour that gained widespread support for such a venture.

Reynolds was wise enough to evoke all the possibilities of such an expedition—nationalistic, scientific, and commercial. He knew that the support of merchants and ship owners would greatly improve his prospects for winning government funding, as these groups could exert tremendous pressure on Congress. Among other benefits of the expedition Reynolds claimed that scientists might find the winter retreat of seals, which would be an economic godsend for the declining whaling industry. But in the process of refining his proposal Reynolds decided that a voyage south to Antarctica would be more realistic than a northern trip, especially as scientists believed that ice formed only near land, and there was less land in the Southern Hemisphere. Besides, compared with the northern polar regions, the Antarctic was virtually unknown and thus provided greater opportunities for exploration. By 1828 Reynolds's campaign had gained a number of converts, the most influential of whom was President John Quincy Adams, and had evolved into an exploration of the commercial possibilities of the South Pacific.[7]

Reynolds had done his homework. He had contacted ships' captains for information, and he had read numerous logs, journals, and Navy Department reports and letters. From this information he had compiled an impressive survey of economic activity in the region. Included within his exhaustive presentation was information about the recent Pacific expedition of the sloop *Peacock* as well as Jones's suggestion that another voyage "would open to our commercial, and national interest, sources of great wealth." Armed with this additional information Reynolds again approached Congress about a mission, and on 21 May 1828, the House of Representatives requested that President Adams send a ship to explore the southern Pacific.[8]

Adams ordered Secretary Southard to fulfill Congress's request as quickly as possible, before that body could change its mind. In response, Southard began examining the numerous applications for the scientific and naval positions available and had Commo. Isaac Chauncey rebuild the *Peacock*. The secretary also detached Lt. Charles Wilkes, a twenty-seven-year-old New Yorker from a prominent and influential family, to Europe to gather the astronomical instruments the expedition would need.[9]

Southard chose Jones as commander of the expedition against the unsolicited advice of Wilkes. The lieutenant of only two years, a self-proclaimed scientific expert who thought he had gained Southard's confidence, arrogantly reviewed the navy's entire list of officers and concluded that he alone had the experience and scientific expertise to command this important expedition. Wilkes also maintained that the "flaming Jacksonian" Jones had gotten his appointment only because of his association with the Hero; he insisted that Jones would not be "anything remarkable."[10]

Although Wilkes had a poor opinion of Jones's capabilities, the young lieutenant understood the navy's chain of command and the behavior expected of junior officers. Wilkes was publicly and professionally politic, although in private he could be and often was otherwise. He didn't fool everyone. Reynolds believed that Wilkes was "exceedingly vain and conceited," and Southard contended that the lieutenant had to be constantly watched. Jones, too, soon came to realize that Wilkes had his own ambitious agenda. Publicly Wilkes showed deference to both Southard and Jones in his attempt to gain promotion and favor, but ultimately he wanted command of the mission for himself. Ten years later, in 1838, his efforts would finally pay off and he would secure that command.[11]

The planned voyage, albeit dangerous, offered an unparalleled opportunity for promotion and advancement. Midshipmen, lieutenants, whaling captains, artists, doctors, and journalists all sought appointments. For Jones, the expedition would provide the honorary rank as well as the pay of a commanding officer; it would also improve his chances for promotion to captain. Prompted by these considerations, Jones traveled to New York, where the Peacock had been readied under Chauncey's supervision.[12]

Soon after Jones's appointment as its commander, however, the South Pacific Exploring Expedition was engulfed by the political deadlock that accompanied the waning months of Adams's presidency. Andrew Jackson, the "Hero of New Orleans," had won a comfortable victory in the recent election, and power was soon to pass to him and his supporters. Anything that smacked of Adams, including the expedition, was anathema to them. The Navy Board of Commissioners, knowing where their bread was soon to be buttered, began expressing hostility to Secretary Southard's appointments, many of which had been made either without consulting Jones or against his recommendation. This political wrangling disenchanted Jones and prompted him to consider resigning his appointment. But reason prevailed. Within two months Andrew Jackson would be president, and Jones speculated that the general would surely remember the sacrifice he had made in Lake Borgne in 1814. Jones continued his preparations and directed Wilkes to gather scientific

instruments, even though he did not believe the expedition would sail
before the next session of Congress convened in August.[13]

Jones was overly optimistic in his assumption about the departure date;
the expedition did not sail for another ten years. During February 1829
Jacksonians in Congress defeated funding measures for the expedition.
Although saddened by the news of the defeat, Jones continued his normal duties, hoping that the succeeding administration would not associate him with Adams or the blackballed mission. Jackson's newly appointed
secretary of the navy, North Carolinian John Branch, eased Jones's mis-
givings when on 17 March 1829 he signed Jones's promotion to captain.
Since the secretary's appointment had been confirmed by the Senate
only eight days earlier, General and now President Jackson most likely
did advance Jones's career.[14]

Jones's promotion did not end his money problems. In early February
1829 he had made financial preparations for his prospective voyage by
negotiating a three-thousand-dollar loan with the Washington branch of
the Bank of the United States, using some of his land for collateral. He
planned for his wife to use the money for expenses while he was away at
sea. The conditions of the loan required him to repay the bank five hundred dollars a year during his three-year or longer absence. The money
would be drawn annually from the Navy Department, and the remainder of the loan would be due within sixty days of Jones's return to the
United States. But when Congress refused to approve the mission, the
bank recalled the note. In a polite but firm reply Jones maintained that
he was not required to repay the entire loan immediately. Contending
that he did not want "to create difficulty," he assured the bank that
"*each* and *every* section of the contract by which [he was] *morally* or
lawfully bound [would] be faithfully executed." The contract had been
legally filed with the Fairfax County Court, and he planned to fulfill the
spirit and letter of the contract's provisions, especially since it benefited
him financially.[15]

With the expedition canceled, Jones sought another assignment, but
he knew there was intense competition among many officers for the few
available positions. After learning of a suitable vacancy in mid-June, he
asked to replace Capt. Alexander S. Wadsworth as inspector of ordnance
for the navy, a position he had held earlier in his career. Secretary
Branch granted his request, and Jones began a job that he would hold
for almost five years.[16]

The ordnance branch, like most divisions of the U.S. Navy in the years between the War of 1812 and the Civil War, lagged woefully behind its European counterparts. In 1824 French artillerist Gen. Henri J. Paixhans had developed the shell gun, which fired a hollow missile filled with powder. The shell exploded on or soon after impact, rendering even the strongest wooden warships utterly vulnerable. The Stevens family of Hoboken, New Jersey, had performed successful experiments with shells some ten years earlier than Paixhans, but neither the navy nor the government had expressed interest in technological innovations then.

Jones, as inspector of ordnance, reported directly to the three-member U.S. Navy Board of Commissioners, which advised the secretary of the navy on all matters related to construction, equipment, and repair. The inspector was the board's expert on guns, small arms, powder, and ammunition, and as such Jones was required to examine, test, store, and mark all guns and ordnance stores for the department. Jones was neither a John A. Dahlgren nor a Matthew F. Maury, both of whom made significant technological contributions to the service. While Jones did not develop a new type of gun or shell, however, he did systemize the testing and cataloging of weapons and he introduced a method of organization that vividly illustrated the navy's ordnance shortcomings.

Although he was based at the Washington Navy Yard, which under the command of Commo. Isaac Hull was slowly being transformed from a storage facility for seagoing vessels to a naval gun factory, Jones's work frequently took him to navy yards and foundries throughout the country. He also traveled widely to serve on courts-martial and on boards of inquiry as requested by the secretary of the navy. In addition, he regularly wrote thoughtful replies to departmental circulars, and in doing so demonstrated his understanding of seemingly difficult and controversial issues.[17]

Working out of his home allowed Jones to keep a constant eye on his domestic affairs, something he had not done since before his trip to the Pacific. In 1829 Mary gave birth to another son, Mark Catesby, the middle name continuing the Jones family tradition of giving sons the name carried by the child's father and paternal grandfather. By summer Jones had finally settled his late sister's estate by dividing the slaves among the heirs. He acquired several of those slaves, increasing his own holding to twenty-six (twenty-three of whom were adults), and he secured five more horses (increasing his herd to nine). Jones aggressively applied manure secured from the livestock that stopped at the tavern and stagecoach depot on his property to increase his clay-based soil's production of grass and grains, and it began paying dividends.

In the spring of 1830, at a public auction, Jones and his brother Roger finally secured legal right to the family estate, which had been tied up in probate since their mother's death. The two, without opposition, paid only $343.13 for the 1,325 acres of land they had been occupying. Soon after acquiring legal title to the land Jones informed one of his tenants that she would have to vacate her premises; he intended to increase his revenue from that piece of property.[18]

Jones traveled to and from Valley Forge on navy business and supervised the preparation of his land for planting. During the previous winter he had applied lime and plaster (gypsum), which he secured cheaply in nearby Georgetown. Together with the manure, these additives greatly improved his soil. Also that spring Jones began a revealing experiment. He set aside one acre of land and for the next seven years planted different crops and measured their productivity. In 1831 he sowed Dutch and winter red-top turnips, and the crop yielded six hundred bushels that sold for $150. Surprisingly, the turnip crop produced his best single-year income on that plot. In later years Jones rotated wheat, clover, and corn but never earned more than $52.50 for any single harvest. He lamented that in 1833 the wheat "lodged and did not fill well"; in 1835 he had "another bad wheat year (blossoms washed off by hard rains)." Although his wheat did not fare well, the clover he planted in 1834 and 1836 thrived, and ultimately the two crops sold for $100.50. After this lengthy experiment Jones posited that fertilizing land was essential for enhancing its productivity, and that lime helped reduce the acidity of the soil and stimulated production. By using these additives, he concluded, a farmer could resurrect acreage that "was utterly worthless" and make a profit of about $50 per acre per year.[19]

Had Jones planted all his available land with turnips in 1831 perhaps he could have settled most of his outstanding accounts. But his experiment was with only one acre. The remainder of his land was sowed in wheat, corn, rye, oats, and clover, none of which produced the revenue needed to clear his debts. Ultimately he was forced to borrow money from Georgetown's Bank of the Valley to meet his obligations. Perhaps it was these financial troubles that prompted him to join with eleven other officers during the spring of 1832 to petition Congress for increased salaries. Their petition extolled their sacrifices and pleaded, unfortunately to no avail, for financial relief.[20]

Jones was becoming annoyed with a bureaucracy that delayed or denied decisions on his pension and on increases in salary. In September 1832 he tried another approach when he wrote Secretary of the Navy Levi Woodbury asking for an increase in his per diem and travel expenses. Such an increase would help offset his current loss of revenue, especially since he traveled extensively while performing his duties as inspector of ordnance. Woodbury reminded Jones that Congress fixed those expenditures and any changes had to be approved by special legislative action. Woodbury did tell Jones that he could file a petition to be submitted to Congress.[21]

In January 1833 Jones began his most important mission as inspector of ordnance. The commissioners sent him to naval stations at Portsmouth, New Hampshire; Charlestown, Massachusetts; Gosport, Virginia; Brooklyn, New York; Philadelphia, Pennsylvania; and Washington, D.C., to test every weapon that the department had stored at those facilities. Realizing that this job would be far too much work for one person, Jones asked the secretary if Cornelius K. Stribling, "an experienced and intelligent lieutenant," could serve as his assistant. Stribling's help would "insure *uniformity*" and provide the navy with another ordnance specialist, as well as lessen his own workload. Woodbury agreed.[22]

Jones gathered the cylinder gauges, weights, and other equipment he needed to examine the ordnance. Unfortunately there were no gauges at the Washington Navy Yard, and it would be almost three months before one could be cast at the West Point Foundry. Jones also compared the navy yard's measuring weights with ones located at the Philadelphia Mint. After balancing the yard's weights, Jones departed for Portsmouth.[23]

The job of an ordnance officer was arduous, tiring, and demanding. And because of its importance, Jones believed that ordnance officers should be paid at the same rate as those of similar rank on shore duty. He argued that it cost more to be an ordnance officer than any other position he had ever held. Working among "greasy arms, rusty guns and in dusty foundries and gun smith's shops" soiled and stained his clothing. The "abuse to clothing [was] far greater than [for] any other officer in the navy." Nonetheless, as inspector he had to appear at the various establishments dressed in full uniform to maintain the dignity and respect of the service.[24]

At each navy yard Jones took an inventory of all ordnance and stores before categorizing them by type. Although inspecting ordnance may sound like a simple duty, it was not. At most facilities Jones had to clean rust from guns and shot before he could begin properly testing each weapon. Jones deplored the conditions under which the navy's guns were held. In New York he found the yard's guns stored in a location that left most of them exposed to ocean spray from breaking waves. Some guns, to his amazement, were even completely submerged when the tide was unusually high. How could the service be expected to rely on these guns, he wondered, and why was the navy surprised when they failed?[25]

Once a weapon had been cleaned, Jones closely examined it for even the slightest imperfection and noted any that were present. Next, he recorded and designated the weapons by their type or class (e.g., 24- or 32-pounders) and marked each with an index number painted on the gun's breech. He also labeled every weapon within each class with an alphabetical letter painted on the gun's pomiglion or cascabel (the rear part of a gun consisting of the base of the breech, ring, fillet, neck, and knob). The alphabetical classification indicated that every gun of that class would fit on the same carriage and could be interchanged for the same type of gun on a ship's deck. Jones noted every gun that had a flaw or displayed inferior workmanship or casting and marked each with a special designation as unfit for the navy; in the margin of his final report Jones explained why he condemned each weapon. This meticulous process, repeated in each navy yard, provided him with the data to report on the status of specific guns within the service and added considerable legitimacy to his inventory.

Those weapons that passed inspection, Jones said, should be placed on wooden skids or ways, or on granite skids as in the case of the Charleston yard, and elevated three to four feet above the ground. Ideally they should also be placed under cover and protected from the elements. Guns that remained uncovered should have the touch holes, vents, and barrels plugged with soft pine to prevent water from settling in the weapons' bore and seriously damaging them. Jones also made special note of the coatings used to preserve guns exposed to the elements. Of the different types he observed, he maintained that "black lead" paint was best suited for iron guns because it was easily applied and removed when a new coat was needed. "Common cold tar" could also be used as a suitable treatment should paint be unavailable, he reported, but many officers and gunmen objected to using tar because of the difficulty in removing it when the gun was needed. In no instance did Jones recommend lacquer; when workers removed lacquer from weapons it flaked off thick scales of metal, leaving the gun's surface rough and uneven.

The commissioners had initially instructed Jones to inspect the shot stored at each navy yard as well as the guns, but by mid-August 1833 that order had been rescinded. Such work would take far too much time from his other, more important duties. Nonetheless, Jones made a superficial examination "without gauging or handling" the shot and offered a provisional opinion. Shot, he maintained, should be sanded, painted with black lead, sorted, and stored under cover. Such a task would require much time, however, and in his opinion would be "useless" unless a lieutenant at each station was given this responsibility and held accountable for its completion.

Once the weapons had been tested, Jones began examining powder samples from every barrel stored at each yard. On his trip north he had stopped outside Wilmington, Delaware, at the Du Pont Powder Works to compare weights from the Washington Navy Yard with those at Du Pont's factory. He had been instructed to weigh six ounces of powder from the yard and compare it with Du Pont's avoirdupois ounces, which had been proved at the Philadelphia Mint. When he found that an ounce of powder from the navy yard was 35.5 grams heavier than Du Pont's avoirdupois ounce, he was forced to spend almost three days adjusting his instruments.[26]

Jones filled the chamber of an éprouvette—a short mortar, usually set at a forty-five-degree angle, that projects a 24-pound solid ball—with first a troy and then an avoirdupois ounce of powder. Much to his surprise he discovered that the troy ounce, containing more grams of powder, did not allow a cannonball to rest against the bottom of the éprouvette. This created a vacuum between the powder and the ball, and the resultant explosion was "much diffused and of course much diminished." He repeated the experiment several times, under different conditions and with a variety of powder samples, but in every instance the outcome was the same. As Jones anticipated, he achieved consistent results when he used an avoirdupois ounce; one ounce of powder propelled a cannonball from thirty-two to seventy-five yards depending on environmental conditions and the powder sample itself. By the time Jones had finished his tests he had concluded that the range a ball was thrust depended on the quality of the powder sampled, and that powder with an unusually high sulfur content generally hurled a cannonball one-third less distance. He expressed serious concerns about the quality of the gunpowder produced by the Du Pont works, but it did not have the "foulness" he had initially believed it to have.[27]

At the conclusion of his experiment Jones had inspected 1,453 "great guns" and 789 "cannon and gunades," 499 of which were smaller than 18-pounders. The intricate inspection allowed him to observe the advantages of long, medium, and short weapons as well as guns of varying caliber. Not surprisingly, he reported that long guns of lower caliber were much better suited to naval warfare than medium, short, or light guns of high caliber. As an example he compared the *Constitution* with its long 24-pounders with the *Brandywine,* which was outfitted with medium 32-pounders. He argued that if the two ships encountered one another in battle, the *Brandywine* would be at a disadvantage after firing only two or three shots. The strain placed on the light 32-pounders' "breeching and bolts," even with reduced powder charges, made them more susceptible to "busting" during the heat of battle. Although his was not an original argument, Jones maintained nonetheless that shorter guns, regardless of their weight, were not as accurate as long guns. The *Constitution*'s long 24-pound guns could bear a heavier powder charge, were capable of propelling shot with greater velocity and accuracy, and would therefore cause more damage.[28]

Of the long, heavy guns cast since 1815, Jones believed that all were "without fault" except the long 42-pounders; their chase was too short and the turn of their breech rendered them useless during an ordinary fight. He argued that if those cannon were to remain as a part of the navy's permanent arsenal, they should be recast on a new pattern. Jones also concluded that the navy's new medium 24-pounders suffered many of the same defects as the medium 32-pounders. Finally, he judged any gun smaller than a 12-pounder unfit for the navy unless it was to be used as a pivot or chase gun in schooners and other small vessels. Jones was especially critical of any gun that did not have at least two hundred pounds of metal mass for each pound of shot it projected. Two years later, in response to a House resolution, Secretary of the Navy Mahlon Dickerson asked Jones to test the efficiency and safety of medium and light guns. Jones criticized these weapons again, but also suggested that a naval board conduct more extensive tests.[29]

Jones's final report was the first systematic account of navy ordnance, and although it contained no drawings of guns, it vividly illustrated the need for improvements in the way that weapons and ammunition were stored. The comprehensive report concluded with a detailed chart cataloging the weapons at each yard—their class, length, and weight, as well as the diameter of their bore and trunnions. Although his report provided the condition of every gun in each yard, he did not offer commentary on the guns aboard the twenty-two ships still at sea or in commission. Nonetheless, the report was the most complete and comprehensive account of Navy Department ordnance in the service's forty-year history. It could well be Jones's most important, and most overlooked, contribution to the navy. His thoroughness apprised the service of its ordnance shortcomings and ultimately provided an opportunity for technologically minded ordnance officers, such as Dahlgren, to begin breaking down the stagnant bureaucracy opposed to change.[30]

The navy ignored Jones's ordnance recommendations. He had spent months testing and retesting guns and powder, and compiling and comparing statistics for his exhaustive report. But almost as soon as Jones submitted it, Capt. John Rodgers requested that he condense it into a brief abstract showing only the number of operative and defective guns by class in each yard. After a week of extracting the data, Jones responded with two one-page summaries that necessarily oversimplified his important conclusions. The longer report with its poignant observations and important assessments was filed away in the departmental records.[31]

In the spring of 1834 Jones decided that after almost five years he had served in the ordnance position long enough. He believed it would be better for his career to go to sea, preferably as commander of the Pacific Squadron. Although Alexander S. Wadsworth had just been given command of that station, Jones nevertheless offered Secretary Levi Woodbury compelling reasons why he should be the station's next commander instead of Wadsworth. During the following spring Jones again petitioned Woodbury for the Pacific station, apparently having read in the newspapers that Wadsworth wanted to return home.[32]

At the same time Jones was seeking sea duty, he also continued pressing Congress for payment of a disability pension he felt he deserved for the wound he had received at the Battle of Lake Borgne. Jones first applied for the pension during the summer of 1815, but his request was first lost and then continually postponed. He asked for twenty-five dollars per month but received nothing until July 1828, when attorney Richard Coxe helped him win from the Navy Department a ten-dollar-a-month pension beginning from the previous 14 February. Some three years later, in January 1831, then Captain Jones still had not received even the ten dollars per month from the navy.[33]

Jones informed Congress that when he had been wounded in 1814 he had held the official rank of lieutenant, even though he was acting as a lieutenant commandant in charge of a squadron of gunboats. Furthermore, his salary at that time was fifty dollars per month, the same amount paid to a lieutenant commandant. He therefore advised Congress that the board's award should equal half of his monthly salary at the time of his injury, or twenty-five dollars per month. Jones also argued that the pension should be granted from the time of his court of inquiry in 1815 rather than from February 1828, the date of his most recent printed memorial.[34]

The commissioners had questioned whether Jones should receive a pension at all in addition to his captain's salary. True, Jones had been wounded and no longer had full use of his left arm, but he was still active in the service and had risen to the navy's highest rank, and Jones himself had always maintained that he was fit for any duty. Therefore the basic question for Congress to decide was whether a captain, "*receiving full pay* [was] yet so *disabled* as to be entitled to a pension." If Jones was disabled and allowed a pension, "*disabled* men would in fact receive *higher pay* than the *ablest* men in the service." According to Michael Hoffman, chairman of the House Naval Affairs Committee, this situation would create in the navy "the most fatal imbecility and discontent." The question was not whether a deserving officer should receive a pension, but rather whether a dangerous precedent might be established. Despite congressional opposition, the commissioners of the navy fund increased Jones's pension to twenty dollars a month—but this was still five dollars a month less than Jones thought he deserved.[35]

Since Jones was not on active duty at the time he did not receive a full salary, per diem, or rations, and this strained him financially. He wrote a personal note to his friend and former navy secretary Samuel Southard, who was then representing New Jersey in the Senate, seeking his support for a pension bill then being considered by Congress. He told Southard in confidence that he had an outstanding obligation of fifteen hundred dollars, and payment was due immediately. If he was "to be dis-

appointed" he needed to know quickly so he could find some other way
to meet his obligations. Congress did not fund his pension from 1815, but
he did receive his twenty-dollar-per-month pension dated from February
1828, and that money helped Jones pay his outstanding debt to the Bank
of the United States.[36]

Jones received unexpected news in May 1836 when Congress voted
$150,000 for a new expedition to explore and survey the southern Pacific.
Given his previous experience, including his Pacific service and knowledge of that region's whaling grounds and commerce, and his constant
pleas for a command, Jones was a natural choice to lead the enterprise.
After a personal interview with President Jackson and Secretary Dickerson, Jones was selected for the position on 28 June 1836.[37]

Jones had first met Andrew Jackson in the spring of 1815 while recuperating from the near-fatal wound he had received at the Battle of Lake
Borgne. The general had won at New Orleans in part because of Jones's
determined defense at Borgne, and Jackson always supported those who
had aided him or shown him loyalty. Jones had done both. In any case,
the choice of Jones as commander was widely acclaimed because he was
popular with his men and highly regarded by the scientific community,
including expedition advocate Jeremiah Reynolds.

From the beginning Secretary Dickerson fought to kill the expedition,
primarily because former navy secretary Southard, Dickerson's Whig
New Jersey enemy, had supported it. Dickerson had no desire to fulfill
his rival's wishes. The secretary also believed that the expedition was
merely an attempt by Jackson at self-glorification, and he despised such
pomposity. During an early cabinet meeting at which the venture was
discussed Dickerson reminded the president that the expedition had
been a pet project of Southard and the Adams administration in 1828,
thinking that this would arouse Jackson's ire and spell certain defeat for
the undertaking. He was surprised when Jackson responded that Southard,
although a scoundrel, had had at least one good idea. Jackson insisted that
the expedition should sail and that Jones should be given the support he
needed to prepare it.

Jones envisioned a grand venture. Two days after his appointment he
requested that the newly rebuilt frigate *Macedonian* serve as his flagship;
in addition he wanted a squadron of two brigs, two schooners, and a
storeship, all specially constructed with additional beams, thicker planks,
and higher quarterdecks to protect the vessels in icebound waters. The

small frigate could comfortably carry the necessary scientists and soldiers as well as the expedition's armaments and equipment. Such a vessel would also awe any islanders the explorers encountered. Jones vividly remembered the impression his small armed sloop had made during his trip to the Pacific in 1826–27.[38]

Over the next several months Dickerson begrudgingly fulfilled his directive while working at the same time to undermine the mission. He initially refused to authorize Jones's request for a frigate and a sizable squadron, arguing that the *Macedonian* was too large to conduct experiments in shoal waters and that foreign exploring expeditions usually consisted of only two medium-sized ships, not a squadron of six. At one point Dickerson actually visited the White House to ask Jackson why the country needed such a large force. He showed the president the *Voyage de la Corvette "l'Astrolabe,"* seven recently published volumes produced by the small scientific expedition led by Frenchman J. S. C. Dumont d'Urville in 1826–29. Yet Americans viewed the upcoming voyage as more than a scientific expedition. It represented a break with the Old World—cultural independence that would coincide with the political independence gained earlier. Jackson concluded that if so much could be achieved with a small fleet, much more could be accomplished with a larger one.[39]

Unhappy with the president's decision, Dickerson remained recalcitrant as Jones pressed his point. Ultimately Jones had to appeal again to Jackson before he gained some satisfaction. In the end the president granted Jones his choice of ships, including the *Macedonian,* which was still on the stocks in Norfolk, but he did reduce the size of the squadron by one schooner. Jones was satisfied with Jackson's orders, but Dickerson was not. He had been publicly challenged by an officer under his control and then overruled by the president. The secretary, a petulant man with a reputation for avenging his political losses, was certainly not happy with Jackson's decision. Regardless, the president claimed to have a "lively interest" in this expedition and he wanted it to sail as soon as possible. As Jackson's secretary of the navy Dickerson had to execute the executive order/wish.[40]

In early July 1836 Dickerson finally gave the order to finish and outfit the *Macedonian.* Several days later he insincerely notified Jones that he would not interfere with the expedition. That certainly was not to be the case. On 12 July he had appointed Jones, Charles Morris, William Shubrick, Lawrence Kearny, and David Connor to a board that would test ordnance at Old Point Comfort (near Fortress Monroe), a task that would take significant time and was certain to infringe on Jones's preparations for the expedition. Jones met with the board only sporadically from early December 1836 until late September 1837, but the subsequent delays sustained by the expedition can partially be attributed to this extra duty.[41]

As Jones fulfilled his ordnance duties he also had to contend with Dickerson's underhanded machinations, which compounded the difficulties of preparing the fleet. The president had given Jones full responsibility for outfitting the expedition, but Dickerson, after consulting with Jones, was authorized to name the officers for the mission, and this is where the major problem developed between the two. Jones, who had risen through the navy's seniority system, did not want to see the practice subverted. The system depended on individuals gaining years of experience at each level before they were promoted to higher rank. An officer's priority at each rank was based on his seniority, or when he was commissioned. The system determined precedence in securing commands and formed the backbone of the service's organization.

Jones had studied the Navy Register, considering both seniority and experience, in order to determine and submit to Dickerson the best-qualified officers for each of the eighty-five available spots. Jones made all of the appointments based on the men's seniority and reported ability because he personally knew none of the candidates. Dickerson, however, did not accept his recommendations. Without consulting Jones he named two of his favorite junior officers, Lts. Charles Wilkes and Alexander Slidell, to command the smaller vessels.

Dickerson had already dispatched Wilkes to Europe to secure scientific equipment for the mission. Jones agreed that Wilkes, who had commanded the Navy's Depot of Charts and Instruments, was a competent scientist and could lead a surveying party. But Jones did not believe that either he or Slidell, who wanted to write an official history of the expedition, should command vessels. He informed the secretary that neither had the necessary seniority for command as there were 102 senior lieutenants above them on the Navy Register.[42]

Wilkes was in Europe when the controversy developed. By the time he had returned to the United States in January 1837, Dickerson had reluctantly acquiesced and the affair had been settled. Dickerson invited Wilkes to join the expedition as a civilian scientist since Jones refused to accept him as a commanding officer. Wilkes refused, arguing that even as a civilian scientist he would have to work in close cooperation with Jones, and that such an arrangement would be impossible given the commander's prejudice against him. Believing that Jones "was not equal to the task" at hand, Wilkes returned to his post at the Naval Observatory.[43]

As for Slidell, Jones thought that the scientific nature of the mission might be compromised "by placing the Rudder of the Expedition in the hands of one whose prominent merit, is that of wielding the pen." Furthermore, "if Belles-lettres attainments" was the primary reason for Slidell's appointment, Jones angrily argued, why not select a more accomplished author such as Washington Irving, James Fenimore Cooper, or James K. Paulding? Dickerson defended Slidell's literary ability and deplored what he regarded as an unjustified attack on that officer's character. He also asserted that several senior captains had given Slidell high marks. Jones seized this opportunity to remind Dickerson that his views often differed from those of his fellow captains. Finally Jones provided his true reason for not wanting Slidell as a part of the mission: Slidell owed his loyalty to Dickerson and would, if given a ship, write a biased account of the expedition—or more precisely, one unfavorable to Jones.[44]

When Slidell learned that he had become the center of a controversy he asked Dickerson to furnish him with copies of Jones's letters on the subject. The secretary foolishly surrendered documents on the condition that the affair not be played out in the newspapers. Slidell initially agreed, but after reading Jones's disparaging comments he launched a campaign of scathing invective in the *Army and Navy Chronicle* to defend his honor. Jones, Slidell retorted, was "an inexperienced and unpopular commander" who had gained control of the expedition because of his political connections. When Jones read that assertion he immediately contacted Southard for information about his appointment to the 1828 expedition. Southard told Jones that he had been chosen because it was in the best public interest, not because of "an improper influence of members of Congress or others." Slidell further charged that the lieutenants Jones chose for the expedition had either refused to join or were on other assignments. He concluded by asserting that he had more service at sea than Jones did.[45]

Jones became increasingly irritated as he read Slidell's charges. He was angry not only at the lieutenant but also at Dickerson for making the papers available to him. In one reply Jones contended that certain parties (Dickerson and his cohorts) were trying to discredit or even destroy the expedition. In another, Jones, trying to atone for his "stiffness," nonetheless insisted on the established privilege of choosing his own officers. He told Dickerson that if he had to accept Slidell he would be saddled with an officer whom he did not trust.[46]

Dickerson, who had initially avoided the controversy, now entered the public arena with his own attack on Jones. The secretary insisted that he had given Slidell copies of the correspondence so that he might defend himself against Jones's criticism. Yet, surprisingly, Dickerson also reprimanded Slidell for his attack on Jones's service record. It was a shame that the navy's dirty laundry was being aired in a public forum, but since it had happened, Dickerson was forced to paint the best possible picture of the quickly deteriorating situation. Meanwhile Slidell traveled to Washington, supposedly thinking that a duel would be the only means to redress the affair. Having second thoughts, he instead wrote Jones a short, sarcastic note asking "how far [Jones] considered himself responsible" for the violent attack on his honor and reputation.[47]

Jones's answer to Slidell did not address the issue of responsibility. He contended that Slidell had thrust this controversy on the public rather than settling it in private or within naval circles. When challenged in public, Jones had simply defended himself in the most truthful manner. He told the lieutenant that he had brought this controversy on himself because he had ignored traditional rules of chivalry and honor, and he must now suffer "the verdict of that tribunal" before which he stood "self-arraigned." Slidell could not allow Jones the final word; he responded with a caustic reply that further damaged his character and the reputation of the service. Slidell's note was the final exchange between the two officers, but several months went by and many newspaper articles and editorials were published before the affair finally ended.[48]

Jones became increasingly frustrated during the fall of 1836 as he traveled frequently between New York, Boston, Philadelphia, and Norfolk to supervise the modifications and repairs to the ships and to serve on the ordnance board. After weeks of constant delays he reported that the preparations were lagging behind and "in a state of comparative suspension." The ships remained laid up and out of commission. Meanwhile the president, Congress, and the American public anticipated a momentary departure. To the public it appeared that Secretary Dickerson supported the expedition, but in reality he was doing everything in his power to ensure that it never sailed.[49]

Finally, in early 1837, Jones had the opportunity to put his squadron to sea. He subjected four ships of the squadron (the flagship *Macedonian* remained behind) to an eight-day cruise off Norfolk to test their sailing qualities. Although pleased with their seaworthiness, Jones acknowledged that they were slow. He received an alarming report from the commander of the bark *Pioneer,* however. Lt. Josiah Tattnall, who had previously taken that vessel on an eighty-day voyage to Vera Cruz to return Mexican general Antonio López de Santa Anna, emphatically reported to Jones that the ship was "totally unsuited" for any expedition. Since the other small vessels were similarly built, rumors quickly spread that the entire squadron was unfit. Jones denied that the *Pioneer* was unfit for the expedition, leading to spirited correspondence between the two naval officers. Tattnall ultimately resigned from the expedition, but not before repeating his views to Secretary Dickerson.[50]

Dickerson asked the recently inaugurated president, Martin Van Buren, to convene a board of navy officers to inspect the ships. The president agreed, and the board quickly reported, much to Tattnall's and Dickerson's chagrin, that with minor repairs the vessels would be adequate for their intended purpose. It was not a ringing endorsement, but the board members had supported their fellow captain. Once the adjustments had been completed the ships took on supplies, food, and scientific equipment.[51]

A more pressing concern for Jones was Dickerson's unwillingness to provide sailing orders for the squadron. Neither Congress nor Secretary Dickerson offered any information about the expedition's objectives, duration, or destinations. More than a year had passed since the initial authorization, and Jones still had not been given instructions for the mission. Jones saw the nationalistic possibilities of the mission, and on 1 June 1837 he sent Dickerson a list of eleven recommendations that he believed should guide it. Dickerson accepted most of these, making only minor changes. The expedition, Dickerson declared, should visit both "the coldest and warmest climates" during its three-year voyage; otherwise, the secretary provided no more instructions until November, when he sent Jones a detailed description of the expedition's objectives and route. Dickerson also finally appointed the scientific corps, another issue that had been greatly debated in naval circles, the press, and Congress. Last, he reminded Jones that the primary objective of the venture was the "great interests of commerce and navigation. The advancement of science is . . . of secondary importance."[52]

Jones had already spent months as commander of the expedition, and every minute had been agonizing. His travels had weakened him physically, and his arguments with Dickerson, his problems trying to recruit men for the cruise, and the need to defend himself in print from charges by Slidell and Wilkes had taken a psychological toll.[53] Finally, in early October 1837, all the problems appeared to be solved, at least for the moment. Jones, unfortunately, was unable to celebrate his accomplishment; he was in bed, sick and exhausted from his unending battles. Jones arose from his bed long enough to read "General Order, No. 1" to the men, and the *Macedonian* departed Norfolk to rendezvous with the other vessels of the squadron off the Brooklyn Navy Yard. Jones praised the men and officers for their diligence and patience but also reminded them of the dangerous nature of the mission they were undertaking. Several publications, including the *Baltimore American,* took the opportunity to praise Jones and his subordinates as news of the general order and the departure of the *Macedonian* aroused renewed interest in the expedition.[54]

When the frigate arrived in New York on 17 October, Jones immediately took up residence—at his own expense—in a suite at the Hotel Astor. For several weeks he had been suffering from health problems, which had been greatly aggravated by his constant bickering with Dickerson. He had also spent seven thousand dollars of his own money during the eighteen months he had been working on the project. Further compounding his financial woes, Jones had signed a surety and assumed responsibility for the four-thousand-dollar debt of a cousin who had accepted the postmastership of Roanoke, Virginia. His declining health and pressing financial problems greatly burdened him, but Jones believed the squadron would soon be under way. Moreover, the bed rest at the hotel would provide a momentary respite, giving him renewed strength for the problems he faced ahead.[55]

Unfortunately, the break would be much longer than Jones anticipated, and it also failed to provide relaxation. Two weeks passed, and Jones still had not received sailing orders from Dickerson. The secretary did not forward them until 9 November, more than three weeks after Jones had arrived in the city. Jones also faced further personnel problems. Without Jones's prior knowledge or approval, Secretary Dickerson suddenly named Walter Colton, a popular chaplain in the service, to serve as both historian and chaplain, and appointed Lt. James Glynn, who was already commanding the *Consort,* as the expedition's geographer

and hydrographer. Jones protested bitterly the dual appointments, especially because both men expected extra pay for their service. He claimed
that these commissions encroached on his privilege as commander. Dickerson, however, maintained his decision despite Jones's objections.[56]

Then came the final straw. The secretary ordered Jones to seal, before
witnesses, all materials and specimens collected during the expedition.
This last requirement, according to Jones, was too much, as it "not only
questions my *honor,* but impugns my *honesty.*"[57]

By mid-November Jones was too sick to leave his bed except for one
ill-advised trip to the navy yard. Doctors attended him constantly. He
suffered an extreme soreness in the chest and hemorrhaging from the
lungs, and he was coughing up blood. The modern diagnosis based on
those symptoms would be tuberculosis, for which there was no available
cure other than bed rest, an accommodating climate, and occasional
horseback riding to break up the congestion in the chest. Doctors told
Jones that he would probably die if he went on the expedition. The fleet
surgeon specifically recommended that he return to his home as soon as
his health and the weather permitted.

Jones wrote to Dickerson on 14 November 1837 to resign his command. His poor health was the primary, although not the only, reason for
the resignation. Certainly Jones had been plagued by problems that
demonstrated his shortcomings, but he did everything in his power to
make this trip because it was his first chance to command a squadron.
But the illness weakened him and made him less able to fight Dickerson,
and ultimately forced him to give up his chance for command and glory.
In later years he would ask for a command as a means to redeem what
he perceived to be a reputation sullied by the events surrounding the
expedition. Privately he wrote that "the deed is done and . . . the die is
cast. *I stay at home.* 'Home sweet home, there is no place like home.'"
Dickerson tried to persuade him to remain with the expedition, but
before his letter arrived in New York, Jones had relinquished command
to Capt. Charles Ridgely. On 5 December 1837, Jones departed for northern Virginia.[58]

Still too ill to take formal leave of his men, Jones left his written farewell
with Capt. James Armstrong of the *Macedonian.* The note thanked his
men for their faithful service and devotion during the constant disap-
pointments and delays. It must have touched them deeply, for thereafter
they resigned from the expedition en masse. They had reenlisted under

Jones's command, perhaps because they truly liked him or admired his stormy personality. The sailors demanded that either the squadron depart immediately or they be discharged. Dickerson had no choice but to accept their resignations.

The secretary was pleased to have Jones out of the way. He confided to his diary that had the expedition sailed under Jones's command it would have been a fiasco. Jones's resignation, "however[,] will make infinite confusion, as no one will take command in such vessels as he has had constructed, or such arrangements as he has made." Those were prophetic words. When the Twenty-fifth Congress convened a few days later that body immediately demanded an explanation for the constant delays. Dickerson, expecting a congressional investigation, had tried to forestall the biting onslaught of public opinion by quickly securing another commander. He offered the command in turn to Capts. William Shubrick, Lawrence Kearny, and Matthew C. Perry, and to Master Commandant Francis Gregory, but all refused for various reasons. In March 1838 President Van Buren, disturbed about the continuing delays, transferred responsibility of the expedition to Secretary of War Joel Poinsett. Within two months Poinsett had solved most of the pressing problems. He reduced the size of the squadron, made it purely scientific in nature, and named Lt. Charles Wilkes its commander. Finally, on 18 August 1838, after twenty-six agonizing months, the much-reduced and strictly scientific mission sailed for the South Pacific.[59]

Perhaps Jones was *not* the officer best suited to command the mission. He could be arrogant, proud, easily insulted, and contentious. Jealous of his prerogatives as commander and determined to maintain the seniority system, Jones refused to compromise and too often engaged in public acrimony. He was a fine deck officer at a time when the navy relied on independent-minded officers to make the correct decisions in moments of crisis. He took responsibility for his decisions regardless of the consequences. But in this instance he did not consider himself responsible for the problems, and he certainly did not intend to be blamed for them.

Jones had not been politic or patient during the preparations for the expedition. His inept handling of the Slidell imbroglio and his constant bickering with Dickerson also demonstrated obvious deficiencies. When he worked alone, Jones generally performed well and successfully carried out his tasks. Yet he ran into problems when he had organizational control over many men and officers, several ships, thousands of dollars, a broad range of supplies and equipment—all in a politically charged crucible. He appears also to have been incapable of wading through the mounds of mind-numbing details associated with the operation.

Ultimately the expedition illustrated Jones's worst qualities, and its failure represented a major crossroads in his life. When he remarked that "the die is cast" Jones did not truly understand the significance of his own words. Until that time he had been able to rely on his association with Jackson and his family's political connections when his career seemed to stagnate within the seniority system. Thereafter he would have to fight more vigorously for ship commands and appointments. Unfortunately, his attempts to clear his name during his last two cruises would further stain his reputation. Jones could not have known that this episode represented the beginning of a downward turn in what previously had been a very promising career.

Midshipman Thomas ap Catesby Jones, circa 1807.
Courtesy Naval Historical Center

Captain Jones, most likely painted after his promotion to captain in 1829. *Courtesy U.S. Naval Academy Museum*

Commodore Jones, most likely after being named commander of the Pacific Squadron in 1842. *Courtesy Naval Historical Center*

Mary Walker Carter Jones. *Courtesy of the Lewinsville Presbyterian Church, McLean, Virginia*

Sharon, Jones's home from 1819 until his death in 1858. *Courtesy of the Fairfax County, Virginia, Public Library*

Gunboats similar to those Jones served on during his duty on the Gulf coast capturing French privateers on the Mississippi River in 1808. Drawing by Capt. William Bainbridge Hoff. *Courtesy Naval Historical Center*

The Gallant Attack and Capture of the American Flotilla near New Orleans, Dec. 1814, in Lake Borgne, by the Boats of the Squadron under the Command of Capt. N. Lockyer. Painting by Thomas L. Hornbrook. *Courtesy U.S. Naval Academy Museum*

USS *United States*, Jones's flagship during his first command of the Pacific Squadron. *Courtesy National Archives*

View of Monterey, capital of Alta California, as sketched by Lt. Joseph Warren Revere of the U.S. Navy. *From A Tour of Duty in California* (1848)

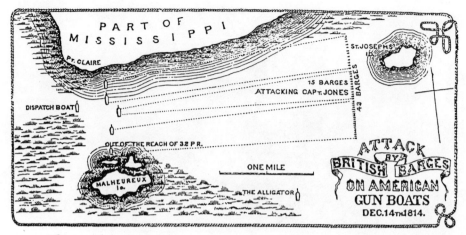

The attack by British barges on Jones's squadron of gunboats, 14 December 1814. *From Pictorial Field-Book of the War of 1812, by Benson J. Lossing (1869)*

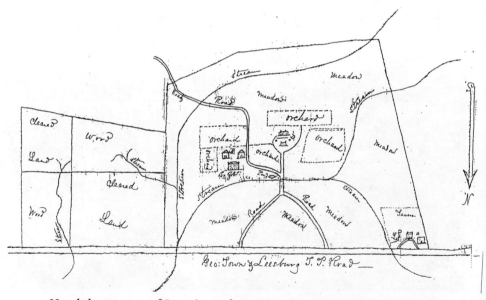

Hand-drawn map of Jones's northern Virginia estate. Exhibit "B" in file of Mary W. Jones, claim no. 21622. *From the Southern Claims Commission case files, National Archives, 1877–1883, Record Group 217, box 353*

The old Lewinsville Presbyterian Church, which Jones helped to found. Photo, date unknown, given to S. R. Pearson. *Courtesy of the Fairfax County, Virginia, Public Library*

The USS *Ohio,* bearing the pennant of Commodore Jones during his second command of the Pacific Squadron. *Courtesy Naval Historical Center*

❧ 6 ☙

THE HERO OF MONTEREY
Pacific Command, 1838–1844

*J*ones returned to Sharon in mid-December 1837 and immediately retired to his bed. He was still terribly sick, but happier now because he was no longer suffering from the cold weather, departmental backbiting, and frustrations that had accompanied his attempts to ready the squadron for service. Although he had abruptly washed his hands of the expedition, over the next several months he still had to answer many questions about goods purchased while he was its commander. Specifically Secretary Dickerson wanted to know about 150 pistol knives, ten thousand pounds of tobacco, and other goods totaling some five thousand dollars. The accusatory tone of the secretary's letters further incensed Jones, but he nonetheless answered in a deferential manner because he needed the secretary's assistance, even if he was reluctant to admit it.[1]

Along with his resignation Jones had forfeited his four-thousand-dollar-a-year salary as a commanding officer. He was subsequently placed on unpaid leave, which would soon become unbearable. He had to regain his health so he could return to active duty, or at least be ready and awaiting orders. Not surprisingly, his health began slowly to improve, but it was not because of the prevailing medical treatment for lung ailments, which in the 1830s consisted of flannel undergarments, "a change of climate, a milk diet, [and] vigorous and daily exercise on horseback." While

Jones truly enjoyed horseback riding in the fresh Virginia air, this alone did not cure him; rest and relaxation did, however, allow him to recuperate slowly. By late February 1838, less than three months after his resignation, Jones reported to Dickerson that he was again healthy and ready for another assignment—and also, not incidentally, the twenty-five-hundred-dollar annual salary it would bring.[2]

The forty-eight-year-old Jones thought that once he had regained his health he would be back to normal. But that would not be the case; he had recurring bouts of the lung disease for the remainder of his life. In fact, Jones was very premature when he reported to Dickerson that he was "healthy." He was not well at all, and his unwillingness to rest produced additional setbacks throughout 1838 and 1839. Jones did not return to active duty until the spring of 1841.[3]

While recuperating at Sharon, Jones turned his attentions again to farming. He had not been a full-time farmer for more than two years, and the farm needed his efforts. The Panic of 1837 had rocked the nation, and the economy was in desperate straits. Unemployment skyrocketed; the price of cotton and other farm commodities dropped; and banks refused to extend credit—most, in fact, demanded immediate payment of loans. The nearby town of Alexandria, Virginia, suffered greatly as houses became vacant and dilapidated, cattle grazed in the streets, and even George Washington's famed Mount Vernon fell into disrepair. Hard-pressed farmers and businessmen in Jones's neighborhood suffered likewise, and most came to realize that they could not prosper on their depleted lands. But neither could they sell the worn-out lands or afford to part with fertile acreage at depressed prices. Farmers unwilling to adapt could not survive in the business climate of the panic years.

In January and February 1838, while "pelting storms" raged about his house, Jones contemplated his own operations and drafted a thoughtful essay on the benefits of fertilizer that was later published in Edmund Ruffin's *Farmers' Register*. His article described how manure, lime, plaster, gypsum, and other chemicals could restore the most barren lands, even the former tobacco lands that Virginians traditionally abandoned. Jones's past efforts had been immensely successful, and many—even northerners—began to notice that his lands yielded more than expected. Moreover, the high price of farmland in the Northeast, combined with the growing markets in the area surrounding the District of Columbia and the agricultural innovations of Jones and some of his neighbors,

taught northerners that farming could again be profitable in northern
Virginia. By the late 1840s northern immigrants had moved into Fairfax
County in such numbers (more than twelve hundred) that land and com-
modity prices greatly increased.[4]

In 1839 Jones proudly reported that his agricultural endeavors had
been so successful that he had increased the size of his farm to 420 acres
(from 100 acres) and had made capital improvements worth more than
ten thousand dollars. He also owned twenty-three slaves, some of whom
he leased out to other farmers, ten head of livestock (mostly horses and
mules), and all the farming equipment he needed for his operations.[5]

Jones also understood the importance of industrial technology, especially steam-powered railroads and water-powered manufacturing. In
1838 he had acquired land along the Great Falls of the Potomac River.
The falls, where the Potomac River descends eighty-five feet in elevation
over a distance of one and a half miles, was located but fourteen miles
from the capital city, and in this new manufacturing age the river offered
a bountiful untapped source of power. During the 1830s the land surrounding the Great Falls changed hands several times, with each owner
or corporation presenting grandiose plans for an industrial center and
town. But by the end of the decade only a single sawmill used the power
offered by the falls. It was obvious to Jones that the falls could power
much more than one mill.[6]

In early January 1839 Jones joined with William A. Bradley and Hall
Neilson, both Fairfax County entrepreneurs, to incorporate the Great
Falls Manufacturing Company. The three men successfully petitioned
the Virginia legislature for permission to use the waterpower of the Great
Falls to manufacture cotton, wool, flax, hemp, paper, copper, brass, and
iron. In addition, the state government also granted the company, to be
initially capitalized at between $100,000 and $1,000,000, the right to cultivate mulberry trees and to produce and manufacture silk. Two months
later Henry Fairfax, Thomas R. Love, and William W. Ball joined with
Jones and Bradley as trustees to incorporate the town of South Lowell
on three hundred of the three thousand acres of land owned by the
Great Falls Manufacturing Company.[7]

Jones and the other trustees named their new endeavor for Lowell,
Massachusetts, which had come to represent the ideal republican industrial center—a town created to promote rather than destroy the country's
traditional social fabric. South Lowell would attempt to use the same

techniques to promote the trustees' real estate venture, not their manufacturing project. According to a civil engineer hired by the trustees, valuable waterfront land along the falls offered "extraordinary capacities and advantages . . . for extensive manufacturing and milling operations." The engineer concluded that the river also had enough water, year-round, to power between fifty and two hundred mills depending on the system of dams and sluices constructed. If all the plots along such a source of potential power could be sold, the trustees would become wealthy and all of Jones's monetary problems would disappear. Yet neither Jones nor any of the other trustees had the necessary capital during the lean financial times of the late 1830s and early 1840s to carry out such plans for the company and town. The trustees' designs would ultimately lie dormant for many years until local and national conditions improved.[8]

The venture never provided the financial security Jones and the other trustees anticipated. In 1846 and again in 1848 the company secured charter extensions from the Virginia legislature, yet no major developments occurred. Four years later, in 1852, an enlarged body of trustees secured a broader grant from the legislature allowing the company to build a railroad from the falls and to sell waterpower and land, but this did not change the corporation's fortunes either. In 1854 the company, in an attempt to secure a government contract to provide drinking water to the District of Columbia, bought the land around the falls from Jones, Bradley, and Neilson. Although this ended the three men's association with the unhappy enterprise, the Great Falls Manufacturing Company somehow managed to stay afloat until the 1880s.[9]

Throughout 1839 Jones pleaded with new navy secretary James K. Paulding for an active assignment. In January he learned that the Pacific Squadron needed a commander and insisted that he was the best-qualified officer for the position; he had served in the Pacific and knew the area and its pitfalls. But Paulding offered the post to Jones's close friend Alexander Claxton. If Jones had to lose out to another officer, he could best tolerate it being to his friend. Jones then asked Paulding for the command of the African Squadron, but the secretary told him that he had given it to Matthew Calbraith Perry. Jones was so angered by that news that he spewed expletives about Perry to the alarmed secretary. Yet Jones felt some justification for the outburst because Perry was Alexander Slidell's brother-in-law and a close friend of Charles Wilkes; he had been a part of the Slidell-Wilkes cabal during the events surrounding the exploring expedition, and Jones held him at least partially responsible for the affair.[10]

The secretary politely told Jones not to feel as if he had been overlooked if the department chose another officer. After all, Paulding maintained, appointments were based on qualifications as well as seniority—an assurance unlikely to comfort Jones. Jones felt that his failure with the exploring expedition had tarnished his career, and he needed an opportunity to redeem himself. He politely asked Paulding for command of the Baltimore Navy Yard or the position of inspector of ordnance. Either position would do nicely because he could reside at his home and considerably reduce his expenses. Jones desperately needed to save money at this time. He told the secretary in confidence that his embarrassment with the expedition and lost pay had cost him $7,000. Furthermore, the auditor of the post office was demanding the $5,462.78 surety and interest he had signed for his cousin W. F. Jones. Jones candidly admitted that he could not pay his debts without "great sacrifice." Lacking a position, he would have to borrow money or sell some of his property at the low rates it brought during the panic years. But Paulding had to tell Jones that he could offer neither position because both had already been filled.[11]

Finally, in October 1840, Jones wrote Paulding that he could no longer "remain passive under the cloud of official disapprobation" overshadowing his career. He had been passed over for command for almost three years. During that time virtually every position in the service had become vacant; yet all had been given to others. Some posts had even been assigned to officers junior to him. In such circumstances, Jones could only come to the "irresistible conclusion" that some unknown influence had been "exerted to [his] great detriment and professional disparagement." Jones wanted to know the reason for his "virtual suspension of rank and ostracism from duty," and would not be satisfied until Paulding ordered an official investigation.[12]

Jones's accusations verged on paranoia. He had apparently been grumbling about the injustice done to him since the summer of 1838, and more than two years later he still harbored the belief that someone was clandestinely sabotaging his career. With each passing year his sense of persecution grew more acute. Paulding, feeling compelled to address the allegations, responded that Jones had already been a squadron commander and that others deserved the same opportunity. As for an investigation, the secretary discreetly skirted a prolonged and complex inquiry by refusing Jones's request and assuring him that this did not reflect poorly on his ability or his standing in the service.[13]

Although melancholy about his future prospects, Jones and his family celebrated a moment of happiness a few months later in Richmond when he and his brother, Adj. Gen. Roger Jones, and seven other army and navy officers were granted ceremonial swords for their distinguished service during the War of 1812. The Virginia Assembly had originally voted the swords to Jones and his brother in February 1834, yet the awards had never been made. Over the next four years the state legislature voted swords to the other officers, but these were not presented either. By 1840 tensions between the United States and Great Britain had reached a fever pitch because of the disputed northeastern boundary and the McLeod affair, and Virginia, like many other states, chose at that time to recognize its heroes from the second war of independence.[14]

The *Richmond Enquirer* called George Washington's birthday, Monday, 22 February 1841, "one of the brightest days in the annals of our city." At daybreak the Fayetteville Artillery of Richmond fired a solemn salute to initiate the occasion. Through the brisk, cold morning air the sun "spread its bright rays over the face of nature" as about six thousand witnesses gathered at the Virginia capitol. At 10:00 A.M. the Public Guard escorted President-elect Gen. William Henry Harrison from his accommodations to the governor's mansion, where the recipients and other dignitaries had gathered. Meanwhile, off the south portico at the lower end of Capitol Square, the Public Guard, the Richmond Artillery, the Washington Grenadiers, the Richmond Blues, the Chesterfield Troops, and the Richmond Light Dragoons, all in beautiful dress uniforms and silver-gilt helmets, stationed themselves in a crescent formation. Banners and drapes hung from every building around the square and "the whole scene," according to witnesses, "was singularly striking and animating."[15]

At eleven o'clock Governor Thomas Walker Gilmer, President-elect Harrison, Vice President–elect John Tyler, and those to be honored appeared on the portico. Only three of the honorees were there in person (the Joneses and Capt. Hugh Nelson Page); navy captains E. A. F. Lavallette and Charles Morgan, army major Thomas M. Nelson, marine colonel Archibald Henderson, and deceased Capt. R. H. Bell and Col. George Armistead, both of the army, were represented by family or friends. Governor Gilmer began the ceremony with an eloquent oration

extolling the virtues of those being honored. He then turned to each offi-
cer or representative and presented a beautiful rosewood case containing a ceremonial sword engraved with a relief of the participant's most
important exploit on one side of the scabbard and a list of his victories
on the other. The swords, ornately crafted with precious metals and intricate engravings by N. P. Ames of Springfield, Massachusetts, offered a
heartfelt tribute to Virginia's native sons. Each representative accepted
his sword and then publicly offered thanks.[16]

The *Southern Literary Messenger* noted that "a new generation has
sprung up since the last contest with our ancient and powerful foe; and
it may not be amiss to recall to the minds of our youths, some of those
heroic deeds, which held in check . . . the lofty pretensions of British
pride." Jones, taking center stage after his brother Roger, swelled with
pride because, as he admitted, "unlike [his] compatriots in war . . . [his]
efforts were not crowned with victory." In fine rhetorical style akin to
that which he had learned at Ogilvie's Richmond Academy more than
thirty years before, Jones concluded that the sword was a symbol not of
his participation at the Battle of Lake Borgne, but rather of his pledge
"for renewed and increasing devotion to my country and to her cause, so
long as that cause may be Liberty and Union."[17]

When the honorees had all given thanks to their fellow Virginians
Harrison reviewed the militia units and the dignitaries then retired to
nearby Military Hall for a lavish reception where Harrison, Tyler, Roger
Jones, and Governor Gilmer all gave rousing patriotic speeches. By
five o'clock that afternoon most of the important guests had left Military
Hall for a momentary rest; that evening the Joneses and their wives
joined five hundred of the most influential members of Richmond society at the "Governor's Evening Fête." It was a night filled with dancing,
laughing, and great entertainment—"one of the completest *jams* ever
witnessed in this city."[18]

That day was especially important to Jones not because of the award
but because it provided him the opportunity to meet and talk candidly
with Harrison, Tyler, and a number of other important dignitaries,
including Abel Parker Upshur, who would soon become Tyler's secretary
of the navy. During those conversations Jones probably explained his
accomplishments as well as the trials and tribulations that had beset his
career, and he more than likely elaborated on his recent ostracism at the
hands of the Van Buren administration. But all that would end, Jones

was certain, on 4 March 1841 when Harrison assumed the presidency and George E. Badger of North Carolina took over at the Navy Department. Almost as soon as the decorations from the inauguration had been stored away, Jones sent a letter informing Badger that he was ready for active service. He also instructed the secretary that some of his "brother officers" believed that he had a claim to the Pacific Squadron.[19]

Jones was reassured a few weeks later when Badger replied that he would be given consideration for a position. That possibility gave him great hope because the previous letters from the department had only explained why he was *not* to be given a command. Jones quickly dashed off a long letter reviewing his qualifications and reminding the secretary that the Pacific station would soon be available and he would be willing to accept it. Jones must have sent the letter to the secretary via Harrison, because attached to it was a note from the president instructing Badger to explore the matter further. But Harrison never had the opportunity to become Jones's benefactor; he died on 4 April 1841, one month after his inauguration, and John Tyler, another of Jones's acquaintances, became president. Some three weeks later, on 26 April, the Tyler administration recalled Jones from his professional exile and Badger told him to be ready to assume command of the Pacific Squadron. It had been three years in coming, but Jones had finally gotten the position he wanted. He expressed his sincere thanks to Badger for the show of confidence.[20]

Throughout the spring and summer Jones watched the mail with great anticipation and worked to put his financial and domestic affairs in order. His wife, Mary, would need money to keep the household going and provide for their younger children Mary Lee, Mark Catesby, and Martha Corbin while he was away. He needed to make plans, too, for the fall harvest and for planting crops in the following years; he would have to determine which crops would be planted on each plot of land. Planning for a three-year cruise was difficult at best, and there were many details to be foreseen and completed. Not surprisingly, given his previous money problems, Jones must not have been able to secure loans for all the money Mary would need because she sold nine slaves during his absence.[21]

Mary had learned how to handle the family estate during her husband's absences. The couple had been married almost twenty years, and she had run the farm while he was in the Pacific and when he traveled on various assignments in the United States. But Mary also possessed the social graces necessary for women of her status, as evidenced by a wedding she and her brother-in-law Roger hosted on the evening of Thursday, 26 May 1842, while her husband was in the Pacific. That formal occasion, attended by several ladies and members of Congress as well as former president John Quincy Adams, celebrated the union of Charlotte Galbraith of Dublin, Ireland, to Henry Dana Ward of New York City.[22]

During the elegant ceremony a dreadful storm poured "heavy rain" on Sharon and cloudy skies obscured the moon, making for "a pitch-dark night." The downpour and muddy roads forced the guests to remain at the Jones estate for the night. Mary made sure that the visitors were as comfortable as possible, given the cramped accommodations. Mr. Adams, who shared a room with Congressman Abraham Rencher, where they slept on beds placed on the floor, remarked that he had a peaceful night's rest and arose to "the music of mockingbirds and robins" from trees surrounding the house. After dressing the following morning, Adams walked around the grounds and talked with some of the others who had also awakened early. He was favorably impressed with his hostess and with Sharon and its grounds, and he confided to his diary that "Commodore Jones's seat is a paradise in the wild, under his cultivation."[23]

On 11 September 1841 Badger, along with every other cabinet member except Secretary of State Daniel Webster, resigned after President Tyler's second veto of a Whig-sponsored bank bill. Two days after the resignations Tyler nominated fellow Virginian Abel Parker Upshur as navy secretary. Every day during his first month in office Upshur met with several navy and marine officers, including Jones, to determine the role the service should play.[24]

In early December Upshur informed Jones that his squadron would consist of his flagship, the frigate *United States;* the sloops-of-war *St. Louis, Cyane, Dale,* and *Yorktown;* the schooner *Shark;* and the storeship *Relief,* a total of only 116 guns. Moreover, the secretary defined the boundaries of the Pacific station as "all the west coast of America, and westward from the meridian of Cape Horn to the 180th degree of longitude; and southward between those meridians to the South Pole," an area Jones believed was far too large to patrol adequately with such a small force. Jones drafted a plan that would enlarge the squadron and require a minimum of seven ships, exclusive of the flagship and its tender. He proposed to station them off the coasts of Chile, Panama, Mexico, California, and the Pacific Northwest, and two among the Hawaiian Islands to protect American interests in the Pacific. The ships would change stations every four months, meaning that each ship would stop at each station twice in a three-year period. Jones also foresaw the importance of steam-powered ships in the Pacific; he maintained that two steamers could perform the work of more than three sailing ships. But the Navy Department never approved the plan, and even after the loss of one of his sloops (*St. Louis*), Jones's pleas went unheard.[25]

Jones's orders from the secretary were straightforward and reflected the uncertainty that prevailed in the Pacific in 1841: "The unsettled state of the nations bordering on this coast . . . renders it, in the first instance, necessary to protect the interests of the United States in that quarter." The borders of the Oregon territory were still unsettled, U.S. relations with Mexico remained tense over the role Americans had played in the Texas revolution, and rumors circulated that Great Britain planned to acquire California from Mexico, perhaps in settlement of Mexico's 1.5-million-pound debt to the British. This possibility aroused Americans who believed that California belonged by natural right to the United States.[26]

Officially Upshur advised Jones to use "great prudence and discretion" and to respect the rights of all nations with interests in that quarter. Yet before the *United States* departed Norfolk on 9 January 1842 Jones and Upshur met unofficially several times for candid discussions of affairs in the Pacific. Although what was said at these meetings remains unknown, they may have allowed Upshur to speak off the record with his fellow Virginian without the fear of provoking a congressional inquiry or an international incident. Upshur may also have offered Jones explicit guidance on departmental policy during his prolonged period of absence and explained the finer points of U.S.-Mexican and Anglo-American relations.[27]

The Pacific cruise would be something of a family affair for Jones as his oldest son, Meriwether, and his second cousin Walter Jones were both midshipmen aboard the *United States*. His slave and constant companion, Griffin Dobson, served as his steward. Jones viewed the cruise as an opportunity both to redeem his honor and to promote his religious beliefs. Since 1833 he had been one of thirty directors of the American Seamen's Friend Society—a nonsectarian organization conceived to instill morality in the individual and convert the world to Christianity—and this stint as commander would provide the chance to launch his crusade against the perceived evils aboard ships. Near the start of the cruise Jones circulated a temperance pledge to the officers and men of the squadron; not surprisingly, this had little effect. In February 1843 six sailors engaged in a drunken fight and were court-martialed and sentenced to be flogged. After the punishment had been administered Jones read to the men of the fleet a long discourse on the evils of spirits. Seaman William Meyers confided to his diary that the long, boring sermon indicated that Jones had a "deranged state of mind." A few days after the flogging Meyers sarcastically noted "that 3 first signers of the Temperance Pledg[e] Comore. Jones, Capt. Armstrong & Capt. Stribling were drunk last night." Although that was only a rumor, it must have brought a grin to those who had been forced to listen to Jones's haughty sermon a week earlier.[28]

When the *United States* arrived at Rio de Janeiro in early March 1842, after a twenty-five-day voyage from Funchal, the crew immediately began procuring food and water, repairing rigging and spars, and scraping the sides of the ship for the run around Cape Horn. Eighteen days would pass before the ship departed for the Pacific, and the interlude offered time for rest and recreation. It also provided young officers a chance to settle questions of honor by the "code duello." Dueling, a custom borrowed from European navies, allowed midshipmen to prove their courage by challenging perceived insults—and almost anything could be considered an affront.[29]

Jones had strong feelings against dueling even though it had been a prevalent custom in his own family. His uncle Meriwether, with whom he had lived in Richmond before joining the navy, had fought many duels and died from a wound suffered during one. Another uncle, Skelton, had also been involved in many duels and supposedly was disturbed later in life about the many men he had maimed and killed. In 1820 the courageous Stephen Decatur, Jones's first commander at Norfolk, had been killed by James Barron in a duel at Bladensburg, Maryland. Being a military man, Jones understood the necessity of fighting for honor, but he believed a man should fight for the honor of his country, not for anger or resentment.

When Jones learned that several midshipmen had gone ashore to settle their disputes with pistols, and that two of them, Alonzo C. Jackson and Angus Baldwin, had even fired three shots at each other before deciding that their honor had been satisfied, he immediately recalled all officers to the ship. He then sent a letter down to the steerage, where the midshipmen bunked, that he expected all twenty-eight young men to read and sign. By endorsing the statement the midshipmen pledged not to participate as principals or seconds in any duel or fight with anyone aboard the *United States* while they were on the present cruise. Anyone who refused to sign could either resign his commission or be denied shore leave for the remainder of the cruise. Although there was much grumbling, twenty-one, including Jackson, signed the document without delay; five other midshipmen, including Baldwin, signed later; the remaining two, George Harrison Hare and T. B. Shubrick, refused, and the former even sent a letter of complaint to Secretary Upshur. Jones told the two officers to leave the ship and return to the United States aboard the brig *St. Mary.*[30]

Jones learned the following summer that Upshur disapproved of his actions. He especially objected to Jones's demand that Shubrick either sign the dueling pledge, resign his commission, or be confined to the ship. Upshur wanted to know "under what law of your country, or what grant of power by that country to you, this thing was done." Shubrick, Upshur angrily argued, had been "placed there [on the ship] by this country & you had no right to displace him." He also maintained that Shubrick's resignation had been "*forced* from him" by Jones; Shubrick "had done nothing to deserve it." Upshur agreed in principle with Jones's intentions but opposed the method by which he had enforced his will. Jones had lost his battle with the department, but no duels occurred for the remainder of the ship's cruise. Midn. (later Rear Adm.) Samuel R. Franklin considered Jones one of the better officers of the day. He commented some years after the incident that "on the whole, Commodore Jones did well, and may have saved lives which otherwise would have been uselessly sacrificed, for youngsters do not always fight with pocket-pistols." Twenty years later, in 1862, Congress saw the wisdom of Jones's actions and passed an act that prohibited dueling, making it a court-martial offense.[31]

On arriving in Valparaiso on 6 May 1842, Jones learned that the rest of the squadron was anchored at Callao, Peru, under the command of Capt. John H. Aulick. The newly commissioned Aulick, commander of the sloop *Yorktown,* had taken control of the squadron after Commo. Alexander Claxton's death and had expected to remain as the senior officer. Apparently Aulick had been promised command of the squadron for at least a year by the new president of the Board of Navy Commissioners, Lewis Warrington. It was widely known in naval circles that Warrington disliked Jones and opposed his appointment as commander of the Pacific Squadron. In fact, Jones had been told that in one instance a member of Congress in the process of criticizing Jones for the constant delays in preparing the exploring expedition pointed to Warrington, then seated in the House gallery, as his source of information. In any case, Aulick now treated his superior with a chilly disrespect that was noticeable to the other captains of the squadron. After only five days Jones relieved Aulick of command on the official grounds that the *Yorktown*, a third-class sloop, was unsuitable for a captain. When Aulick protested, Jones showed tolerance and understanding by writing a frank personal response admitting that Aulick's recent conduct had contributed greatly to his dismissal. Should Aulick want to protest the decision, Jones would be willing to settle the affair publicly in Washington. Apparently discretion prevailed and nothing else came of the affair; Aulick returned to the United States and shortly afterward assumed command of a navy yard.

On 23 June Jones put the entire squadron to sea for two months to practice fleet maneuvers. He instructed all the vessels to tack, wear, and make and shorten sail together in harmonic precision. It was an exciting cruise because most of the officers had never participated in such exercises. Moreover, the exercise vividly illustrated the importance of ships operating in unison. The maneuvers also clearly demonstrated the need for a uniform system of signal codes. Most commodores either employed their own codes or used none at all. In fact, a lieutenant aboard the flagship informed Jones that he had served in the Pacific before and the commodore had hoisted signals only twice during the entire cruise. Armed with such information, Jones designed and submitted to the Navy Department a set of uniform signals. Like many of his suggestions, the memorial was filed away and ignored.[32]

When Jones took his station at Callao, he learned firsthand of the uncertainty that Upshur had tried to convey during their previous meetings. Two months earlier a French squadron had departed from Valparaiso for an unknown destination. Jones and British admiral Richard Thomas believed the French were planning a settlement in California. In a report to the secretary Jones wrote that "California is deserving the attention of our Government," and that any European colonization attempt would "be disastrous to our . . . interests." This rumor of an impending French settlement, combined with a flurry of activity in early September, heightened tensions and helped to precipitate Jones's subsequent actions.[33]

On 5 September a mail steamer arrived at Callao from Panama, and soon thereafter HMS *Dublin*, Thomas's flagship, weighed anchor with sealed orders. Jones, knowing that the British regularly advertised when their ships would sail, suspected that Thomas's secretive departure indicated colonization designs. The steamer also brought information that led Jones and other observers to believe that the United States and Mexico were already at war.[34]

Troubled by the war news and the hasty departure of the British squadron, Jones traveled the eight miles to Lima to confer with the American chargé d'affaires, James Chamberlayne Pickett. While he was meeting with Pickett, dispatches arrived from John Parrott, the U.S. consul at Mazatlán, Mexico. Enclosed with the dispatches were two newspapers. A copy of the Mexican *El Cosmopolito* dated 4 June 1842 contained letters on the subject of Texas from the Mexican government and Waddy Thompson, the U.S. minister to Mexico. The tone of these notes and Parrott's suggestion that they would cause a breakdown of relations between the two countries substantiated Jones's belief that if war had not yet begun it was close at hand. A Boston newspaper ran an article from the *New Orleans Advertiser* of 19 April claiming that "according to authentic information . . . Mexico has ceeded [*sic*] the Californias to Great Britain for seven millions of dollars!" After carefully considering all the available information, Jones and Pickett concluded that the reports could be accepted at face value. The two men decided that if war with Mexico had indeed begun, Jones would be justified in forestalling British occupation of California. Jones returned to Callao to ready his ships.[35]

Jones intended to keep his plans secret, but his unusual activities and the hasty departure of the British squadron aroused curiosity. In addition, the *Cyane*'s cargo—fourteen dozen spades, thirty-two axes, one hoe, one pickax, one dozen hatchets, and 1,045 pounds of bar iron, peculiar merchandise for a naval vessel—raised questions about the upcoming mission. An unfortunate lack of wind delayed Jones's departure until the afternoon of 7 September, giving the British ships a two-day head start. Nonetheless, Jones planned to put to sea, crowd on sail, and reach California before the British. Once in California he would disembark his force, build defenses onshore, and prevent the British from landing. Britain's claim of a treaty of cession would be nullified by Americans' occupation of the land. Jones planned to make a defensive seizure and quoted Emmerich Vattel, the noted eighteenth-century authority on international law, that "defensive war requires no declaration, nor even, on urgent occasions, an expressed order from the sovereign," for justifi cation. Jones pressed forward with all possible speed, ignorant of the fact that the true British destination was the Mosquito Islands off the Atlantic coast of present-day Nicaragua.[36]

Jones left a letter behind at Callao for Com. John S. Nicholas, commander of the *Yorktown*, which was on a cruise to the south, explaining his intentions. One day out from port, Jones backed topsails long enough for his fleet commanders to board the flagship. He presented Capt. James Armstrong of the *United States*, Com. Cornelius K. Stribling of the *Cyane*, and Com. Thomas A. Dornin of the *Dale* with the information that had brought the fleet to sea. Jones then asked, "Is the rumor of war between the United States and Mexico . . . and the cession of the Californias . . . to Great Britain, sufficiently probable to justify the withdrawal . . . of our naval force from the coast of Peru and to Chile, to send . . . to California?" The commanders unanimously answered, "Yes, without doubt."[37]

Jones's second question was more ambiguous: "Under what circumstances would it be proper for us to anticipate Great Britain in her contemplated military occupation of California?" After careful deliberation the officers agreed that "in case the United States and Mexico are at war, it would be our bounden duty to possess ourselves of every point and port in California that we could take and defend." Furthermore, they concurred that if the "views of the late President Monroe, in his celebrated message to Congress, December 2, 1823," were still "received as the avowed and fixed policy of our country, . . . we should consider the military occupation of the Californias by any Power, . . . as a measure so decidedly hostile to the true interest of the United States as not only to warrant but to make it our duty to forestall . . . Great Britain." Shortly after the officers reached this conclusion, the *Dale* left the squadron and headed for Panama with dispatches for Washington while the *United States* and the *Cyane* proceeded to the coast of California to act as circumstances dictated.[38]

On the cruise north to California the *Cyane* and the *United States* became separated and did not rejoin until they neared Monterey, Alta California, on 16 October. Jones noted during his journey that he did not see a "single strange sail" north of the equator. Surprisingly, this did not prompt him to question the rumor that war had begun. The northward passage was unusually slow due to obstinate head winds, which forced the ships to sail west after crossing the equator almost to the Sandwich Islands before they could put about and head to the northeast.[39]

The prolonged journey worked to the advantage of Jones and his crew because it allowed time for gunnery training and small arms practice, which, according to one report, continued both day and night. Alonzo C. Jackson of the *United States* later informed a relative that on every calm day the crew transported a barrel two miles out to be used for target practice. During the practice, he said, a whole broadside, consisting of twenty-six guns, would be fired simultaneously, "a thing that is very seldom done." Midshipman Franklin recalled that a company of one hundred men chosen to drill daily with muskets sharpened their cutlasses to a razor edge and improved their marksmanship by firing at a bag suspended from the foremast. This display of firepower and drill made a vivid impression on all present and developed the backbone for any decision Jones and his squadron had to enforce.[40]

On 18 October, a few hours out of Monterey, Jones issued an order publicly notifying his command: "We are now approaching the shore of California, the territory of Mexico, the enemy of our country, whose flag it is our duty to strike, and hoist in its place our own." Jones informed his men that they not only had to take Monterey, they "must keep it afterwards, at all hazards." Jones stressed that while the Mexican soldiers should be treated as enemies, the innocent civilians must be reconciled to the change and, if possible, brought over to the U.S. side. The United States, he maintained, must appear as the "protectors of all, and not the oppressor of any." To fulfill these expectations Jones established regulations that prohibited maltreatment of the inhabitants and plundering of any kind. Once the orders had been read to the crew the commanders selected landing parties to go ashore and take possession of Monterey.[41]

On the morning of the 19 October 1842, the *United States* and the *Cyane* rounded Point Pinos off the southern tip of Monterey Bay. The two ships, having hoisted the British Union Jack as part of their disguise, sighted the Mexican bark *Joven Guipuzcoana*, and a chase ensued. Jones ordered the flagship to fire a shot across the bow of the Mexican vessel, and this convinced the frightened commander to stop. Joseph F. Snook, the English commander of the Mexican vessel, claimed that he was involved only in the coastal trade and knew nothing of the international diplomatic situation. Unwilling to take any chances, Jones disregarded Snook's plea to be released and instructed the *Cyane* to take the prize in to Monterey.[42]

Jones ordered the flagship to hoist the Stars and Stripes and then sailed alone into the harbor. At 2:45 P.M. the frigate dropped anchor off the castle of Monterey, "a dilapidated work mounting eleven guns." Jones raised a white truce flag and waited anxiously for several hours, expecting a visit at any moment by some American or neutral party from whom he might obtain "disinterested information." When no one came forward, Jones became suspicious. He had the flagship's guns primed, loaded, and ready for offensive or defensive action. Still no one came. By 3:30 the *Cyane* had anchored beside the flagship and Stribling had its guns readied for action. Finally, a small boat flying Mexican colors approached Jones's flagship. Not yet wanting to reveal his intentions, Jones asked the Mexican officers a series of questions, but the Mexicans were so nervous he could not learn anything from them. They "had never heard of any difficulties between Mexico and the United States," they told him, and they "knew nothing of war."[43]

Not satisfied with this information, Jones summoned the mate of the nearby American merchant ship *Fame*, who claimed that the vessel had been delayed for almost a week in the Sandwich Islands because of war rumors. Yet he remarked that nothing had occurred since his ship arrived in Monterey, although he had heard a report that the British planned to seize Upper California and guarantee Mexico's possession of Lower California. This story, combined with a flurry of activity in the Mexican fort, confirmed what Jones had heard in Callao, and he decided that "the time for action had now arrived."[44]

By four o'clock that afternoon, with Jones's private secretary, Henry LaReintrie, acting as interpreter, Captain Armstrong of the *United States* had gone ashore under a flag of truce and demanded the surrender of Monterey. Papers for the capitulation had apparently been prepared in advance because there were copies in both English and Spanish. Additionally the date, place, and signature lines had been left blank, probably so they could be used in different towns if necessary. The existence of these forms has fueled speculation that Jones's actions were premeditated before he left the United States and that he would have seized any point in California, but it may have also reflected his desire to save time and gain control of Monterey before the British arrived.[45]

Jones offered straightforward and simple terms of surrender and gave Juan Bautista Alvarado, the acting governor of Monterey, eighteen hours to make his decision. Alvarado, initially willing to surrender the port without question, later equivocated and turned the problem over to Don Mariano Silva, the city's military commandant. Silva quickly concluded that the city's defenses—twenty-nine regular soldiers, eleven pieces of artillery, and a castle in serious disrepair—were no match for the Americans' guns; the only sensible recourse was surrender. Shortly after 11:00 P.M. two Mexican officials boarded the *United States* to surrender Monterey. The parties agreed to sign the formal articles of capitulation the following morning at 9:30 and to raise the U.S. flag at 11:00 on 20 October 1842.[46]

Thomas O. Larkin, an American merchant from Monterey, accompanied the Mexicans as their interpreter later that evening when the commission boarded the flagship. During the negotiations Larkin asked which side had declared war. One of the American delegates responded that the declaration was conditional and on the part of Mexico. Surprised, Larkin retorted that he had onshore several papers of "late dates," some as recent as 20 August 1842, that made no mention of strife between the two countries. Larkin went ashore to find the papers but failed to produce them, leading Jones to believe that he had been attempting some kind of subterfuge. Jones concluded that the need for action was even more urgent than he had previously believed.[47]

The Mexican commissioners, José Abrego and Pedro Narváez, "appeared impatient to surrender the country." They boarded the flagship two hours early to sign the formal articles by which the U.S. forces would land and take possession of Monterey. The landing party, composed of 150 sailors and marines, then went ashore; Jones's son Meriwether was one of the midshipmen who accompanied them. The marines proceeded to the town, where they received the arms and took the barracks of the Mexican troops, while the sailors occupied the castle that overlooked the harbor. The entire conquest ended without incident except for the shouting, the cheers, the music, and the thirty-six-gun salute that accompanied the raising of Old Glory above the newly named "Fort Catesby." The Mexican troops and a number of suspected spies were confined. Jones reported that the operation had been "conducted in a most orderly manner."[48]

The afternoon and night of 20 October passed without incident, and all but one division of marines returned to the ships. On the following morning Commodore Jones went ashore to inspect the town and fort now flying the Stars and Stripes. Once he landed, the pomp and ceremony abruptly came to an end. Jones's secretary had finally found the papers Larkin had mentioned the previous day. Dated as late as 22 August 1842, they mentioned nothing of hostilities between the United States and Mexico or the cession of California to Great Britain. Jones, suddenly realizing his mistake, called an immediate conference with Armstrong and Stribling, and they agreed that the only course of action was to restore Mexican authority and try to mend relations. At 4:00 P.M. the marines lowered the American flag and, with as much pomp as had accompanied its raising the day before, rehoisted the Mexican flag. The troops were reembarked, and property that had been seized was returned.[49]

The reaction of Monterey's inhabitants to the invasion varied, mainly because they were such a diverse group, including Anglo-Americans, Mexicans, foreigners, and native Californians. At first many of them had seemed frightened, but with Jones's proclamation that there would be neither looting nor violence and that native rights would be respected, fear gave way to admiration for the Yankee invaders. As Larkin recounted in 1844, "the fear and apprehension of the lower class of People here was at its height, drawing their recollections from the horrible atrocities commetted [sic] by the Spaniards, and they expected to see the same enacted here." Many of the town's public officials found themselves suddenly summoned away on urgent business when they heard the news of the invasion. Yet they returned as hastily on hearing that the Americans "did not shoot at sight, then scalp their victims with a great knife, as many . . . believed was the habit of the fighting Yanquis." As a result of the orderly landing, Larkin reported that "the people are not afraid of the next squadron, perhaps many are anxiously waiting its arrival." More important, because there was no incident of questionable conduct during the occupation, the people generally seemed to view the marines as "a fine body of Young men" whose departure would leave a void along the coast of California.[50]

Several incidents raised the prestige of the bluejackets in the eyes of the Californians. For example, when one marine made a purchase and then borrowed a pitcher to obtain water, he actually paid for the item and returned the pitcher. According to Larkin, Mexican troops rarely paid for anything. While the ships remained in Monterey the men mingled with the inhabitants ashore, either "hunting wild Deer or dancing with the tame Dear, both being plenty in and about Monterey," noted Larkin. The flagship had an excellent German band that provided the impetus for a number of balls—"as many Balls as there were Sundays"—

and some sailors who had never danced before learned on this occasion. Larkin called attention to the fine discipline of the men and to the speed and precision of the American ships during an emergency. This impressed the male population, he said, while it took only the young men in uniform to entice the females. Larkin also pointed out that there had never been better order.[51]

One story neither Larkin nor Jones chose to recount concerned Meriwether Jones, the commodore's son, who was sent ashore for the ceremonial lowering of the American flag and the rehoisting of the Mexican flag. Young Jones dramatically exclaimed that he could not strike the American flag and then proceeded to get so drunk that he rolled down a small cliff. This must have been especially embarrassing for Jones given his crusade against alcohol.[52]

Both Jones and Larkin tried to conceal their embarrassment over the premature seizure of Monterey by concluding the incident with many banquets and dances. Larkin's primary fear, that the landing would stir up hostile feelings toward the United States among the natives and foreigners of California, proved to be unfounded, and he was relieved to find that it had just the opposite effect.[53]

The Californians, as distinguished from the Mexicans, "showed a very imperfect sense of how much they had been injured by this insult offered to Mexico." Subsequent relations with them were no less cordial than before, and the incident passed without further consequence. Even so, Larkin feared that if the navy did not leave behind a ship, Governor General José Manuel Micheltorena would "let loose, his army of Cut throats and robbers, (in retaliation for the insult this territory has received) to plunder the property." To prevent this, he petitioned Commodore Jones to station a ship off the coast to protect the innocent. No incident occurred to justify this precaution, but Larkin nonetheless felt much more at ease.[54]

Although the affair had been settled without rancor in California, it had serious repercussions at the national level. The government in Mexico, with the help of the Mexican press, criticized the barbarity of "Thomas APE Jones," creating an atmosphere in which the Tyler administration had to suspend negotiations for the purchase of California. Some Mexican officials even suggested that the incident could be invoked to legitimize the cancellation of all U.S. claims against Mexico, but cooler heads prevailed. Waddy Thompson, the U.S. minister to Mexico, tried to convince the Mexican foreign minister, José María Bocanegra, that it was no dishonor to surrender to a superior force, and that since no public or private property had been damaged, relations could be normalized. Should any claims arise, Thompson pledged that they would be paid in full by the U.S. government. In Washington, Secretary of State Daniel Webster and Mexican minister to the United States Gen. Juan N. Almonte exchanged sharp notes. After considerable discussion all the diplomatic parties involved agreed that Jones should be recalled and reprimanded for his actions.[55]

While the diplomats settled the affair at the national level Jones worked on the Pacific coast to harmonize relations. The flagship remained at Monterey until 22 November, one full month after the American flag had been hauled down, and then departed for the Hawaiian Islands; Jones transferred his pennant to the *Cyane* and remained in Monterey until 11 December. During that time Jones worked diligently to improve his and his country's damaged image. He wrote to his friend Virginia congressman Henry Wise, explaining what had happened and referring him to the official report that Jones had submitted; in one letter Jones hoped that the "wrong will rest on me and not the government." He also confessed to Wise that he had not known the true international state of affairs when he acted. It is possible that Jones wrote to Wise, an influential congressman as well as a friend, because he knew his fellow Virginian would defend his reputation and assert that his actions were an honest mistake, thereby removing any blame from the Tyler administration.[56]

One week after the seizure of Monterey Governor Micheltorena invited Jones to a conference at the village of Los Angeles to settle the affair. A date in January was set for the conference. Before meeting with the governor Jones contacted Harvard graduate Dr. John Marsh, a naturalized Mexican citizen who owned considerable land in California, to learn everything he could about the region. Marsh sent him a lengthy discourse on California history that vividly illustrated the disorder the region had recently experienced. Jones also met secretly with Abel Stearns, a prominent American businessman who had married into a prominent California family. In late December Col. Manuel Vallejo, the former commandant general of Alta California, treated Jones and his staff to a lavish party that included a cannon salute, rodeo, Indian dances, and footraces at his home in Sonoma. Soon after meeting with Vallejo, Jones visited vintner Jean Louis Vignes at Aliso, and the Frenchman gave wine and brandy to Jones and his officers, as well as several barrels to be taken to President Tyler.[57]

When the *Cyane* anchored off San Pedro, the port for Los Angeles, on the afternoon of 17 January 1843, Jones found one of Micheltorena's aides awaiting his arrival. The Mexican officer carried a note from the general inviting Jones and his entourage to a reception at the settlement of Los Angeles, some thirty miles away. After a lavish dinner on the following afternoon Jones, accompanied by Commandant Stribling, Dr. Clymer, and Mr. LaReintrie, departed for the interior in a fine carriage; Purser Gibson, three midshipmen, and Jones's slave Griffin Dobson followed on horseback.

During the ten-league trip inland from San Pedro Jones noticed the splendid gold and silver braids and decorative badges on the Mexican officers' uniforms as well as the "gaudily caparisoned" horses of the twenty-five lancers, a sharp contrast to the sober dress blues of the American officers. Being a farmer, Jones also noticed that the convoy traversed an arid and parched plain without trees or shrubs as far as the eye could see. Not foreseeing the importance of irrigation, Jones concluded that the lack of water and vegetation "destined [these lands] to become a desert waste, unfit for man's habitation." But he did notice black mustard plants that stretched eight or nine feet tall and innumerable flocks of birds, including several varieties of "the sweet little skylark, which abound[ed] on the shores of [the] Potomac!" Arriving at Los Angeles shortly before nightfall, the Americans were taken to the home of Abel Stearns, where they were greeted by almost twenty American citizens from the area. Later, General Micheltorena and his staff appeared in full military dress, and the general told Jones that after their interview the following day he would host a party for the Americans.[58]

When Jones arrived for the noon meeting with Micheltorena he was not sure what to expect or what the general would demand. After the usual courtesies and conversation, Micheltorena began by reading aloud in Spanish a list of formal articles to be signed by him and by Jones. These eight provisions, drafted only days after the Monterey incident, blamed Jones for the outrage in October and insisted that the American fleet at San Pedro fire their guns in a salute to the Mexican flag. Moreover, the articles instructed Jones to pay fifteen thousand dollars to the California treasury for the trouble created by the general alarm. He must also provide a complete set of military musical instruments and fifteen hundred infantry uniforms for those ruined during the Mexicans army's forced march to Monterey. As Micheltorena read, Jones's secretary slowly translated the passages and the general's intentions became apparent. Jones was astonished at what he heard; the provisions were preposterous, and he certainly could not sign them in the name of his government. Rather than create another diplomatic incident, Jones told the general he needed to have a fully translated copy of the articles before he could comment officially. The meeting ended and Jones retired to Stearns's spacious Spanish-style mansion to prepare for the party later that evening.[59]

Shortly before eight o'clock that night one of Micheltorena's aides delivered quadruplicates of the articles in both Spanish and English. Jones finished dressing for the ball and then studied and discussed the provisions with Commandant Stribling. As he read, Jones became more and more incensed, and soon "feelings of disgust mingled with commiseration" overwhelmed him. His first impulse was to return the papers without comment and to have no further communication with Micheltorena. Instead, Jones decided to attend the ball to learn more about the character of Micheltorena and Mexicans in general.

The party was a grand occasion despite a tumultuous downpour that turned the streets into a quagmire. Jones thoroughly enjoyed himself as he danced the evening away with Stearns's wife, Doña Arcadia Bandini de Stearns, and her beautiful sister. When Jones left the party at 2:00 A.M. he felt that he understood much more about the gracious Mexican manner and about Micheltorena personally. He had discovered that the general had literally been sent into California exile by General Antonio López de Santa Anna and hoped that the way he handled the Monterey affair might win for him renewed acceptance in Mexico City.[60]

On the morning of 20 January Jones graciously thanked Micheltorena and Stearns, his host. He informed the general that he did not have the authority to sign the articles but promised to pass them along to his superiors in Washington. Micheltorena asked Jones to remain until he could prepare official dispatches, complete with copies of Jones's correspondence, for the Mexican government. Jones agreed and spent a second night in Los Angeles. At about 1:00 P.M. on 21 January, Jones, LaReintrie, and Dobson departed amid the beating of drums, the firing of cannon, the ringing of bells, and a formal salute from Micheltorena. The trip had been necessary to repair strained U.S.-Mexican relations along the California coast, but it had also been entertaining and informative. Jones had learned much about Micheltorena and the differences between Cal-ifornians and Mexicans. At five that afternoon Jones arrived at San Pedro, where he ate dinner with Englishman John Forster, and within three hours the *Cyane* departed for Mazatlán.[61]

When Jones arrived at Mazatlán in early February 1843 he found the *United States* and the sloop *Yorktown* already present. After a month-long stay in the port, the three ships departed for Valparaiso. The south-ern trip proved quite difficult. The fleet encountered calm seas and no winds, ultimately forcing Jones to place the men on short rations for more than a month. One seaman remarked that it "was a trying time, and there was no telling what our sufferings might have been had not a kind providence favoured us with a breeze." Finally, on 27 April, the fleet arrived in Valparaiso.[62]

When the squadron reached port Jones heard that he was to be relieved by Commo. Alexander J. Dallas, who was then on his way to the Pacific. The order from the Navy Department was said to be dated 24 January 1843 but had not yet arrived in the Pacific because of the slow nature of communications. Jones's contemporaries asserted that it was news of his recall that prompted Jones's decision to proceed to the Hawaiian Islands and claimed that the maneuver represented nothing more than an attempt to retain his command. Some historians agree. It may be true, yet Jones also sincerely believed that events in Hawaii justified his decision.[63]

At Valparaiso Jones learned from passing ships' captains about the unauthorized British seizure of the Hawaiian Islands by Capt. Lord George Paulet. The news must have given Jones some satisfaction, considering his own recent unauthorized seizure of foreign territory. Apparently in consequence of the self-interested misrepresentations of British consul Richard Charlton, Paulet had presented a series of demands to King Kamehameha III. When the Hawaiian monarch did not fully meet the British demands, Paulet took over on 25 February 1843 and held the islands as a British territory. Paulet apparently had no governmental authority for the seizure; thus his actions represented a British version of Jones's Monterey affair.[64]

Jones did not sail immediately for the Hawaiian Islands. He remained in Valparaiso for a time, expecting his replacement via Cape Horn at any moment. Yet no official word came. In early June, Jones took the flagship to Callao and waited seventeen more days for Dallas to arrive via Panama. Eight months had passed since his seizure of Monterey and he still had received no official notice of his status. Jones knew, moreover, that Paulet had held Hawaii for four months, and that every day he waited for official news the British grip over the islands strengthened, a prospect that concerned Jones greatly. On 21 June 1843 Jones gave up waiting for his replacement and departed for the islands he had not seen since 1827.[65]

On 22 July the *United States* anchored off Hilo and Jones learned that Capt. Lawrence Kearny and the *Constellation* had arrived at Honolulu some sixteen days earlier. Kearny had protested Paulet's actions—as Jones would have done—and had met with King Kamehameha as a sign of U.S. support. Kearny's contact with the king angered Paulet and created a hostile, tense situation that was abated only by of the appearance of Rear Adm. Richard Thomas of the Royal Navy on 26 July. Thomas disavowed Paulet's actions as soon as he arrived and on 31 July returned the government to the Hawaiian monarch. Not coincidentally, Thomas had departed Valparaiso at the same time as Jones, so he realized that there were two U.S. frigates in the islands. The restored Hawaiian monarchy proclaimed the first ten days of August an occasion for celebrating its regained independence.[66]

Jones remained in Hawaii for eleven days while he learned more about the situation. Missionary Titus Coan informed him that Captain Paulet had gone "directly to the prisons, and . . . turned loose a company of infamous men and women, to spread pollution through the community." Jones sympathized with the Christians on the island who had to face such wickedness and vowed to do all within his power to fight the evil that was overtaking the island. He agreed to use the flagship's fine band to entertain the islanders at a meeting, after which he presented to about two thousand people a rousing sermon on the evils of drink. Coan concluded that Jones was still "the same firm and fearless friend to truth and of universal improvement that he was when he visited [in] 1826."[67]

Armed with information about recent events in the islands Jones made the one-day trip to Honolulu on 3 August. There he found Kearny's *Constellation* lying outside the harbor; the frigate had too much draft to cross the bar that commanded the port. The flagship and the *Cyane* also remained outside the harbor, joining Paulet's and Thomas's frigates and a British sloop. It could have been a tense situation had Thomas not overturned Paulet's actions. Instead, Jones discovered that the islanders were in the fourth day of celebrating the Hawaiian monarchy's restoration and he allowed his crew to join in the festivities. During his sixteen days in port Jones met with Thomas, Paulet, and other British officers; with the acting U.S. consul William Hooper; and with island officials. He attended a dinner aboard Thomas's flagship and reciprocated on Saturday, 13 August, by hosting a luncheon meeting for King Kamehameha and Admiral Thomas aboard the *United States.* Ten months earlier Jones had been prepared to fight to prevent the British from taking possession of California. Now he worked diligently to establish harmony between the British and American factions on the island, and between the Hawaiian monarchy and British officials. Jones understood the importance of Hawaii to future American commerce and expansion, and he was trying to win the respect and friendship of the islanders. As he departed, he drafted a letter suggesting that the Navy Department should establish a "naval depot" in Honolulu; he reported that "the local council have agreed to the landing of our naval stores and provisions free of duty." Jones apparently had won the trust of the island government, and in doing so had brought the islands one step closer to the United States.[68]

Before departing, Jones issued orders for all deserters from American ships to be rounded up and returned to the ships they belonged to or be signed aboard the *United States.* One seaman who mustered unwillingly aboard Jones's flagship on 17 August 1843 was Herman Melville, who had deserted at Nuku Hiva from the whaler *Acushnet* before making his way to Hawaii. He had been working as a clerk for an English mercantile company in Honolulu and had signed a one-year contract extension in early June. There is no indication why Melville violated his contract and returned to sea. Perhaps it was because of Jones's orders, or perhaps a Hawaiian turned him in, in accordance with the 1826 treaty Jones had previously negotiated. Regardless, Melville returned to a profession he intensely hated, and he transferred some of his rancor to Jones; he disparagingly referred to Jones as "Commodore J" in *Moby Dick,* and as "the high and mighty commodore" in his novel *White Jacket.*[69]

Still having received no official communications, Jones decided to return to Valparaiso via the Marquesas Islands and Tahiti. Kearny meanwhile would return via California. When Jones arrived at Nuku Hiva on 6 October, he found a French fleet commanded by Rear Admiral Dupetit-Thouars, who informed Jones that Commodore Dallas had arrived at Callao the previous July to replace him. This was the first official news Jones received of his recall. After enlisting several seamen discharged from a whaler because of misconduct and taking on more water and food,

Jones immediately left for Tahiti, where he landed on 13 October. At
Matavia Bay he found Thomas's flagship, the French frigate *Thetis*, several whalers and trading vessels, and a letter from Dallas ordering Jones to
return to the United States as soon as possible. A week later Jones set off
for the coast of South America. After an uneventful thirty-three-day voyage the *United States* anchored at Valparaiso.[70]

Dallas had left several letters in Valparaiso for Jones before taking off
in hot pursuit of the *United States*. The irate Dallas, insinuating that
Jones's voyage to the islands was a deliberate attempt to maintain his command, instructed Jones to proceed to Callao and wait. Before departing
Chile for Callao two weeks later Jones responded to Dallas's charges.
That "the activity of [the Pacific] squadron should strike you with surprise is not very unnatural, when compared with the indolence of my
predecessors," he wrote. Jones maintained, moreover, that he had come
to the Pacific "to correct abuses, and to set an example of activity." Perhaps, he mused, tongue in cheek, "your success may be as great as mine
has been, though I hope your reward may be very different." On arriving
at Callao, Jones found Kearny's *Constellation* and more curt letters, but
not Commodore Dallas.[71]

Jones waited for Dallas at Callao for thirty-eight days. He wondered if
he should continue waiting for Dallas, as one letter suggested, or immediately return home, as another had ordered. Jones decided that since
Dallas had already assumed command of the squadron he would return
to Washington in accordance with Secretary Upshur's instructions. At
3:30 P.M. on 21 January 1844 Jones addressed his men for the last time
and then handed the ship's log and other important papers to Captain
Armstrong. It must have been a sad occasion for Jones as he watched his
broad red pennant lowered; the ship fired a thirteen-gun salute and the
men gave three hearty cheers as he, Dobson, and LaReintrie left the ship
and boarded the *Constellation* for home.[72]

Dallas arrived in Callao a month later and learned, much to his chagrin, that Jones had escaped him again. Still fuming, he wrote a vitriolic
letter to the Navy Department accusing Jones of insubordination and
demanding that he be court-martialed. The months of seething and searching for Jones had exacted a heavy toll on Dallas. Less than four months
later, in early June, he suddenly died aboard his flagship. Ironically, Jones's
path would cross Dallas's again. When Jones returned as commander of
the Pacific Squadron four years later in 1848, his first assignment was to

oversee the disinterment of Commodore Dallas's body from Lima. Jones must have gotten some satisfaction as he ordered the coffin placed on the storeship *Erie*, which sailed astern the flagship; Dallas was again chasing Jones across the Pacific Ocean.[73]

When Jones arrived back in Washington in 1844 he learned that much had changed in the Navy Department. Upshur had moved to the State Department and Thomas W. Gilmer had assumed the duties of secretary of the navy, then both men had died on 28 February 1844 when the "Peacemaker" gun exploded aboard the *Princeton*. Virginian John Y. Mason had been appointed to replace Gilmer, and he had to settle the Monterey affair as well as Dallas's charges of insubordination. Jones felt compelled to address Dallas's charges formally. Instead, Mason chose to discard both complaints. The secretary reasoned that Dallas had been correct in assuming command of the squadron when he did, and that Jones had acted properly by not relinquishing command until he had formal confirmation of his recall. As far as the department was concerned the affair was over. Jones was not censured for his premature seizure of Monterey, and his prolonged voyage to the islands could be explained by Upshur's recall letter, which instructed Jones to "return to the United States in such mode as may be most convenient and agreeable."[74]

Before he left the Navy Department Secretary Upshur had agreed to recall Jones, but he had made it clear to Secretary of State Daniel Webster and President Tyler that he would not jeopardize morale in the navy by humiliating "an able and well-intentioned commander." This was surprising because Jones was hardly one of Upshur's favorites. Yet in the end Upshur staunchly defended Jones, a fellow Virginian. Perhaps the secretary felt partially responsible for the events at Monterey, thinking he had misled the commodore during the several informal conferences the two had held before Jones left for the Pacific.[75]

The House of Representatives did take action against Jones once news of the seizure of Monterey reached Washington. Ex-president John Quincy Adams, who led the attack, believed that Jones's actions were not, as some claimed, the efforts of a misguided officer but rather part of a grand scheme. Adams confronted Webster on 25 March 1842 at the State Department for three hours trying to gain information concerning the affair. Webster maintained that the administration was not responsible for the incident; the commodore's actions, he said, were a "freak of his own brain, without any authority or instructions whatever." But Webster refused to answer Adams's questions concerning the government's attempt to acquire California, avoiding the issue by claiming that his answers would reveal sensitive information. Adams did not believe him; he rationalized that "it would have never entered into the head of Jones to commit such an outrage upon a nation whom he believed able to resent it." Jones must have been following orders.[76]

The investigation by the House Committee on Foreign Affairs exonerated Tyler and Webster and concluded that the seizure of Monterey "was entirely of [Jones's] own authority, and not in consequence of any orders or instructions given to him by the Government of the United States." Although Jones was officially saddled with the responsibility, the complicity of President Tyler is not beyond question. Tyler was involved in financing Duff Green's secret mission to London in 1843 to settle the Oregon question, and his involvement in that affair was hidden from the Senate and the public. According to Silas Reed, who claimed to have been with the president when the news of the seizure reached the White House, Tyler had "hinted" to Jones before his departure to beware of French and British movements and, above all, not to "let them gain a 'preemptive' right to any of the California harbors." After hearing of the abortive seizure, Tyler supposedly remarked, "Jones has got me into trouble, and I have done the same with him. I will, however, have to disavow his act to Mexico, but will make it all right with him."[77]

Shortly before leaving office Tyler, working through Mason, did make it all right with Jones. The secretary informed Jones that despite his recall, the president perceived "evidence of ardent zeal" in Jones's service to his country. There would be no "punishment of any description for conduct actuated by any such elevated principles of duty," and Jones would be given a new command as soon as possible. Within two months new navy secretary George Bancroft would offer him another assignment.[78]

Because the Navy Department did not publicly exonerate or defend Jones, the prevailing belief among those in the service was that he had been punished. Moreover, any officer who made an incorrect decision such as that in the future could expect the same fate. One midshipman serving on blockade duty at the beginning of the Mexican War in 1846 remarked that "the humbug policy of our government in regards to its Navy has made timid men of our Captains—afraid of consequences save a few such as the hero of Monterey (C. A. Jones)." One Californian saw events differently and surmised that "it often takes an indiscreet enthusiast to incite others to action. The action of Com. Jones may have been ominous." Certainly the seizure demonstrated the lengths to which the U.S. government would go to prevent California from falling into British hands. Jones's actions also showed how easy the capture of California would be. In this view, Navy Department officials knew exactly what had happened in Hawaii after the Monterey incident because Jones had informed them in several letters. And the secretary could not publicly praise his actions in Hawaii for fear of insulting Mexico, or at least exacerbating the poor relations with that country.[79]

The "hero of Monterey" had to wait for his mistake to fade from public memory before he could expect to be restored to command. This was particularly difficult for an officer who had spent his entire career glorifying his own successes—his selfless sacrifice at New Orleans, his opening of diplomatic relations with the Pacific Islands, and even his untiring work with naval ordnance. He had done all the department had asked of him and more, without a modicum of public gratitude. Throughout his career Jones believed that his government did not appreciate his services. His advancement to the highest rank in the navy was no reward but rather what had been expected based on the prevailing system of seniority. While his promotion surely demonstrated confidence in his abilities, it did not provide the public recognition Jones believed he deserved, especially after the humiliation he suffered in his involvement with the South Seas Exploring Expedition. Jones had wanted badly to restore his reputation after that affair, yet his actions at Monterey had the opposite effect. After his return in 1844 he knew that he needed another command to rectify the impressions created at Monterey. In Jones's mind his first Pacific command had been necessary to improve his reputation after the South Seas Exploring Expedition imbroglio. Ironically, his second command in the Pacific would not revive his fortunes but rather would help to bring about his ultimate downfall.

～7～

JONES OVERSTEPPED
HIS AUTHORITY

Pacific Command and California, 1844–1850

*M*onths before Jones returned to his home in northern Virginia the *Daily National Intelligencer* reported his mistaken seizure of Monterey in an article entitled "An Untoward Occurrence." But after printing Jones's long letter of 10 September 1842, the editor reminded the newspaper's readers that "naval commanders . . . serving in remote seas, charged with high and responsible trusts—protectors and defenders of the flag of the Republic—are often constrained to act decisively and promptly, according to their view of facts and circumstances seen only by the lights shed around them at the time." The "lights" Jones had seen on the coast of South America in 1842 had prompted him to seize Monterey, and he believed until his dying day that he had made the correct choice based on what he knew. Even so, Jones knew that he would have to secure another sea command to redeem himself. Unfortunately, his next command would brand him forever as an inflexible tyrant watching over a squadron of "prison ships."[1]

Jones desperately wanted the support of the public as well as formal approval from the Navy Department and the president for his actions. He told Secretary Mason after his return that unless the department restored him to duty, his case would be a lesson to every other officer in the navy. Thenceforth it would be better for officers to be prudent "than to follow the impulse of patriotism." In fact, the Tyler administration did privately approve of the seizure while publicly downplaying the incident to harmonize relations with Mexico. The succeeding Polk administration would do likewise. Meanwhile, the Navy Department silently approved of Jones's patriotism, even allowing him to publish his correspondence relating to the affair. Secretary Bancroft, Mason's successor, also assured Jones that he would receive another command when one became available.[2]

As Jones awaited his next assignment he again took an active role in farming operations at Sharon. Before his trip to the Pacific he had conducted extensive experiments with soil additives and had concluded that crushed bone was better suited for the depleted lands of northern Virginia than any other putrescent manure. It was also more durable and cheaper, a plus for the cash-poor farmers of the area. Jones had been performing similar experiments for more than twenty years, and his efforts were gaining widespread attention. Northern farmers who had moved to northern Virginia seeking cheaper land sought out Jones for his expertise. One New Yorker claimed that Jones's operation "has become the pattern farm of the entire region." Other northern farmers were "pleased with the prospects before them." Jones certainly felt pleased with his own farming prospects—his livestock, land, and slave holdings were increasing—even if he was not completely happy about his professional prospects. Yet those, too, could change.[3]

During the spring of 1845 George Bancroft appointed Jones to a board of examiners convening at the shore school at the Naval Asylum in Philadelphia. Mathematician William A. Chauvenet had created a two-year course of instruction for midshipmen there that included subjects ranging from law and foreign languages to steam mechanics and sailing. The Navy Department required each midshipman to have four years of service at sea before enrolling. Once students had completed the courses, a board of officers administered written and oral examinations in seamanship, geography, math, and practical navigation. Although it was not the equivalent of West Point, the program did represent the beginning of formal education for navy officers.[4]

Bancroft supported the school in Philadelphia, but he wanted a permanent naval academy. He persuaded Secretary of War William L. Marcy to transfer the deserted army post of Fort Severn at Annapolis to the Navy Department, and also instructed the board of examiners to consider sites for such an institution and to recommend a course of study.

Bancroft had carefully selected the board during the spring of 1845, and correctly believed that his choices—Commos. Thomas ap Catesby Jones, George C. Reed, and Matthew C. Perry; and Capts. Isaac Mayo and E. A. F. Lavallette—were reform-minded officers who supported the concept of an academy. Equally important, Bancroft knew that all were respected by their peers.

The board suggested that naval cadets, aged thirteen to fifteen, be appointed in the same manner as those who attended West Point. Their coursework would also be identical to that at West Point, except for the abstruse study of calculus and service aboard a practice frigate and steamer stationed at the academy. Midshipmen would take an annual exam given by the school's academic board and three officers chosen by the secretary of the navy. After two years of study, the students would spend three years at sea and one year aboard the practice frigate before they were eligible to take the lieutenant's exam. The board's report was thoughtful as well as thought provoking. Two of the professors from the naval school offered similar recommendations in their own reports. The board concluded that this new institution should be the future source of the naval officer corps.[5]

In late July 1845 Bancroft instructed the officers to consider another question: promotion in the higher ranks. This was such a controversial issue that Bancroft decided to expand the board to twenty members. Promotion had always been determined almost exclusively by seniority. If an officer escaped dismissal or death, he would slowly advance when vacancies in the higher ranks became available, and ultimately would be promoted to captain, the navy's highest rank. Although Jones had been only thirty-nine when he achieved that rank in 1829, by 1845 promotions to captain averaged but two a year, and the lucky officers were nearly fifty years old. Bancroft estimated that if things continued at the present rate, the navy would soon not have a captain younger than seventy. Most officers acknowledged that this system kept exceptional young officers relegated to lower ranks until they had passed the prime of their lives. It also prompted many technology-minded officers to resign rather than remain subservient to unqualified commanders wed to the old ways or traditions. Neither scenario was good for the service.

The board's discussion of the promotion question was heated and stormy. The officers initially agreed overwhelmingly that promotion should not be based on seniority alone. But the system they proposed was as antiquated as, and much more complicated than, the one they were trying to replace. Their proposal would throw the issue of promotion into the Senate as a last recourse, making it a political question with all the attendant nuances that would entail. Bancroft had also instructed the board to recommend for promotion three commanders, three lieutenants, and six passed midshipmen. During discussion of this topic senior officers Charles Stewart and Jones vigorously protested the board's decision to make their choices by secret ballot. Stewart, arguing that a secret ballot was akin to the hated Star Chamber because officers had to give no reason for their vote, championed the system of advancement by seniority alone as the only non-political means for promotion. Jones agreed with some of Stewart's objections, but he opposed the system of promotion by seniority alone, feeling that this system stifled reform of the service and personal advancement. Jones cast blank ballots in protest throughout the proceedings.[6]

In early October 1845 Jones spent an evening with Bancroft and used the occasion to press for his reassignment as commander of the Pacific Squadron. He reminded Bancroft that his guiding maxim had always been: "He who does not stand up for his own rights is an unsafe depository for his country." Bancroft declined to discuss the matter and firmly told Jones that his appointment was not possible at the moment because it would undermine relations with Mexico. That was not the answer Jones had wanted to hear. He reminded Bancroft that the Tyler administration had cleared his name. President Tyler himself had said that if the country went to war, there was no one better suited to command the squadron than Jones. He also informed Bancroft that he had learned that the Pacific station was to be given to an officer junior to him. If so, in his mind there could be no question that the department viewed the Monterey affair as a stain on his career.[7]

Bancroft tried to convince him that such was not the case, but Jones refused to be mollified. Only a sea command would prove to him that he was not in disgrace. Less than two weeks later Bancroft offered Jones command of the unpopular African Squadron. With that offer Jones could no longer complain that he was being punished for the Monterey affair, but instead of accepting the post he declined it, claiming that he needed to remain in the United States during the winter of 1845–46. In its upcoming session Congress would again consider his request for reimbursement, and the Supreme Court was scheduled to rule on a case involving a financial loss he suffered while acting as surety for a relative who died owing money to the government. In fact, Jones did not want to sail the fever-ridden waters off the coast of West Africa chasing slavers. It was a position in which commanders gained no glory, no reward, and no thanks. Duty off Africa would take him out of the public eye and offer no chance for redemption. But Bancroft had called Jones's hand, and Jones could no longer complain that he was being slighted.[8]

Although he still wanted the Pacific Squadron, Jones knew that he would have to accept quietly almost any duty the department offered. When Jones learned that his friend and former commander William M. Crane had died in mid-March 1846, Jones asked for the now-vacant position of inspector of ordnance. Bancroft acquiesced because Jones had held the position twice before. The job again allowed Jones to remain at home, oversee his farming operations, and work to win favor with Bancroft and the Polk administration.[9]

Late in the spring of 1846, as President Polk asked Congress to declare war on Mexico, Jones found himself engrossed with religious concerns. His aunt Martha Corbin Tuberville Ball had donated two and a half acres of land for a church at Barrett's Crossroads, near present-day Vienna, Virginia, and Jones helped to organize and start the Lewinsville Presbyterian Church. Contributors from northern Virginia and the District of Columbia donated money, and the Winchester Presbytery sent Levi H. Christian to minister to the congregation. The church—a colonial white-frame structure with two potbellied stoves in the corners and a slave gallery above the vestibule—was completed for $650 and opened its doors to a congregation of seventeen members on 3 January 1847. Jones became the first trustee and was also the superintendent of the Sunday school. Since the church had accommodations for slaves, Jones instructed his own slaves, including Griffin Dobson and his family, to attend weekly services. Dobson's children also attended the "colored school" taught by the minister.[10]

The church represented a lifelong dream for Jones and Mary; her stepfather, Rev. William Maffitt, had proposed such a church two decades earlier. Mary Jones was also the sister-in-law of the Reverend Thomas Bloomer Balch, who had been working since 1844 to establish a church at Lewinsville. Jones had toiled vigorously for Christianity throughout his career in the navy, and for the remainder of his life he would work for this "family" church in Lewinsville. In April 1849 he signed as a trustee when the church gained legal possession of the land from the

Ball family. When the congregation built a parsonage, barn, and school-house, Jones and two others co-signed the loan. During his last years, when he was constantly beset by financial problems, Jones always donated food and wood for fuel and sent his slaves to assist the minister with daily chores. His last charitable act to the church came in the form of a codicil to his will in which he required his executors to pay the out-standing debt incurred during the construction of the parsonage.[11]

While Jones was busy building his church, U.S. military forces con-quered California and New Mexico. In the first three months of 1847 Gen. Zachary Taylor's volunteer forces defeated Santa Anna at the Bat-tle of Buena Vista and Gen. Winfield Scott used army and naval forces to besiege and capture Vera Cruz. Only two months before Scott's attack Jones had suggested an increased offensive role for the navy, including the use of heavy naval guns against the Mexican castle at Vera Cruz; Scott employed a similar plan in his attack. While others were reaping glory in combat, a sullen Jones remained at the Washington Navy Yard working with ordnance, far from the fighting. In November and Decem-ber 1846 he served on a joint army-navy board that reported favorably on Hale's rockets, but his old enemy Commo. Lewis Warrington, president of the board and chief of the Bureau of Naval Ordnance, successfully opposed adoption of the weapon.[12]

Jones wanted desperately to return as commander of the Pacific Squadron; he knew the war might be his last chance for glory—and per-haps also his last chance to redeem his faltering career. Finally, in late April 1847, fellow Virginian John Young Mason, who had replaced Ban-croft as navy secretary, told Jones to ready himself for command of the Pacific Squadron. Apparently Mason had just received a confidential let-ter from Capt. W. B. Shubrick, commanding the ship *Independence* at Monterey, containing an angry request to be ordered home. Mason had sent Commo. James Biddle to supervise naval operations along the Cali-fornia coast, prompting Shubrick to conclude that the department had lost confidence in him. "Commodore Jones," he angrily told Mason, "would gladly come out and finish the cruise of this ship." Biddle asked Mason not to recall Shubrick because such action would effectively end that officer's career. Thus Jones would have to wait until late October before he could replace Shubrick.[13]

While he waited, Jones acted as president of the second Board of Exam-iners at the Naval Academy in Annapolis, where his son Meriwether was then a student. Jones, along with Commos. Foxhall A. Parker and John D. Sloat and Capts. Bladen Dulaney and Hiram Paulding spent six days supervising tests in gunnery and steam, French, natural philosophy, astronomy, math, and chemistry. After the professors had graded the exams, the board ranked the students by the average of their scores; Meriwether was thirty-first in a class of fifty, with his highest score in gunnery and steam. For the next twenty-three days, beginning on 15 July, the board interviewed the midshipmen, who had to produce the journals they had kept during their cruises and letters from their commanders. The officers then administered an oral exam in seamanship, which consisted of a wide variety of questions emphasizing practical knowledge. Before determining their fate, the board investigated the students' "moral conduct" and financial indebtedness. Those who satisfied the board's scrutiny, including Meriwether, became passed midshipmen of the class of 1847.[14]

The officers who composed the board seemed like gods to the young midshipmen. They had the power to end an aspiring naval officer's career before it even began or to ensure that the student took the correct steps to succeed. Like most of his contemporaries, Jones could be gracious and helpful. He could obtain foreign wine to repay a political ally when necessary; and he could use his influence to gain favor or to secure a departmental exemption, as he did in 1847 for his nephew Walter Jones, who was allowed to complete his examinations and other requirements the following year. Jones also could, and did, strike fear in the hearts of those young, naive men. One midshipman foolishly informed Jones that the steerage—the area where the midshipmen slept—was uncomfortable. Jones supposedly howled: "Uncomfortable, sir, uncomfortable! Why, what blanked fool ever joined the Navy for comfort?" Another who later became a rear admiral admitted that the "mere name of Commodore Ap. Catesby Jones still frightened him." This image of Jones as a heartless disciplinarian is the one that survived in the minds of the younger officer corps, the group that carried forth the traditions and ceremonies of the age of sail into the age of iron and steam.[15]

By the end of September 1847 the Stars and Stripes flew above the halls of Montezuma in Mexico City, and still Jones awaited his Pacific assignment. Although the war had virtually ended, the treaty concluding the conflict would take months to negotiate and sporadic fighting continued. Jones knew that with each passing day his chances for professional redemption dwindled. Finally, on 16 October 1847, Mason instructed

Jones to proceed to the Pacific to blockade Mexican ports south of the Gulf of California and divert all trade to ports under U.S. occupation. Knowing Jones's aggressive and contentious nature, Mason also reminded him that California had already been conquered and told him to cooperate harmoniously with land forces. Jones read those instructions closely because he did not want to take another misstep. Before departing he requested that the department forward copies of *Wheaton's International Law* and *Niles' Weekly Register* to aid him in any future diplomacy.[16]

On 25 October Jones and his entourage, which included Capt. Cornelius Stribling, who would become his flag captain; his son Meriwether, who acted as his private secretary; and his body servant, Griffin Dobson, departed Norfolk aboard the steam frigate *Cumberland*. Fifteen days later the ship anchored off Chagres, Panama, and the group disembarked, crossed the isthmus, and boarded another steamer for Valparaiso. The entire trip took only fifty days; it was the quickest Jones had ever made. He had been unsure about the potential of steam-powered ships, but afterward he praised their "inescapable importance." He especially believed that they could be "reasonably well adapted to [the Pacific] coast" because they shortened distances and therefore improved communications. The navy, he contended, needed more steam-powered vessels.[17]

As soon as he boarded the *Ohio* in Valparaiso Jones encountered problems. Supplies were difficult to secure on the Pacific coast, and those that were available were scarce, of poor quality, and generally very expensive. Adding to Jones's difficulties, the civilian storeship *Matilda* from New York arrived later than expected, ultimately delaying the departure of the squadron by a full month. Jones became incensed when he learned that this "disaster" arose because the ship's owner delivered his private cargo before bringing supplies to the squadron. Even worse, much of the ship's cargo was worthless. The shoes were unsuitable (Jones condemned one thousand pairs) and the "duck clothing," frocks, and trousers were "worse than useless for the Navy." It was an inauspicious beginning to the cruise.[18]

After Commo. Alexander Dallas's coffin had been sent off to the United States, the *Ohio* departed for Mazatlán. Mason had informed Jones that Mazatlán had been conquered and he "confidently expected" that the city would be held. Jones knew that Shubrick had recently captured San Blas and Tepiti. With the war quickly coming to an end, the operations at Mazatlán might be his only opportunity for action. On the northward trip,

Jones maneuvered his ships in fleet formation while the men exercised the ships' guns. When the *Ohio* joined the *Congress*, *Cyane*, and *Southampton* off Mazatlán on 15 May 1848, Jones learned to his dismay that the war was over. His task would now be to restore order to the region.[19]

Although news of the war's end had reached the port, no one was certain of the provisions of the treaty or what could be expected with peace. "*Hostile feelings*" toward the Yankee conquerors had not disappeared, and Jones anticipated the worst once U.S. forces departed. Many Mexicans, believing that the United States planned to acquire Baja as well as Alta California at the war's end, had aided the Americans during the conflict. Rumors that Mexico would retain Baja California created a panic among these sympathizers. Foreseeing untold atrocities should the territory be returned to Mexico, Jones sent Lt. H. A. Wise with a letter to the American peace commissioners at Guadeloupe Hidalgo, urging them to secure either all of Baja California or at least a clause in the treaty to protect these allies from reprisals. He regretfully learned when Wise returned in mid-June that the commissioners had done neither.[20]

Once Jones received official news of the peace, he made plans to return Mazatlán to Mexican authorities. The evacuation ceremony held a certain irony as the victor had to lend powder and guns so the vanquished could fire formal salutes. The Mexican military and government appeared powerless, but Jones knew that as soon as the U.S. forces departed the situation would drastically change, and both groups would exact their revenge on the helpless civilians. Without approval from Washington he decided to use money from the Military Contribution Fund—money raised from import and export taxes collected at harbors occupied by U.S. forces during the war—to reimburse those Mexicans loyal to the United States who wanted to remain. "Disaffected citizens" who chose to leave would be relocated to Alta California.[21]

During July and August the *Ohio* visited the ports of La Paz and Guaymas to investigate the extent of the refugee problem. Jones appointed Captain Stribling as the navy's commissioner to hear and adjust claim payments, which were to be divided into three classes. The first category consisted of Mexicans whose property had been confiscated by U.S. occupation forces; these were to be paid in full. The second group included those loyal to the United States who chose to remain and who lost property to vengeful Mexican soldiers or officials; these would be paid in full up to two hundred dollars, and in part above that sum. The third class consisted of those who chose to relocate and had to leave property behind; these would also be paid in full up to two hundred dollars and in part above that amount. By the end of August Jones reported that "350 souls," including former governor Don Francisco Pallacios de Miranda and other respectable citizens, had left Baja California for Monterey.[22]

Jones described to the Navy Department the action he had taken and hoped Mason and President Polk would approve. "I have averted the most diabolical schemes for bloodshed and rapine," he proudly exclaimed, "and by so doing prevented revolt and secured for Mexico . . . her sovereignty over Lower California." He had also spent more than thirty-seven thousand dollars from the Military Contribution Fund to transport "refugees with the wrecks of their fortunes & household effects, without the extraordinary expenditure of a single dollar from the national treasury." He took pride in this feat, and although his use of the external fund would later be questioned, Mason declared that Jones had done "honor to the American character." He had not been fortunate enough to see combat and win glory, but he had capitalized on his limited opportunity and made correct decisions—and afterward, true to form, extolled their importance. Unfortunately for him, it would be his only occasion to boast; the remainder of his tour would offer nothing but personal misfortune.[23]

While in La Paz earlier that summer Jones had received an interesting letter from Monterey that forewarned of the chaos he would find when the squadron arrived off the coast of Alta California. Gold had been discovered, and within weeks gold mania had infected Hawaii, the Oregon territory, and Mexico. Hundreds of fortune seekers were flooding into the harbor at San Francisco. Col. Richard B. Mason, the military governor of California, and Lt. William T. Sherman quickly toured the mining region to determine the legitimacy of the stories. Mason's report, combined with Thomas O. Larkin's letters to Secretary of State James Buchanan, proved that the craze was no hoax. These reports also helped create the great gold rush of the spring and summer of 1849.[24]

Gold mania actually began to infect the Pacific Squadron months before the flagship arrived off California. Throughout July and August 1848 Jones complained of a shortage of carpenters; this was a prelude of events to come. Also, shipboard discipline had become lax, insubordination was more frequent, and desertion had increased considerably. Jones initially tried to restore order and tighten regulations by appealing to his men's sense of duty. He addressed the crew with a long speech about obeying superior officers—an address that midshipmen had to copy verbatim into their journals. Yet the ordinary methods of discipline that Jones had used with success before were insufficient during this turbulent time. More stringent measures were called for—such as keeping the ships continuously at sea.[25]

Perhaps more disconcerting than the discipline problem was an item of news that Jones received from San Francisco. On Thursday, 13 December 1846, Com. John B. Montgomery of the sloop *Warren* had sent a small boat ashore to transport money and supplies to nearby Fort Sacramento. The boat never returned, and Montgomery soon learned that the nine crewmen had killed his son William Henry Montgomery, who commanded the vessel; his son and secretary John Elliot Montgomery; and the boat's pilot before fleeing to the gold fields with fifteen hundred dollars of public money. Montgomery sent one of the ship's officers along with Governor Mason and Lieutenant Sherman to the gold fields in an unsuccessful attempt to identify the "mutineers and murderers." Jones thought this episode was an exception, the worst he could expect. But as he learned more about the events occurring in California, he became convinced that nothing "can exceed the deplorable state of things . . . growing out of the maddening effect of the gold mania." He would have preferred otherwise, but he realized that the squadron needed to be on the "coast until the whirlwind of anarchy and confusion . . . [was] superseded by . . . some legal government, potent enough to enforce law, and to protect life and property."[26]

During the summer of 1848 Jones faced a dilemma. It would be impractical to keep his ships constantly at sea, but if he did not, he would be hard-pressed to prevent desertions. He considered discharging in California those men whose enlistment had expired, assuming that this would greatly improve his crew's morale. It would also strengthen the California economy, because many of the men had trades that would make them productive members of society. Although the men would probably run to the gold fields as soon as they were discharged, they would likely return to the service once the gold frenzy had run its course. Secretary Mason rejected Jones's proposal for mass discharges as a means to maintain discipline and prevent desertion, suggesting instead an occasional discharge only as a reward for good conduct.[27]

Another more drastic solution, and ultimately one Jones briefly employed, was to offer large cash rewards for the return of deserters. While in Monterey in mid-October Jones announced "A New Gold Discovery" totaling forty thousand dollars, which would be paid in installments for the return of navy deserters. Reward money, he believed, was much more certain than the fleeting prospects in the mining districts. Mason rejected this proposal as well, telling him that such payments would "not be advisable."[28]

Jones did not yet know the secretary's reaction to his plans for discharging seamen and offering rewards for deserters, but he did understand the need for immediate and drastic action. On the trip north to Monterey, Jones had issued Special Order No. 2 to his officers. This brief memorandum detailed their duties and the procedures they should follow once the ship arrived off California: the *Ohio* would anchor no closer than three cable lengths from land, which would discourage men from jumping overboard and trying to swim to shore; small boats could go ashore during daytime but were prohibited from doing so after sundown; and those boats that went ashore could not remain any longer than necessary to land people or supplies unless they were securing water or stores. In each instance armed officers and sentinels were to watch for and shoot to kill anyone trying to desert.[29]

The junior officers despised the order because it also restricted their shore leave. Some claimed it infringed on their rights as officers, and many responded by submitting verbal and written requests for furloughs. Jones, naturally, refused to release so many officers because it would have left his ship critically short-handed. Next, he received a number of resignations, which he forwarded to the Navy Department for the secretary's decision. Until that was rendered, the officers would have to continue in the service. The restrictions on officers' liberty, combined with the department's unwillingness to accept their resignations, destroyed morale in the squadron and prompted officers to carry out their duties halfheartedly.[30]

The *Ohio* remained at Monterey for a month (9 October–9 November) before departing for San Francisco. During this time Jones experienced a rash of desertions by both junior officers and seamen. Many sailors fled even though their enlistment was about to expire and the navy still owed them money. It was easy to understand why these low-paid sailors took such a chance. With lots of luck and a little labor, prospectors could fill their pockets with gold that could be sold for twelve dollars an ounce in San Francisco and as much as eighteen dollars an ounce in New York. Or they could work as laborers in the gold region and command high wages, upward of eight dollars a day.

Governor Mason confirmed that "laboring men at the mines can now earn in *one day* more than double a soldier's pay and allowances for a month." An experienced carpenter or mechanic could command the staggering wage of fifteen to twenty dollars a day. The price of labor was so high, Mason said, that only those earning thirty to fifty dollars a day could afford to hire a cook or servant. William Rich, the army paymaster at Monterey, accurately described the labor problem in California when he remarked: "The pay of governors, judges, & etc., as allowed in the United States, will hardly compare with that paid to salesmen and shop clerks here." Common vegetables were almost prohibitively expensive. Any deserter with initiative could prospect for gold; work as a laborer, cook, or servant; or even grow vegetables and prosper in California.[31]

By the time the *Ohio* arrived at San Francisco on 20 November, Jones's problems had reached epic proportions. His crews were deserting and his officers were dissatisfied and rebellious; some were even refusing to follow what they considered harsh, odious orders. Jones had always had good relations with his sailors; they had respected him because he appeared concerned for their welfare. His junior officers had considered him a stern disciplinarian, but they generally regarded him as a just and fair commander. Now he had been branded a despot who kept zealous watch over a squadron of prison ships anchored safely in an American port, far removed from danger or enemies.[32]

Two episodes in particular infuriated Jones and convinced him that his junior officers were not following his orders. On 18 October 1848 a boat pulled alongside the *Ohio* to unload supplies, and the seamen cast a line to secure the vessel. All of the sailors but one jumped aboard the flagship. As the lone crewman prepared the boat to be hoisted, someone opened a porthole and eight men jumped into the boat, cut the lines, and rowed away. The deck officer ignored—or claimed he knew nothing of—the escape until the boat had rowed out of sight. A second episode occurred on 14 November, when a group of men convinced a "faithless sentry" to lower a small boat that had been hoisted under the *Ohio's* bow for painting and repairs. When the boat hit the water, the sentinel shimmied down the rope and five men sprang from an open porthole and began rowing into the darkness before the deck officer knew what had happened. In this instance the officer fired shots, striking one of deserters in the leg, but the sailors escaped nevertheless. This group of deserters committed a series of crimes before they were finally captured and executed. Jones believed that both episodes could have been prevented by diligent deck officers committed to fulfilling their duty.[33]

Jones asserted that neither Captain Stribling nor any of the lieutenants except Charles M. Armstrong and George F. Emmons tried to prevent men from deserting the *Ohio*; Jones praised Armstrong for having *"not* lost sight of your true position in the chain of military discipline." He candidly declared in a letter to the secretary after the 18 October incident that "some of the officers" were "a little tainted" by the gold mania, mentioning three lieutenants in particular: Joseph F. Green and John B. Marchand of the *Ohio,* and T. Augustus M. Craven aboard the *Dale*. Along with his remarks Jones also sent Mason a copy of a confidential letter in which he responded to complaints filed by the three lieutenants. Green and Marchand had questioned the restrictions on junior officers in such an offensive manner that Captain Stribling refused to hand their complaints to Jones. In fact, Stribling told Jones that if he read the letters he would have to court-martial the lieutenants. Craven, a former editor of the *United States Nautical Magazine* and a grandson of Thomas Tingey, wrote that he vigorously opposed the limits placed on officers, especially since he believed the restrictions would not curb desertion of seamen.[34]

Although Stribling had insinuated that he could settle the controversy with Green and Marchand, Jones wrote the three lieutenants a letter explaining the necessity of the order and indirectly questioning their patriotism and sense of duty. Craven remarked to his private journal that "the document was so carefully worded, and its special pleadings so artfully woven, that it was evidently intended as a net behind which the commodore should partially screen himself and in which he might catch the unwary." He decided to remain quiet for the moment and "make [his] complaints at home." Unfortunately for Jones, his confidential assessment of Craven, Green, and Marchand became public knowledge long before the men returned home.[35]

When the affair began, Jones had suggested that if the three lieutenants withdrew their charges against him and their objections to Special Order No. 2, all would be forgotten. It would have been a simple solution to an increasingly complex problem. All three refused, even though Jones threatened to court-martial them for spreading malicious falsehoods. The episode eventually grew to such proportions that it alienated Jones from Captain Stribling and the other junior officers as well. Eleven of the twelve junior officers aboard the *Ohio* (only First Lieutenant Armstrong refused) signed an affidavit proclaiming that Green and Marchand had opposed the order not because they were tainted by gold mania but because they believed it infringed on their honor. Without the support of his junior officers Jones had no choice but to drop the matter. Even so, he bull-headedly forwarded copies of all of the materials to Secretary Mason and awaited the secretary's opinion on what action to take.[36]

What happened next is not exactly clear. Apparently someone in the Navy Department allowed Jones's letter disparaging the lieutenants, which also discussed conditions in California, to be printed in an eastern newspaper; within weeks a copy of the publication found its way to the lieutenants on the West Coast. The young men were understandably outraged because Jones had unjustly and publicly maligned their reputation and honor. Green and Marchand responded with a formal complaint accompanied by their signed affidavit. They wanted to be recalled from the Pacific so they could bring charges against Jones in Washington for "malicious falsehood," and they requested an immediate investigation of the libel charge against them. Jones viewed the lieutenants' response as arrogant and contemptuous. He considered bringing them before a court-martial, but given the attitude of his officers he knew he could not expect a conviction. Without the support of his junior officers Jones would have been better served to settle the issue as quickly as possible.[37]

Although Jones did not convene a tribunal in this case, the number of courts-martial in the fleet steadily increased. Jones told Mason in April 1849 that cases had been ongoing continuously since February and there appeared to be no end. Every seaman and officer seemed to have a complaint against someone. The trouble became more acute when the storeship *St. Mary* arrived in early April. After that Jones was forced to adjudicate charges and countercharges involving virtually every sailor and officer aboard the ship. During the proceedings he learned that the captain's incompetence and drunkenness had produced much of the discontent and disorder.[38]

Another troublesome concern for Jones involved Lt. Fabius Stanly, who had arrived on the coast of California aboard the *Warren* in December 1846. Stanly had served in the Pacific for thirty-two months and had participated in the engagements at Mazatlán. In October 1848 he asked Jones for a leave of absence, apparently because he wanted to visit the gold fields. But the department had instructed Jones to refuse such requests, and Stanly's petition would be no exception. In early March 1849 Stanly went ashore on the advice of the fleet surgeon to have a tooth extracted but missed the "sundown boat" and did not return until the following morning. When he finally boarded the *Warren,* Stanly reported to the captain, who curtly told him to prepare a written statement explaining his absence. Stanly angrily responded, "Captain Long, I have made my report, you may put it in writing yourself, sir." Soon thereafter Stanly faced a court-martial, which found him guilty of absenting himself overnight without permission and impertinence to his superior officers. Stanly protested the court's ruling and the reprimand he received, and wrote the secretary of the navy for permission to return home so he could press charges of tyranny against Jones. Stanly's complaint had to be forwarded through the squadron's channels of command, and Jones was the last to see the letter before passing it along to Mason. Not surprisingly, Jones attached a note that questioned Stanly's motives and insinuated that his actions and his letters vividly illustrated "his fevered imagination," which Jones admitted he had at times suspected.[39]

Midn. Isaac G. Strain aboard the *Ohio* created another problem for Jones. Citing Navy Department regulations, which stated that commanding officers on duty within the United States could not convene courts-martial, Strain insisted that the commodore had acted outside his authority. Jones, also citing navy regulations, responded that commanding officers on duty outside the United States had the power to convene such tribunals as was necessary and proper for maintaining order. Jones insisted that California was not yet part of the United States, and thus was a foreign station. A court subsequently found Midshipman Strain guilty of conduct unbecoming an officer and of showing disrespect for a superior officer. Jones revoked Strain's midshipman's appointment and dismissed him from the squadron. He also issued to Strain a strong reprimand that was read to all the officers of the squadron; the eight-page discourse was posted and all midshipmen had to copy it into their journals. Meanwhile Strain traveled to Washington to protest his case before Secretary Mason.[40]

Stribling offered little assistance to Jones in his time of need. His only suggestion was that Jones take the squadron out of California waters until the gold fever subsided. Jones would not hear of it. He was "mortified, nay deeply humiliated," that any officer, especially a fleet captain, would suggest shirking duty in the face of discontent and desertion. The

navy had to remain, not only to maintain a semblance of order and stability, but also to provide a safe means for moving California's gold to the
East Coast. Since there had been two episodes of mutiny, murder, and
piracy, Jones decided to keep his squadron intact and use the storeship
Lexington to transport $300,000 of gold to New York. He estimated in
November 1848 that $3 to $5 million worth of gold had been mined in
the region that year, and he predicted that in 1849 miners would recover
an estimated $15 million more. Moreover, he warned that "two-thirds
must find its way to the United States" to pay for clothing and food for
those in California. With that much at stake Jones conceded that the
squadron must remain on the coast until stability prevailed.[41]

It appeared that order would not soon return to California. The gold
rush had stripped San Francisco of its civil government and most of its
inhabitants. Crime, including murders and robberies perpetrated by
army and navy deserters, was rampant. In one violent episode a group
known as the Hounds rioted, destroyed property belonging to foreigners,
and brutally killed a man; a court convicted the group's leaders, and
Jones impressed them aboard the flagship. One observer wryly remarked
that "this restored order in the city," at least temporarily. Even so, between
1849 and 1856 California had more than one thousand murders with but
one conviction. But military rule, however fleeting, could be appreciated
only a short time before some began to consider it tyranny. California
needed a stable, permanent government, and Jones wanted to ensure that
it would be American, not British or French.[42]

In November 1848 Jones met personally with Governor Mason to discuss what action military forces should undertake in California. This
was ironic in view of the fact that Jones could barely maintain order in
his own squadron. How could he or the navy expect to restore peace to
the California countryside? After a long meeting the two officers decided
that should Congress not send instructions, they would help the people
appoint delegates to frame laws and create a provisional government; the
military would assist, yet not usurp, civilian authority. At the same time
Jones reported to the Navy Department his view that the U.S. government should take advantage of "the golden *harvest* of this . . . undiscov-
ered 'El Dorado'" and make sure that California did not slip from its
grasp. Unfortunately, Congress sent no guidance, for the question over
California had become inescapably linked to the growing sectional
debate over slavery. The region remained in limbo.[43]

Jones pondered his own dilemma as a slave owner as Congress debated the question of slavery in California. While the squadron was off the coast of Guaymas in the summer of 1848 his slave Griffin Dobson had asked to buy his freedom. Antislavery sentiment had pervaded the squadron, and apparently several white and free black crewmen aboard the *Ohio* felt that Dobson should be a free man. Like most slaveholders, Jones attributed his servant's desire for freedom to the interference of outside agitators, who "would not let him [Dobson] have any peace." Moreover, they offered, if Jones would agree, to contribute the money so Dobson could immediately purchase his freedom. Jones was worried about losing the services of his servant, steward, and sometime cook, the man whose assistance he relied on because of his debilitating old wound. Dobson was also a constant companion who had been by his side for years. Ultimately, "Griffin being a faithful servant, and seeing how unpleasantly he was situated, [Jones] consented to the proposition." Jones contended that someone had offered him as much as one thousand dollars for Dobson as late as October 1847, but in this instance he agreed to take only four hundred, which was contributed by several crewmen and high-ranking officers. The only stipulation was that the sale would not take effect until they returned to Virginia—ensuring Dobson's assistance for the remainder of the cruise.[44]

In truth, Griffin Dobson was probably already technically a free man. The provisions of Jones's sister Betty's 1822 will had stipulated that her slaves be held in trust by her designated descendants until the American Colonization Society could transport them to Africa. If the slaves had not been colonized within ten years, however, she wanted them to be "absolutely and unconditionally emancipated and free." After 1833 Dobson should therefore have been free. There was only one problem: Virginia law required freed slaves to leave the state. Had Dobson previously proclaimed his freedom, he would have faced immediate expulsion. With his family at Sharon in 1833, and later with a wife and children who were slaves there as well, Dobson probably chose to continue with Jones so that he could remain with his family and near his friends.[45]

In any case, Dobson's sale was concluded before either he or Jones received news of the California gold strike. When they arrived on the California coast, Dobson realized that his big chance was at hand. In May 1849 he approached Jones and requested his freedom. Perhaps Dobson anticipated that the high wages then being paid for labor in California would give him the opportunity to raise money to buy the freedom of his wife and children. Whatever Dobson's motive, Jones reluctantly agreed to release him so he could proceed to the gold fields to seek his fortune.[46]

Dobson and Jones were both well aware of the conditions in the gold region because they had visited them. In the fall of 1848 Jones had made preparations for an extensive tour. He had instructed the *Ohio*'s carpenters

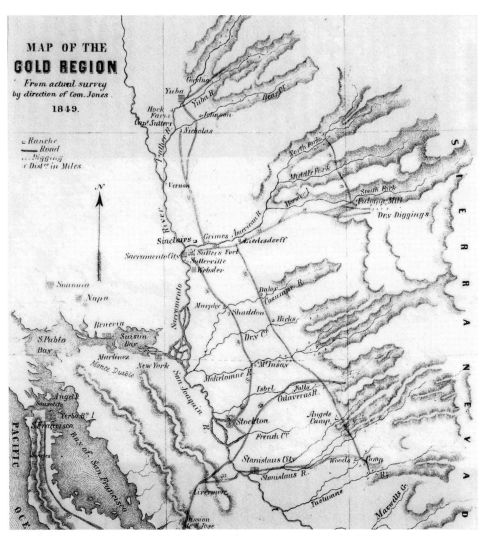

Map of the California gold fields drawn from a survey directed by Commodore Jones, 1849. From *California and Oregon*, by Theodore T. Johnson (1851)

to repair a horse cart for the journey and sail makers to shape a canvas for covering for it. Armorers manufactured tools for digging gold and iron bands to strengthen two money chests. A party of sailors went ashore to train horses and gather riding equipment. Jones took an active role in the preparations, but he had to postpone the trip because of the increased desertions. Even so, he sought out additional information on conditions in the region and on two occasions sent reports to Washington with Lt. Edward F. Beale, who had personally profited when he traded one hundred grains of quinine for an eight-pound nugget of gold.[47]

Jones did not visit the gold region until November and December 1848, when he and Governor Mason made an extensive tour of the district. Before leaving the ship Jones collected money from the ship's officers which he combined with a substantial quantity of specie from the Military Contribution Fund; Jones contributed $1,200, Purser Samuel Forrest added $1,000, and the wardroom officers collectively raised $2,000. Jones intended to use the funds to buy gold dust at discounted rates in the gold fields, then transport it to Mexico or the East Coast and sell it for a higher price per ounce, to the financial benefit of anyone who invested. More important, Jones maintained that the purchase would provide much-needed currency for the California economy. Placing the money under the care of a third party, Jones assembled one lieutenant, one midshipman, a surgeon, Griffin Dobson, and marine guards—a representative party totaling about fifteen—to view the opportunities and perils present in the fields. During the trip Jones paid more than $20,000 for slightly more than 1,808 troy ounces of gold. The gold, bought at prices ranging from $10.00 to $12.50 per ounce, was subsequently transported to the Philadelphia Mint, where it sold for $18.50 an ounce.[48]

In July 1849 Jones made his second and last trip to the mining district with Mason's replacement, General Persifor Smith, and Georgia congressman Thomas Butler King, then acting as President Zachary Taylor's emissary to California. This tour, more ceremonial than Jones's first, traveled as far inland as the North Fork of the American River and gave King the chance to examine the gold region personally before reporting directly to President Taylor. But it was not an enjoyable trip for Jones. King insisted that they travel during the hot middle part of the day rather than in the mornings or evenings as Smith and Jones suggested. In fact, King himself nearly died from dysentery. Jones offered his expertise freely to King during the expedition, but his greatest contribution was bringing a supply of food and distributing it to starving miners in the foothills of the Sierras. He had seen the hardships during his first trip and wanted to alleviate as much of the suffering as possible, a group of miners supposedly gave him a gold cup in return for his thoughtfulness.[49]

By early 1849 Jones had decided to give up command of the Pacific Squadron and return to the United States. He had experienced a host of problems, and more were soon to appear. Early that spring a bout of scurvy plagued the *Ohio* as a result of the crew's confinement aboard ship and the lack of fresh vegetables. Jones moved ashore and sent the flagship to Hawaii for shore leave and fresh supplies. The diplomatic situation in Hawaii had worsened over the five years since Jones's last visit, and the arrival of the American warship further strained tenuous relations for Anthony Ten Eyck, the U.S. commissioner. Apparently Eyck had written and published disparaging letters about King Kamehameha III and his ministers, and the king consequently suspended him. Jones was concerned but reluctant to intervene. Although England and France frequently sent warships to the Pacific Islands to "coerce an adjustment" when difficulties arose, Jones believed that the United States should not use such heavy-handed diplomacy, especially since "all the right is not on our side of the controversy." He concluded that nonintervention was the best alternative because it would preserve relations and the country's "national honor and dignity."[50]

If Jones was disinclined to intervene in Hawaii during the spring of 1849, he was more than willing to meddle in California affairs. In February 1849 citizens of San Francisco, at his and Mason's suggestion, had held a mass meeting and elected a fifteen-member legislative body empowered to govern in the absence of any other authority. Jones heartily approved of the initiative and thereafter used the navy to support the fledgling government. General Bennett Riley, who arrived on 12 April bringing news that the U.S. Congress had still not acted on the California question, assumed control—not as military governor of California but as the leader of the existing Mexican-based civilian government. Claiming that the assembly created in San Francisco had no authority, Riley called elections to fill vacant offices and select members for a constitutional convention, to begin meeting on 1 September. Not surprisingly, Riley's plan received vocal opposition.[51]

Riley hoped by taking aggressive action he would deflect criticism from the U.S. government for its handling of the situation in California.

He wanted to restore order and prevent the region from moving away from the United States. Some of the inhabitants suggested that California ally itself with France or England or even declare its independence. Jones reported to the Navy Department that quick action was needed on the California question. Whether the free-state constitution they drafted in the fall of 1849 was good or bad, Californians adopted it almost unanimously, and although Jones remarked that he was a "Southern Man with Southern Principles," he suggested that Congress accept the document. Jones sternly criticized those who suggested independence and implied that he would do everything within his power to ensure that California became part of the United States. This insinuation incurred the wrath of many, including the editor of the *Daily Journal of Commerce,* who derisively charged that Jones would even use the naval force at his disposal to interfere in California affairs. In response, the *Daily Pacific News* came to Jones's defense, championing him as the state's best friend.[52]

Jones wanted to link the fortunes of California inextricably to those of the United States, making each dependent on the other and thus ensuring their union. California was growing at an unbelievable rate as towns and cities sprang up in deserted fields almost overnight. This unparalleled expansion offered speculators the opportunity for quick and liberal profits on their investments, provided they could direct settlers to their ventures. Thomas O. Larkin, Robert Semple (both friends of Jones), and Bethuel Phelps had bought the site of Benecia on Carquinez Strait off San Pablo Bay. They soon began promoting their investment, working tirelessly to make Benecia the port of entry for California, the state capital, and the site of supply depots for both the army and navy. Although they did not secure the port of entry or site for the state capital for their town, Larkin secured army and navy contracts by successfully cultivating General Smith and Commodore Jones.[53]

Almost as soon as Smith arrived in California he bought from Larkin a residential lot and several commercial lots in Benecia. He also asked for a plot of land for the army's quartermaster depot in the city. Likewise, in late January 1849 Jones purchased from Larkin two blocks and ten lots; the latter, bought for fifty dollars apiece, were worth five hundred to fifteen hundred dollars each by May. To show his support, Jones resided in Benecia and brought the entire squadron to a small cove north and west of the city that was soon thereafter called Southampton Bay in honor of the frigate *Southampton.*

Jones saw an unlimited future for Benecia and tried to convince others of the same. He told fellow officer Matthew F. Maury in a self-interested tone that the city was "one of the finest sea ports in the known world." He acknowledged that the Golden Gate could be blockaded by any powerful naval force, and thus could not be held by the United States during wartime without a railroad connection. Jones also hinted to Maury that Benecia should be the terminus of any railroad constructed to the Pacific coast. In a more aggressive—and unethical—attempt to promote growth, Jones approached William Heath Davis and offered to transport via ship his entire business, building included, to a lot in Benecia free of charge. All Davis had to do was construct a large brick building on the site. Jones also gave empty navy meat barrels and surplus salt to Baron Steinberger, who later opened a much-needed butcher shop in the city; thereafter Jones always received the best beefsteaks and roasts available.[54]

Benecia prospered as the army and navy established a presence, and a mint started coining five-dollar coins. In the spring of 1849 Jones learned that a joint army-navy board would soon arrive to determine the location for a naval base. Believing that this offered a wonderful opportunity for Benecia, he instructed the steamer *St. Mary*, with his nephew Midn. Catesby ap Roger Jones aboard, to sound and survey San Francisco, San Pablo, and Suisun Bays as prospective sites. After the survey Jones became even more convinced that Suisun Bay and Benecia offered the best location for a naval base. It had a good shoreline for unloading ships, easier access, and was safer than San Francisco Bay, which was dominated by fog, strong currents, hidden rocks, and shoals. While Jones promoted the advantages of Benecia, however, he also invested heavily in San Francisco; he loaned to David Chandler $10,450 on eight lots at 5 percent interest per month. Soon after the board arrived in early April 1849 it recommended, much to Jones's delight, Mare Island near Benecia as the location for the naval base.[55]

If Jones had devoted more time and energy to naval operations and administration and less to promoting the city of Benecia and California statehood, he might have avoided some of the troubles that came next. He learned during the summer of 1849 that improperly stored naval supplies at Monterey had spoiled. The storekeeper had also sold large quantities of rancid pork to local inhabitants instead of condemning the meat. Although Jones was not directly responsible, the people of Monterey nonetheless directed their anger at him. Another difficulty concerned the steamboat *Edith*. Intrigued with the possibilities of using steamships for communication purposes, Jones acquired the vessel from the army and invested considerable time and money refitting it as a dispatch boat. On its first trip the *Edith* ran aground and sank, and Jones had to spend another thirty-five hundred dollars to repair the boat. He was not directly responsible for either incident, but ultimately the commanding officer, as Jones should have known, is always given the blame.[56]

Meanwhile, Jones's desertion problem continued, with the men showing increasing boldness. Late on the evening of 11 September 1849 five men from the *Ewing* threw Midn. William Gibson overboard from a small boat and tried to drown him. As the boat rowed toward the Carquinez Strait and the Sacramento River, Gibson hopelessly fought a strong current to get ashore. Fortunately, the captain of an English merchant ship saw Gibson sweeping by and pulled him to safety. Two days later a patrol captured the deserters as they tried to make their way inland to the gold fields.[57]

The court-martial of the five men began on 8 October and ultimately produced more than a thousand pages of testimony and evidence. Jones hoped that the men would be found guilty and that he could use the episode to restore order to the squadron. But he also realized, given the seriousness of the affair, that everyone in San Francisco would be watching the trial; the accused had to receive a fair hearing. Jones therefore hired, at a fee of one hundred dollars a day, the prominent attorney Hall McAllister to conduct the defense. After seven days of startling testimony and able defense, the court found the men guilty of mutiny with the intent to kill, desertion with the intent to kill, assaulting an officer in the execution of his duty, and theft of government property, and sentenced them to death.[58]

Jones knew that the Articles of War required presidential approval for any military execution inside the territorial jurisdiction of the United States. Yet Congress had not declared California a territory or a state. Well aware that it would take months before President Millard Fillmore reviewed the case, Jones concluded that California was a foreign station in which the commander had the authority to reevaluate and approve or set aside sentences. Jones reviewed the case and determined that the ringleaders, brothers Peter and John Black, should suffer the full judgment of the court. At the last minute Jones commuted the sentences of Jonathan Biddy, William Hall, and Henry Commerford to one hundred lashes, loss of pay, and confinement at hard labor for the duration of their enlistment. On 23 October 1849, Jones ordered Peter Black hanged from the *Savannah*'s yardarm while his brother was hanged on the *Ewing*. Jones's bold decision had a dramatic effect—one midshipman commented that "there were no more desertions."[59]

In late June 1850 Jones finally received letters from the Navy Department informing him that Capt. Charles McCauley would soon arrive to relieve him. Jones was finally going home, although not exactly under the circumstances he would have preferred. The recall had a discomfiting tone, for new navy secretary William A. Graham added that he should return to Washington "by the shortest route and without unnecessary delay." Since McCauley had arrived at about the same time as the letters, Jones had not yet had time to settle the squadron's affairs on the coast. He finished his public duties and relinquished his command on 1 July, but he remained in California for two additional weeks concluding personal business. Jones departed on 15 July on the steamer *Tennessee* for Panama, where he crossed the isthmus and boarded the *Crescent City*. He arrived in Washington in late August.[60]

The abrupt tone of his recall greatly surprised Jones. He had constantly informed the department of his actions while in command, and he had assumed that the department approved of everything he did. President Taylor and the Navy Department had supported Jones when he relocated the Mexican refugees to California, and Secretary Mason had approved of how he distributed the squadron, the way he handled the problem of resignations, and his initial attempts to prevent desertions, although he later made suggestions on other ways to curb desertions. Jones had frequently received encouraging letters: the "department has full confidence that your good judgment will carry you safely through" all difficulties, said one; another claimed that his effort to suppress desertions "has been characterized by your usual energy"; another remarked that the department "looks with entire confidence to your successfully meeting and overcoming all difficulties which you may encounter." The department's letters had given him a favorable impression and a false sense of security.[61]

Jones had also received strong endorsements from civilians in California as well as officers attached to the squadron. John Coffin Jones, the former commercial agent in Hawaii, knew much about the growing discontent in California and commented to his friend Larkin that

Commodore Jones was "the best man that could have been sent to command the Pacific Squadron." William Heath Davis offered a similar opinion, remarking that Jones had been selected "not only because of his superiority as a naval commander, but on account of his intelligence, sagacity, diplomatic talent and courage." Even Samuel F. Du Pont of the *Cyane* characterized Jones as "energetic, forthright, assertive, socially inclined, and 'not deficient in magnanimity.'" Moreover, it did not take flattery to win Jones's attention; nor did he dislike a man because they disagreed. Jones would have been pleased with these appraisals, but unfortunately neither John Jones, Larkin, nor Du Pont had much political influence or power in Washington.[62]

Jones had been politically astute in the past, but for some reason he did not realize that all was not well. Apparently forces were working against him behind the scenes in the department and in the capital, and among his own former officers as well. Lieutenant Beale, who had carried dispatches to Washington from the Pacific on two occasions, disliked Jones so much that he anonymously drew a disparaging cartoon that circulated throughout the squadron. While in Washington during the summer of 1849 Beale spread stories that exaggerated the situation in California. He told Charles Wilkes that "some of the deserters have been tried and shot." True, some had been tried, and some had been shot as they attempted to escape, but none had been shot execution style. Regardless, from that discussion Wilkes concluded that Jones had "overstepped his authority (as he did once before)." After receiving news that Lieutenant Craven intended to press charges against Jones later that fall, Wilkes happily speculated that these transgressions would "cost him his commission." Wilkes did not know for sure what would happen to Jones, but he had met Secretary of the Navy Graham and thought highly of his professionalism. Wilkes later recorded in his autobiography that "a courteous reception awaited all who approached [Graham]." Jones, unfortunately, did not experience a "courteous reception" when he returned to Washington in late August 1850.[63]

∼∂ 8 ≻∽

The Decision Is Final
Court-Martial and Aftermath, 1850–1858

*A*t noon on a blustery Monday, 16 December 1850, Thomas ap Catesby Jones appeared before a tribunal of his peers at the Washington Navy Yard. Secretary of the Navy William A. Graham had summoned him to answer charges of misconduct while in command of the Pacific Squadron. Jones was not aware of the extent of the five charges he faced, which were riddled with politics and discolored by personal animosity. He had no idea that the charges were going to bring an ignominious end to his long career.[1]

Much had changed in Washington since Jones had departed for the Pacific in 1847. His friend and ally John Young Mason had left the Navy Department in early March 1849 and returned to Richmond to practice law. William Ballard Preston, who assumed the post with Zachary Taylor's inauguration, had been forced to resign in early July 1850 when President Millard Fillmore reorganized the cabinet. Congressman Edward Stanly and others from the North Carolina delegation had recommended Graham, their former two-term Whig governor, as Preston's replacement, and Fillmore quickly submitted his name to the Senate. Graham was confirmed on 20 July 1850 and assumed his job on 2 August. He promptly engrossed himself in the intricacies of naval administration, studying ships and their operation, technology and strategy, discipline and punishment, officers and their qualifications, and a host of other issues of which he knew little.[2]

Fillmore chose Graham because he was an astute Whig politician who could help assuage southern discontent over the new northern president and the California compromise. Although Graham knew little about the Navy Department, he was a diligent administrator who personally investigated every question he confronted. He also wisely sought out and often incorporated the opinions of respected and informed naval officers such as Matthew F. Maury. And while some historians consider Graham one of the best navy secretaries of the nineteenth century, it should be remembered that he was first and foremost a sagacious politician who had all the biases of his profession. Graham played the Washington game well and paid his political debts and returned favors when necessary, especially if his political or naval officer confidants strongly recommended a particular course of action.[3]

Whirlwinds of change and reform blustered through Washington in 1850. The country's rapid growth forced the Navy Department to reevaluate its policy concerning the size and disposition of the fleet, the implementation of new technologies such as steam and iron, and personnel questions such as the education, training, promotion, and retirement of the officer corps. Although reforms in these controversial areas would represent important structural changes for an antiquated department still wed by tradition to the age of sail, they did not generate the popular outcry from the American public that the issue of punishment in the navy and merchant marine evoked. Flogging, the most common way to maintain discipline in the navy, had been unavoidably compared to the punishment slaves suffered in the South. A naval officer, like a plantation owner, could flog his underlings at a moment's notice for any perceived wrong, and many believed this tyrannical, barbaric abuse of power resulted in the horrible mistreatment of sailors.[4]

The American public had gained its impression of flogging from the writings of Richard Henry Dana, Herman Melville, and others. In 1840 Dana had published *Two Years before the Mast,* the story of a compassionate young New Englander who confronted a despotic captain and witnessed brutal floggings while aboard a merchant ship sailing around Cape Horn. Ten years later, Melville published his novel *White Jacket; or The World in a Man-of-War,* in which he criticized navy floggings as inhumane.

Melville also ridiculed several other aspects of the navy, and even
mocked the fictional officers aboard his frigate the *Neversink*. For example, Melville remarked that his commodore, who can easily be identified
as Jones, was "dumb, for, in my hearing, he seldom or never uttered a word.
And not only did he seem dumb himself, but his presence possessed the
strange power of making other people dumb for the time." The following
year Melville published *Moby Dick*, which depicted Captain Ahab, a man
who hated and was obsessed with killing the white whale that had been
responsible for the loss of one of his legs. Correspondingly Jones hated
the British for the wound he had suffered to his arm at Lake Borgne in 1814
and afterward was obsessed with thwarting their designs; Jones's endless
hatred of the British quite possibly provided the model for Melville's
Captain Ahab.[5]

In late September 1850, less than a month after Jones returned to
Sharon, Congress enacted an antiflogging law for the navy and merchant
marine; supposedly every congressman had a copy of *White Jacket* on his
desk during the debates on the subject. Reformers had finally secured
their victory, but it would be left to Secretary Graham to enforce this leg-
islation, and unfortunately for Jones, his case would provide the first significant test. During his command in the Pacific, Jones had sent letters
to the Navy Department describing the punishments he had administered while attempting to maintain discipline in the Pacific Squadron. At
the time the letters were written the department had approved, but under
this new law Jones's somewhat harsh actions would be considered illegal. The change that labeled discipline as oppression in fact appeared to
Jones to be an ex post facto attempt to convict him for acts that were not
yet considered a crime. Throughout his career, discipline, obedience, and
patriotism had been synonymous with the expectations of a good officer,
and while in command Jones had always tried to fulfill his duties at all
costs. And the department had always supported officers who did their
duty. But when he visited the Navy Department in early September to
meet with Graham, Jones learned that a group of junior officers had
accused him of unfair punishment. Even so, Jones believed that the
department and a jury of his peers—all senior captains—would support
him rather than his accusers.[6]

On that cold December Monday Jones listened as Judge Advocate
James M. Carlisle read a series of verbose and repetitious charges: fraud
against the United States; attempting a fraud against the United States;

scandalous conduct, tending to the destruction of good morals; neglect of duty; and oppression. Within each of these charges Carlisle added a list of specifications that compounded the seriousness of the allegations. For the next month and a half Secretary Graham, acting as prosecutor, and Jones's counsel, prominent Washington lawyer Walter Jones, who was also Jones's cousin, argued the intricacies of the charges and specifications before a board of captains, four of whom were senior to Jones (Capts. Charles Stewart, Lewis Warrington, John Downes, and Henry E. Ballard) and four junior (Capts. W. Bradford Shubrick, Lawrence Kearny, John D. Sloat, and Matthew C. Perry). It was an unusual tribunal because the board was two members short of the customary number. Nevertheless, Jones was confident that he would be acquitted of all charges.[7]

The first charge—fraud against the United States—consisted of five specifications accusing Jones of illegally withdrawing $10,643.09 from the Military Contribution Fund. The money, which had been collected by navy personnel from Mexican customhouses during the course of the recent war, was not part of the U.S. Treasury but rather a fund to be used at the discretion of the commander of the station. As such, Jones had used it to purchase gold dust in California, which he transported to the Philadelphia Mint and sold for $18.50 an ounce, reaping a profit for Jones of almost $8,000 dollars. Afterward Jones returned to the Navy Department the original sum plus the costs incurred in transporting the gold to the East. The profit was turned over to his wife, Mary, and to Thomas R. Love, a Fairfax County, Virginia, attorney and Jones's financial agent. While the transaction was unsavory, there was no law or regulation covering the dubious fund and its handling because it was not Treasury Department money. Jones's actions were highly questionable and unethical, but they were not technically illegal.[8]

The second charge—attempting a fraud against the United States—accused Jones of sending to the secretary of the navy a fraudulent account of the Military Contribution Fund in order to disguise his illegal activities. This count could not be established unless the first charge was conclusively proven; therefore the two were inextricably linked.[9]

The three specifications of the third charge claimed that Jones had acted with scandalous conduct and destroyed good morals. The first and third specifications merely repeated the allegations of the first two charges, that Jones had defrauded and had attempted a fraud against the government of the United States. It was the second specification on which the crux of this count rested. According to Official Dispatch No. 34, dated 25 October 1848, Jones had "falsely, scandalously, and maliciously" written that Lts. Joseph F. Green, John B. Marchand, and T. Augustus M. Craven were a "little tainted" by the "maddening effect of the gold mania." The prosecution contended that Jones, without provocation or justification, had condemned these officers, stained their records, and insulted their professional honor.[10]

Jones's defense did not challenge the first and third specifications because they repeated previous accusations. The second specification—libel—was a different story. The prosecution produced a long list of officers who had served in the Pacific with the lieutenants and who testified that they were of exemplary character. Purser Samuel Forrest testified that all three officers had complained that Jones's Special Order No. 2 was "unjust." Insisting that the officers were "indignant" but not "resentful," Forrest further testified that they "considered [the order] an encroachment on their rights as officers. Lt. Edward M. Yard reaffirmed that statement when he swore that one of the officers had called the order "invidious to his class." Yet, Yard insisted that this officer did not "indulge in such conversation on board" ship. Major Henry Hill of the U.S. Army observed that he "never remarked any lack of zeal, or anything in their conduct, subjecting them to the suspicion of being tainted with the gold mania." Even Captain Stribling concluded that they were "not in the least tainted with the gold mania." After this lengthy line of questioning, the prosecution contended that Jones had no right to cast such unfounded aspirations on the officers in his official communications.[11]

Jones's defense countered that a libel, to be such, must have been written "maliciously and without probable cause." The entire strategy of the defense rested on the events that prompted Jones to act as he did. The situation in California necessitated forceful action lest "anarchy and confusion" reign. Seamen had deserted in unprecedented numbers. Supplies had been blatantly stolen. Insubordination infected the crew as stories of "El Dorado" permeated the squadron. In an attempt to stem the increasing rate of desertion and insubordination, Jones had issued a strict general order, one part of which disallowed watch officers from going ashore. The defense maintained that the three lieutenants hated the constraints so much that they officially complained of its injustice. Jones even insisted that the complaints indicated serious character flaws. Stanly's note, accordingly, exposed "the chicanery of his incoherent and garbled statements"; Jones insisted that Commodores Morris and Shubrick, and Commanders Mclean and Judd could easily "testify to his troubled spirit." Jones also indicated that the other officers were "restive" and their complaints remonstrative.[12]

Their formal complaints had convinced Jones that the three lieutenants had become tarnished with "gold mania." Jones had requested that the three withdraw their objections and apologize for their contemptuous actions. When they refused, Jones had submitted Dispatch No. 34 and copies of the three letters to the Navy Department. Jones had followed standard procedures when he forwarded all correspondence to Washington, yet something unusual had happened to the confidential letter condemning the lieutenants; it appeared in an eastern newspaper and eventually came to the attention of the three in California. The three lieutenants were outraged when they saw Jones's letter and emphatically argued that Jones had publicly insulted their honor. They quickly secured affidavits that claimed they opposed the order not because of gold mania but rather because they considered it an attack on their professional honor as naval officers.[13]

The four specifications of the fourth charge—neglect of duty—appeared to repeat the previous charges. The charge stipulated that Jones had neglectfully removed public money from the control of his pursers or the proper disbursing agents under his command. He had also failed to provide accurate and detailed accounts of the monies within the fund when ordered to do so by the Navy Department. This was another charge inextricably linked to the proper management of the Military Contribution Fund.[14]

The last charge—oppression—could have been the most serious. Its first two specifications accused Jones of oppressively withholding for two months a favorable verdict in the court-martial of Lt. Fabius Maximus Stanly (the brother of North Carolina congressman Edward Stanly). Supposedly Jones had also "oppressively and maliciously" withheld a leave of absence from Stanly for about the same length of time. But the most serious specification claimed that Jones had illegally convened the court-martial that condemned Peter and John Black to death. The prosecution maintained that Jones did not have the authority to convene the court-martial because federal law prohibited naval commanders from doing so in "American waters" without authorization from the president of the United States, and the chief executive had not given that permission.[15]

Jones countered by arguing that he had transferred Stanly "from a sec-
ond-rate sloop, doing guard or harbor duty, to one of the first-class cruising sloops in the world!" Jones could only conclude that Stanly's complaint
was a "strange notion; but indicative, however, of the lieutenant's idea of
naval service." As for the courts-martial, Jones insisted that they had been
legal because California had not yet been incorporated into the United
States and was thus legally a foreign port. Besides, Jones asserted, had the
territory been part of the United States and the executions illegal, then his
crime was murder and he should be tried by a civil rather than a naval
court. The judges deliberated Jones's argument and concluded that he had
"lawfully" convened the courts-martial and carried out their sentences.[16]

Jones's defense attempted to disprove the charge of fraud—this, unfortunately, was his main concern—by describing the anarchy within California and the inflationary nature of the economy. "Every necessary of life
was from 1,000 to 5,000 percent above ordinary prices," Jones claimed,
except for gold, which "was fifty percent below par" because of the
scarcity of coinage. Customhouse officials accepted only specie as payment of duties, which further depleted the amount of coinage in circula-
tion. Even merchant ships carrying items needed for daily life had to
remain at sea until they could amass the necessary specie to pay the
required duties. Meanwhile, onshore the lack of coinage drove prices
and the cost of living skyward. According to Jones the downwardly spi-
raling economy had prompted him, but only after serious deliberation and
consultations, to use the surplus Military Contribution Fund to replen-
ish California's supply of coinage.[17]

The court deliberated for only three days before returning the verdict
on 1 February 1851. The board of officers determined that all the specifications of the first charge of fraud were proven, although their decision
stipulated that Jones did not intend to defraud the government and that
as a result was innocent of the charge. The officers also concluded that
the prosecutor did not prove that Jones had attempted a fraud against
the United States and was thus not guilty of the second charge. The surprise for Jones came on the third count—scandalous conduct tending to
the destruction of good morals. This charge had consisted of three specifications, two of which repeated previous accusations and a third in
which Jones criticized the lieutenants. The court found him guilty of
scandalous conduct, guilty of the four specifications encompassing neglect
of duty, and guilty of two specifications of the fifth charge of oppression.

Finding him guilty of three of the five charges brought against him, the court determined that Jones should be suspended from the service for five years, the first two and a half without pay.[18]

Of the numerous specifications and charges, only two seemed legitimate: that Jones had fraudulently used money controlled by the Navy Department, and that the four lieutenants (Green, Marchand, Craven, and Stanly) had been mistreated by their superior officer. As commander of the squadron, Jones maintained that he had acted in the best interest of the U.S. Navy and had broken no laws. The verdicts against him are full of contradictions. The court did not find him guilty of fraud or attempting a fraud, the primary charges investigated during the proceedings. On the third charge, scandalous conduct, the court found him guilty of improperly using government money, of providing the department with misleading accounts, and of unfairly criticizing the lieutenants, yet acquitted him of any "deliberate falsehood" or "malicious intention." The fourth charge convicted Jones of neglect of duty, even though the court concluded that his actions were "not negligent." The last charge convicted him of oppressing Lieutenant Stanly, yet the court contended that he had not acted "oppressively and maliciously." Jones was innocent when considering the letter of the law yet guilty in the eyes of his judges.[19]

The case exhibited a number of irregularities that were never adequately explained to Jones or his counsel. The first occurred on 7 September 1850, when Secretary Graham asked Jones to explain the charges leveled against him by the lieutenants. Jones responded later that month, with the understanding that the material he provided would not be used in a case against him. Instead, Graham permitted the judge advocate to use Jones's responses to modify the charges and specifications against him, even before Carlisle had been officially appointed to the case. The revised charges were then presented to Jones on 1 November 1850, the same day the department placed him under arrest.[20]

Also exceptionable was Graham's serving as the prosecutor in the case. The secretary ordered the trial, selected the judges and judge advocate for the court, prosecuted the case, and ultimately confirmed the sentence. Graham also introduced Lieutenant Craven—one of the accusers—"as assistant prosecutor of the new charges." Jones expressed concern about the secretary of the navy "throwing the weight of his high moral standing, as well as the influence of exalted official station, into the balance against" him. But he did not make an issue of the irregularity at the time because he did not think he would lose; he believed his fellow officers would uphold tradition and support one of their own, for they too could suffer in like manner. Moreover, according to Jones, Craven's appointment as assistant prosecutor demonstrated "the wishes of the prosecuting Secretary towards his *prejudiced and doomed victim*." Throughout the proceedings Jones insisted that Graham demonstrated an obvious bias against him "rather than the impartial fairness for which his position called."[21]

That the accusers were four junior officers unhappy with their commander further strengthens the contention that these charges had an unusual character. Jones argued that a junior officer generally does not bring charges against his superior "unless there has been a previous falling out." The charges of the four lieutenants appeared to have just such a motivation. Jones had denied Lieutenant Stanly's request for a "nominal duty, that [would allow him] to visit the interior," that would, in other words, allow him access to the gold fields. Lieutenants Green and Marchand had been denied furloughs for a mercantile journey from Mexico to California, a trip that would have yielded a nice profit like the one Jones had made. The rationale for Craven's complaint is not as transparent. Jones knew the Craven family. Although Craven said that relations between Jones and his family were amiable, he had been brought to task for questioning publicly his superior commander. That apparently did not please the family or the lieutenant, as evidenced by his private remark while in the Pacific that he was willing to "'bide my time' and make my complaints at home." In short, each of the four lieutenants had a complaint against Jones, and in 1850 the Navy Department had a secretary willing to listen, especially when one of the accusers was the brother of a congressman and a close friend from Graham's state.[22]

Political and personal animosities as well as the successful crusade against flogging all played important roles in Jones's court-martial and conviction. True, Jones had behaved like an old-fashioned tyrant. Attitudes about naval discipline were changing, but Jones unfortunately did not detect the shift in the winds or understand that he should trim his sails accordingly.[23]

A month after his court-martial Jones wrote a long letter to the *National Intelligence* pleading his innocence. He admitted that he had profited from the gold transaction. He also stated that he had initially planned to turn over all profits to the Treasury. Even though he did not carry through that plan, he pleaded that his actions were not illegal. He had not disobeyed any order; nor had the government lost money in the transaction. The verbose letter did little to win sympathy for Jones. Ten days later, on 13 March 1851, Jones appealed to President Fillmore, again to no avail. During the summer Jones's attorneys—Joseph Bradley, his cousin Walter Jones, and Walter Cole—prepared a short pamphlet containing documents related to the case and printed them for distribution. A copy was sent to Secretary of the Navy Graham along with a long letter from Jones describing his exceptions to the court-martial. Graham initially ignored Jones's bitter protests; when he finally did respond he enclosed a dispatch from the attorney general, who maintained that the secretary of the navy did have the power to approve sentences of courts-martial. Finally, in the summer of 1852, Graham told Jones that President Fillmore concurred with him and the attorney general and that the court's "decision is final." Ultimately, Jones's intricate maneuvers had done more to injure than to aid his cause.[24]

In the months after his court-martial Jones sought out other opinions about his case. On one occasion he informed Graham that "many able jurists have declared [the verdict] to be *without proof.*" Jones certainly believed the ruling was wrong and that he had suffered injustice at the hands of the four scheming lieutenants. He also believed that his name and character had been besmirched. And not least, his salary had been reduced by six thousand dollars. Initially thinking that only the lieutenants had been behind the attack on him, Jones assured Graham that he intended no disrespect to the department, nor did he want to create a public controversy. But it took only a few months for Jones to conclude that he was the victim of larger political manipulations, that he had been "defeated by the subterfuge of Mr. Graham, and the weakness of Mr. Fillmore." In fact, relations between Jones and Graham became extremely tense during the winter and spring of 1852, prompting rumors in the District of Columbia that Jones "threatened to seek a personal redress" from Graham, who had by now retired. Jones politely assured Graham's successor that such rumors were unfounded and that they were circulated by enemies attempting to prolong his exile from the department.[25]

The Jones controversy did not damage Graham's political career. During the summer of 1852 the North Carolinian resigned from the Navy Department to become the running mate of unsuccessful Whig presidential candidate Winfield Scott. His successor, John P. Kennedy, began his own investigation of the Jones case, which had been receiving increased attention on Capitol Hill. North Carolina congressman Edward Stanly and Lt. (later Rear Adm.) Richard Mead continued attacking Jones, bringing new charges of graft in cases involving a naval sawmill and excessive repair costs to the propeller of the steamboat *Edith*. When Jones learned of these new accusations he angrily demanded a congressional investigation. An investigation was conducted, and Congress published an extensive report on the case, but no decision was ever rendered, and the affair died behind a closed committee room door.[26]

As Jones awaited the decision of Congress, Kennedy informed him in late February 1853 that President Fillmore had remitted the remainder of his court-martial sentence; he would be listed as awaiting orders and would soon receive command of the navy yard at Mare Island. Although Jones humbly thanked Kennedy he was not completely satisfied. As long as others perceived him to be "a convicted culprit" he would remain "victim to the malice, revenge, and corruption" of the lieutenants who had conspired against him. The administration that had brought about his downfall had restored him to duty, but only a few days before passing from power. President Franklin Pierce and new navy secretary James C. Dobbin maintained that Jones did, in fact, have the full confidence of the department, yet neither ever reversed the verdict of the court-martial, nor did they give Jones command of the Mare Island Navy Yard.[27]

After being reinstated, Jones successfully petitioned Congress on two occasions for debt relief. In one instance the Senate Judiciary Committee determined that he was not responsible for the four-thousand-dollar debt incurred by his deceased cousin Walter F. Jones, and that he should be reimbursed the money he had paid as a surety; the full Congress approved the recommendation in 1854. The House Committee on Naval Affairs, and later the full Congress in 1856, decided that Jones should be reimbursed the nine hundred dollars he paid to the attorney who defended the mutineers from the *Ewing*. Jones also tried again, to no avail, to convince Congress to reimburse him for expenses he incurred while commanding the sloop *Peacock* in the Pacific in 1826–27. While these were minor victories, they nonetheless eased Jones's sense of indignity.[28]

In July 1855 Jones's last opportunity for command disappeared. Secretary Dobbin had convinced Congress to approve a board of fifteen officers, five from each of the three ranks, to examine the officer rolls and remove all of those not capable of active service. This controversial "plucking" board, as it became known, placed seventeen captains, including

Jones, on the reserve list, furloughed fifteen, and dismissed three. Jones insisted that this action represented a witch-hunt to remove the senior officers of the navy, and in some respects he was correct. The seven most senior commanders in the navy were removed, while number eight—a member of the board—and three other commanders on the board received promotions to captain.[29]

The dismissal prompted Jones to write a series of vitriolic letters, including a long, almost desperate account of his career written in October 1855. In this letter he insisted that he was still fit and able to perform any duty expected of an active officer, and to prove his point he included supporting letters from four doctors, one written as early as 1847. His almost pathetic protest concluded with copies of letters that praised his service while on the New Orleans station some forty years earlier—the high point of his long, controversial career. He and the other dismissed officers protested the board's decision and won individual hearings. In March 1858, after considerable debate, Congress voted to restore the pay Jones lost because of the court-martial. A hearing on his dismissal was scheduled for later that summer.[30]

During his exile Jones had remained at Sharon, a bitter and angry old man. The world had somehow changed while he was in California, and he was no longer the hero who had been revered by a grateful nation in 1815 and awarded a ceremonial sword by Virginia in 1841. During this time he struggled to improve his farm's productivity and prosperity, only to find financial hardship and uncertainty. His farming operations did not provide enough money to support him and wife Mary, son Mark, and daughters Martha and Mary Elizabeth Ball; the latter had come home after her husband deserted her and their young children Ida and Kate. Jones still had some wealth, but it was in the form of land and slaves, neither of which could be easily liquidated. In 1850 his four-hundred-acre farm had been appraised at $24,700, with another $3,900 in livestock and equipment, but this substantial holding began to dwindle after his court-martial. Over the next seven years he had continually to sell lots, including his stake in the Great Falls Manufacturing Company, just to pay debts and provide essentials for the family. In 1840 Jones had owned forty-three slaves; between 1847 to 1850 he had to sell eleven, and in 1852 he sold six more.[31]

Jones's worsening financial situation rather than his magnanimity probably lay behind Griffin Dobson's purchase of his family's freedom in late September 1852. His three years as a free man in the California gold fields had apparently yielded Dobson enough money to buy the freedom of his wife, Cynthia (age thirty), and his five children, Watt (age twelve), Molly (age ten), Beverly (age nine), Henry (age seven), and Edmund (age five). Dobson, identified in the legal contract as "a free man of color of California," paid only twelve hundred dollars for all six members of his family.[32]

While Jones awaited his professional fate he immersed himself in his agricultural experiments. In September 1852 the Chagres Fertilizer Company used a series of letters that Jones had written to plug their product; Jones's experiments had made him something of a local celebrity, and many sought his opinions. His work with fertilizer provided the research data for his prize-winning essay "On the Renovation of Worn-out Lands in Maryland and Virginia," published in the *American Farmer* in March 1854. Later that month the farmers of the county rewarded Jones for his years of painstaking work by electing him president of the Fairfax County Agricultural Society. His naval career might have ended unceremoniously, but his work as a farmer continued to attract considerable admiration.[33]

Jones did not gain recognition as a farmer until the waning years of his life. But by 1857 he was exhausted from continuous battles with the government and far too tired to revel in his newfound fame. He knew that his remaining days on earth were few. He prepared his will and tried to place his affairs in order. He was still short of cash but had not given up hope that the government would pay him for his expenses while in the Pacific in 1826–27. If so, the family would be in fine shape economically. During the summer he traveled to nearby Capon Virginia Springs for his health, but the therapy did little to relieve the pain in his chest and shoulder. Throughout the fall Jones experienced periods when he was "quite feeble," "quite infirm," and "quite unwell," but he refused to show any weakness. The Reverend C. B. Mckee, who visited Sharon in October 1857 and expected to find Jones in bed, instead "found him walking about his place." Although Jones seemed to be improving during the winter and spring of 1858, his health waned in the late spring, finally leaving him unable to get out of bed.

On 30 May 1858, sixty-eight-year-old Thomas ap Catesby Jones died at Sharon of natural causes—most likely congestive heart failure compounded by tuberculosis. Three days later he was buried in the cemetery of the Lewinsville Presbyterian Church in a simple ceremony attended by a small group of family and close friends. The sailing navy had lost one of its most colorful captains.[34]

~❧9❧~

PRECIOUS IN THE
SIGHT OF THE LORD
A Mariner's Legacy

*T*homas ap Catesby Jones entered the United States Navy in
1807 at the height of American Anglophobia and spent much
of the next eight years confronting British aggression on the
New Orleans station. His gunboat assignment on that "inactive, forlorn
station" offered him an opportunity that his successors there would not
enjoy. In 1809, as a nineteen-year-old, he began a six-year stint commanding gunboats along the Gulf coast, where he encountered smugglers,
pirates, privateers, slave traders, and ultimately the British navy. This service demonstrated Jones at his very best—commanding a vessel on an isolated frontier where an officer had to make sound, rational decisions
based only on the facts at hand and then accept the consequences. Jones
proved without a doubt that he was decisive, loyal, and determined to
expand federal authority along that lawless frontier. Later in life he was
always proud to refer to his tour of duty at New Orleans and his sacrifice
at Lake Borgne. It was, in fact, the high point of his long career.

After the War of 1812 Jones received an appointment aboard seagoing
vessels in the Mediterranean and quickly learned that the channels of
advancement in the U.S. Navy were clogged and uncertain. Yet he gained
needed experience with capital ships and fleet maneuvers, and learned
the duties associated with command and naval diplomacy. Once again

he was successful, and by 1820 thirty-year-old Jones had been promoted to master commandant, the second-highest rank in the navy. In the years that followed Jones completed a sensitive diplomatic mission in the Pacific, demonstrated an excellent understanding of naval ordnance and its importance, and was promoted to captain. By 1829 he had reached the pinnacle of success in the navy. He was a thirty-nine-year-old captain working for an administration that vividly remembered and appreciated his valor at Lake Borgne.

The first half of Jones's career exemplifies how one could succeed in the early navy. He received his appointment because of his family's political connections and the threat of war with Britain, but he advanced in rank through diligent service, good luck, fortunate assignments, and proper political and naval alliances (i.e., with Stephen Decatur, Isaac Hull, Daniel Todd Patterson, and Andrew Jackson). The second half of his career, however, coincided with the emergence of Jacksonian democracy and the age of the common man, when birth and rank became less important than ability, expertise, and alignment with the new politics. Despite the changes in the larger society, the navy clung desperately to the old ways, including its system of promotion and assignments based on seniority. Fortunately for Jones, he had already reached the service's highest rank.

Jones was a typical pre–Civil War captain who tried to set himself apart from his fellow officers by frequently recommending reform within the service. As inspector of ordnance he suggested improvements in the types of guns the Navy Department maintained as well as in the ways they were to be stored; his suggestions created a baseline for the development of naval technology. He also recommended and supported the creation of a naval academy, which, in Gilbert Workman's words, "doomed the breed of the man-child midshipman he himself had been." As a flag officer he maintained strict discipline, attempted to prevent dueling and excessive drinking, and used flogging only in the worst cases. His efforts won him the admiration of his seamen and the wrath and disdain of his junior officers. It was some of these younger officers who would be responsible for his court-martial and suspension from the service years later. In addition, Jones suggested basic operational changes such as squadron maneuvers, a system of signals for communications, disposition of ships and size of stations, and the use of steam vessels. The latter helped to break down the autonomy of commanders on distant assignments such as Jones had enjoyed along the Gulf and in the Pacific. As a squadron commander he thought in broad national and strategic terms, always bolstering the position of the United States and working to undermine British influence, especially in California and Hawaii. And although Jones's role in the acquisition of California has been generally overlooked, his efforts there proved conclusively that California had much to offer to the United States and that the nation should work to secure Hawaii as well. His vision of Manifest Destiny stretched even further west as he proposed and hoped to command a U.S. expedition to Japan. Jones's antagonist Matthew Calbraith Perry supplanted him as commander of that celebrated expedition.[1]

Jones was not an atypical naval commander for the mid-nineteenth century, but he was a striking personality in an age in which temperament helped shape the navy. Even so, Jones made no significant, long-lasting contributions to the service. He was a hero of the War of 1812, but not on the same level as Isaac Hull, Oliver Hazard Perry, or Thomas Macdonough. He was interested in innovation, yet he did not offer memorable scientific or technological contributions as did Matthew F. Maury and John Dahlgren. He did not make a voyage that gained the nation's attention as did Charles Wilkes (although he had that opportunity) or Perry. No catchy, descriptive nickname such as "Mad Jack" or "Ready to Hazard" emblazoned him on the rolls of naval history. The only nickname he gained was the derisive "Thomas 'APE' Catesby Jones" given to him by the Mexican press after his October 1842 seizure of Monterey.

If Jones had no lasting impact on the navy, why should he be remembered or studied at all? He is a classic example of the type of officer nurtured by the navy during its early existence; he is representative of a large group of nameless, faceless officers who served their country diligently yet received little or no credit and have been forgotten by time. Jacob Jones, John Downes, Henry Ballard, Jesse Wilkinson, and W. Compton Bolton were all captains of Jones's generation who reached the highest rank in the service but subsequently faded into obscurity. Jones also represents the type of highly competent officer who composed the naval patriarchy of the age of sail: he was a mariner, diplomat, warrior, scientist, and bureaucrat. Given the size of the navy and its broad mandate, officers had to be conversant in many duties rather than specializing in one or two. Moreover, these officers were men who by force of personality, spirit, and energy helped to transform the small defensive, gunboat-oriented navy of the Jeffersonian period into a seagoing force that eventually projected American power on all the earth's oceans.

Although the navy's transformation occurred slowly and did not truly become apparent until the American Civil War, Jones and his brethren nonetheless made important contributions that helped to lay the foundations for that change. Jones was involved in naval diplomacy, ordnance, education, and in promoting the use of technology; but he is not known for his contributions in any of these areas. His historical image is that of a rash, contentious, self-assured, and self-righteous officer unwilling to tolerate insubordination or lapses in discipline—traits representative of his generation of naval officers. In fact, the one full-length study of his career completed in the 1930s is entitled "The Contentious Commodore," and it portrays Jones as a bitter, argumentative officer constantly seeking approval. Jones could certainly be contentious, and he constantly sought approval, but it was just this self-righteous, self-reliant type of officer that the navy nurtured.

Perhaps Jones's health also affected his conduct. The wound he suffered at the Battle of Lake Borgne had a lasting impact on his personality and demeanor; he was unable to use his left arm, and this inadequacy created a festering, lifelong hatred of the British. The wound also made him especially sensitive to criticism; he always had to defend to the utmost his ability and decisions. Certainly Jones used his disability to the utmost as well, making sure to get assistance and compensation for his loss, but it also caused him considerable pain and discomfort, especially in cold and wet climates such as Jones experienced in New York in the fall of 1837. Further, Jones suffered from recurring bouts of tuberculosis, which sapped his strength and determination for long periods, usually striking when his immune system had been strained by other pressing issues such as the preparations for the South Pacific Exploring Expedition. Although these conditions do not excuse his contentiousness, they do offer a partial reason for it.

Jones's economic situation also affected his personality. He had been born into a moderately influential Virginia family that fell on hard times during his youth. The downturn of the family's fortunes and then the unexpected death of his father and mother, which forced him to reside with his uncle, most likely created feelings of insecurity and abandonment, feelings exacerbated when his government also abandoned him at the end of his career. Throughout his life he constantly worked to win the approval of his government, demonstrate his worthiness, and recoup the fortune his father had apparently squandered. He overextended his farming operations in the hope of becoming a great planter. He spent personal money while on official cruises, anticipating that he would be reimbursed with interest; even at the time of his death he believed the government was going to reimburse him for money spent in the Pacific some thirty years earlier. And it was his financial schemes and personal use of federal money in California that ultimately raised questions about his character and helped bring about his downfall. The eight thousand dollars he made on his gold transactions could hardly have been sufficient reimbursement for the court-martial those activities helped to bring about. All told, his quest for wealth prompted Jones to make too many dubious decisions—one of which caught up with him during his second command in the Pacific.

Jones's piety worked to counterbalance his contentiousness and avariciousness. He was a devout Presbyterian and an elder of the Lewinsville Church, which he helped to found. He tried to bring religion to his men and to the island peoples he encountered; every time he was in Hawaii he treated the islanders with Christian charity and sided with the missionaries rather than the merchants or government. At times, however, his faith drove him to extremes. He held services aboard ship virtually every Sunday he was at sea. He launched a campaign on his ships against hard spirits and drunkenness and reportedly would not tolerate any blasphemous language. He always believed sincerely that he was right in his actions, but in most cases it was folly to try to enforce his high-handed regulations aboard ships. Nevertheless, Jones tried to uplift his men, to make them better sailors, citizens, and Christians. He wore his self-righteousness on his sleeve and dared anyone to question his piety.[2]

At home Jones was a devoted husband and father who wanted to provide well for his family. He successfully experimented with scientific farming techniques to improve his farm's productivity. Had Jones never joined the navy his experimentation and drive to succeed would have undoubtedly made him an accomplished farmer. When he spent long periods at Sharon he kept detailed records of his endeavors and wrote thoughtful essays about his findings. His hard work, or more precisely the hard work of his slaves, turned his barren northern Virginia farm into a lush paradise that he wanted his wife, children, and grandchildren to enjoy after his death.

During his life Jones accumulated, through inheritance and purchase, considerable land and slaves—he was often called rich in land and slaves and poor in money—and apparently he saw no inconsistency in the way he treated slaves and the way he treated the Hawaiians he encountered during his Pacific cruises. Both were dark skinned and thus, in his view, inferior beings, but the islanders controlled lands that the United States coveted. As such, Jones treated them with respect and dignity. But he also treated his slaves reasonably well. For example, he made sure that Griffin Dobson and his family were well provided for, that they attended church, and that the children received an education. Yet Jones did keep Griffin Dobson in bondage when technically he was a free man. Jones maintained that it would have been irresponsible for him to free any of his slaves, especially Dobson, when they were unable to provide for themselves; California in 1849 provided Griffin Dobson an unquestioned opportunity to fend for himself. Jones did not give Dobson his freedom without receiving payment. Nor did he permit the freedom of Dobson's family three years later without additional payment. It was not Jones's magnanimity that allowed Dobson and his family to purchase their freedom, but his need for cash.

Jones was, in his own words, "a southern man with southern principles" who had lived his entire life in a slaveholding state. Yet he was not a rabid sectionalist who supported Virginia's sovereignty over the authority of the national government. He served the U.S. government loyally for forty-six years. Had the secession crisis occurred in 1841 rather than 1861, Jones certainly would have remained loyal to the Union. Yet had he lived until 1861 he might well have joined the Confederacy; the federal government had turned its back on him, whereas his native Virginia had rewarded him for his loyal service to the country. Had he lived a few years longer, Jones would have been forced to reconcile secession and slavery with a sense of nationalism, just as he had been forced to do in California in 1849. In that instance national interests were far more important than the issue of slavery. But incorporating California into the American Union was also necessary for Manifest Destiny, for continued continental expansion, and for preventing further European, especially British, encroachment in North America.

Jones did not have to choose between the Union and Confederacy in 1861, but his family did. His son Meriwether Patterson Jones remained in the Union Navy during the war while his nephew Catesby ap Roger

Jones joined the Confederacy. His wife, Mary, daughter Martha, and son Mark remained at Sharon until 1863, when the Thirteenth New York Cavalry and Fifth Pennsylvania Artillery encamped on the farm. The arrival of the Union Army prompted Mary and the children to flee, probably to Prince William County, Maryland, to stay with relatives. Afterward Union soldiers ravaged the estate as well as the nearby Lewinsville Presbyterian Church. When they finally returned after the war, Mary and Martha found Sharon in shambles. The two women had to reside in the Lewinsville parsonage until their house and property could be repaired. One of the interesting twists of the Civil War occurred when Herman Melville visited his cousin Col. H. S. Gansevoort, who commanded the Thirteenth New York Cavalry, at Sharon. Did Melville realize that he was standing on the farm of the hated commodore who had been the inspiration of his books *White Jacket* and *Moby Dick*?[3]

In 1870 Mary sued the U.S. government for the damages Union forces had inflicted on the family farm, but she received only $2,041.36 of her $9,999.70 claim. In 1871 the court ruled that Mary's flight to join Confederate family members indicated support for the southern cause, despite the service record of her deceased husband and her loyal Unionist son Meriwether Patterson, who died in early April 1866. As a result, Mary was not entitled to the full value of the damages she sought. The money she did receive, while helpful, did not ease the family's financial problems. Mark Jones had been forced to sell part of the farm in 1858 to pay his father's debts. In 1869 he sold more, and in 1877 the remainder had to be conveyed to creditor William Fletcher. Mary died on 20 February 1885, a bitter and disillusioned woman living off the charity of her family and a small federal pension.[4]

The saga of Thomas ap Catesby Jones and his family is similar to that of many members of the antebellum southern aristocracy; many families wealthy in land and slaves fell victim to hard times during and after the Civil War. Yet the family's course, as well as that of most southerners, had been set years before the war began. While the events of Jones's last years, including his financial mismanagement, meant little to the ultimate well-being of his family, they were crucial for his historical reputation.

In late October 1855, when he wrote that important letter chronicling his career, extolling his sacrifices, and insinuating that it was time for the nation to provide its thanks, Jones presented a romanticized view of his deeds. The letter was filed away and subsequently forgotten in Navy

Department records, while Melville's stories—portraying dogmatic, authoritarian sea officers who endeared themselves to no one—still attract readers today. This is not to imply that Melville created the modern impression of Jones, for that is not the case; Jones did that himself. But Melville's accounts, combined with Jones's sometimes angry and bitter Navy Department reports—and even his last will and testament, which chastises his "ungrateful country"—all helped to create the view that Jones was a rash, impetuous, and "contentious commodore."[5]

During the first six months of 1858 the navy lost two of its most colorful officers. On 4 March Matthew C. Perry died; his funeral two days later was a civic event in New York City, complete with a funeral procession down Fifth Avenue. Jones's burial ceremony some three months later, on 2 June, was quiet and unassuming, attended only by family and friends. The deaths and funerals of these two officers vividly illustrate the reputations each gained during his lifetime. Perry had spent his entire career encouraging naval reform, and it was he who ultimately opened Japan to American trade. Becoming a national hero in the process, Perry gained his popularity late in his career and took it with him to his grave. Jones had also supported reform and focused America's attention on the Pacific, although on California and Hawaii rather than Japan, but he had won his fame very early in his career, and his own later actions diminished its luster.[6]

As the age of sail gave way to that of iron and steam, so did the colorful and controversial officers who had provided the character and backbone of the service during its formative years give way to a new generation. Standing over Jones's grave is a tombstone inscribed with the expression: "Precious in the sight of the Lord is the death of his Saints." Perhaps no other early naval officer—or self-perceived saint—was as colorful and controversial as Thomas ap Catesby Jones. His death helped to mark the end of a crucial formative era for the U.S. Navy.

·⭑ Notes ⭒·

ABBREVIATIONS USED IN THE NOTES

ASP   U.S. Congress, *American State Papers: Documents, Legislative and Executive of the Congress of the United States* (Washington, D.C., 1832–1861), Class VI: *Naval Affairs*

Autobiographical   Letters from Officers Transmitting Statements of Their
  Statement   Service, June 1842–Dec. 1844, NA, RG 24

CFL   Confidential Letters Sent by the Secretary of the Navy, 1843–Nov. 1860, NA, RG 45:14

CL   Letters Received by the Secretary of the Navy: Captain's Letters, 1805–61, 1866–85, NA, RG 45:M125

Cruise of *Peacock*   Cruise of the *Peacock,* 1826–27, NA, RG 45:25, 1

Duke   Special Collections Department, William R. Perkins Library, Duke University, Durham, North Carolina

Exceptions   Thomas ap Catesby Jones, *Exceptions to the Illegal Organization, Proceedings, Findings, and Sentence, and etc. of the Naval Court Martial in the Case of Commodore Thomas ap Catesby Jones*

Exploring   Records of the U.S. Exploring Expedition under the Com-
  Expedition Letters   mand of Lt. Charles Wilkes, 1836–46, NA, RG 37:M75

FCCA   Fairfax County Court Archives, Fairfax, Virginia

FCL   Fairfax County Public Library, Fairfax, Virginia

FDRL   Naval History Manuscript Collection of Franklin D. Roosevelt, Franklin D. Roosevelt Library, Hyde Park, New York

Hambleton LB   Samuel Hambleton Letterbook, Maryland Historical Society, Baltimore, Maryland

Harris LB   Logbook/Journal *Peacock,* Cruise to the Pacific, 1824–26, Thomas J. Harris Papers, LC

Hawaii	State of Hawaii, Archives Division, Honolulu, Hawaii
HEHL	Henry E. Huntington Library and Art Gallery, San Marino, California
HNOC	Historic New Orleans Collection, New Orleans, Louisiana
HR	Records of the U.S. House of Representatives, NA, RG 233
Ins	Letters Received by the Secretary of the Navy from Inspectors and Assistant Inspectors of Ordnance, NA, RG 45:226
Jones Statement	"Statement of Lieutenant Thomas ap Catesby Jones to Daniel T. Patterson, 12 Mar. 1815," NA, RG 45:HJ, box 181, 1814–15
LC	Manuscript Division, Library of Congress, Washington, D.C.
MCL	Letters Received by the Secretary of the Navy from Commanders, 1804–86, NA, RG 45:M147
ML	Letters Received by the Secretary of the Navy: Miscellaneous Letters, 1801–84, NA, RG 45:M124
Muster	Muster and Pay Rolls of New Orleans Naval Station, NA, RG 45:92, Rolls subseries 2, New Orleans
NA	U.S. National Archives, Washington, D.C.
NASP	*New American State Papers: Naval Affairs,* ed. K. Jack Bauer
NHF-LC	Naval Historical Foundation Manuscripts, Library of Congress
NYHS	New-York Historical Society, New York City, New York
OL	Letters Received by the Secretary of the Navy from Officers below the Rank of Commander, 1802–84, NA, RG 45:M148
OSW	Letters Sent by the Secretary of the Navy to Officers, 1798–1868, NA, RG 45:M149
Proceedings	*Proceedings of a Court-Martial on Commodore Thomas Ap Catesby Jones, U.S.N., 1851,* 31st Congress, 2d session, Senate Executive Document 45
PSL	Letters Received by the Secretary of the Navy from Commanding Officers of Squadrons, 1841–86, NA, RG 45:M89
PUL	Department of Rare Books and Special Collections, Princeton University Library, Princeton, New Jersey
Review	*Review of the Evidence, Findings and Sentence of the Naval Court Martial in the Case of Commo. Thomas Ap Catesby Jones,* by Walter Jones, Richard S. Coxe, and Joseph H. Bradley
RG	Record Group
RNO	Report on Naval Ordnance of the United States, 1833, NA, RG 45:230

SHC-UNC	Southern Historical Collection, University of North Carolina, Chapel Hill, North Carolina
UVA	Alderman Library, University of Virginia, Charlottesville, Virginia
USNA	Nimitz Library, U.S. Naval Academy, Annapolis, Maryland
VHS	Virginia Historical Society, Richmond, Virginia
W & M	Swem Library, College of William and Mary, Williamsburg, Virginia
WLCL	William L. Clements Library, University of Michigan, Ann Arbor, Michigan
ZB File	Thomas ap Catesby Jones, ZB File, Naval Historical Center, Washington Navy Yard, Washington, D.C.

CHAPTER 1. IMPROVING YOURSELF IN YOUR PROFESSION

1. Jones to Secretary of the Navy, 31 October 1855, "Memorial of Commodore Thomas ap Catesby Jones," 32d Cong., 2d sess., Senate, Committee Report no. 431, 1–15.
2. Ibid., 3.
3. Ibid., 7.
4. Jones to Secretary of the Navy, 1 December 1855, ibid., 8–9.
5. Lewis H. Jones, *Captain Roger Jones*, 25, 74–76.
6. Ibid., 25.
7. Ibid., 31; Thomas W. Ray, "Northumberland County," 49–50.
8. J. Motley Booker, "Mt. Zion and Its People," 3–4; Thomas A. Mason, "The Luminary of the Northern Neck," 3978–79; Ray, "Northumberland County," 51–53.
9. Thomas Jones to Mr. Bogle of London, September 1763, John Warden to Thomas Jones, 24 December 1771, Jones Family Papers, LC; *Virginia Vital Records*, 499; Ray, "Northumberland County," 52–54.
10. Thomas R. Wright, *Westmoreland County Virginia*, 44–47; E. M. Sanchez-Saavedra, *Guide to Virginia Military Organizations*, 7, 19, 185; "Northumberland County [Virginia] Committee, 25 January 1775," *American Archives*, cols. 1178–79; receipt for provisions furnished by Col. Thomas Jones, 18 May 1780, Jones Family Papers, LC.
11. John K. Gott, "Genealogy of the Turberville Family," 56, 58; James F. Lewis and J. Motley Booker, "Catesby Jones of 'Level View,' " 5; *Virginia Tax Records*, 365.
12. Certificate of Dr. Walter Jones, 20 May 1789, in *Calendar of Virginia State Papers*, 4:620; Catesby Jones to George Tuberville, 20 February 1792, Peckatone Papers, VHS; Catesby Jones to Robert Carter, 2 April 1790, Carter Family Papers, VHS.
13. *Virginia Vital Records*, 499; Clericus, "Biographical Sketch," 127.
14. L. H. Jones, *Captain Roger Jones*, 53–54; Christopher McKee, *A Gentlemanly and Honorable Profession*, 82.

15. Meriwether Jones to St. George Tucker, 12 May 1800, Tucker-Coleman MSS, W & M; *History of the College of William and Mary,* 92; Thomas Bloomer Balch, "Sharon," 387; Clericus, "Biographical Sketch," 127.

16. Will of Lettice Corbin Tuberville Jones, 15 December 1804, Northumberland County Deed Record Book, no. 17, 255–56; Clericus, "Biographical Sketch," 127.

17. Richard B. Davis, "James Ogilvie," 290; "Recollections of James Ogilvie," 534–37.

18. "Recollections of James Ogilvie," 534; Receipt to Jacob Cohen, 10 January 1804, James Ogilvie Papers, VHS; Meriwether Jones to Roger and Catesby Jones, Thomas Monroe, and Walter Jones, 27 March 1805, Jones Family Papers, LC.

19. Meriwether Jones to St. George Tucker, 12 May 1800, Tucker-Coleman MSS, W & M; Meriwether Jones to James Monroe, 11 August 1802, James Monroe Papers, LC; Meriwether Jones to Thomas Jefferson, 16 September 1805, Jefferson Papers, LC; Meriwether Jones to Thomas Jefferson, 26 October 1805, Letters of Application and Recommendation during the Administration of Thomas Jefferson, 1801–1809, NA, RG 59.

20. Robert Smith to Thomas ap Catesby Jones, 22 November 1805, OSW; Robert Smith to Thomas Jefferson, 22 November 1805, Thomas Jefferson Papers, LC; Jones to Smith, 27 November 1805, Letters from Officers Acknowledging Receipt of Commissions and Warrants and Enclosing Oaths of Allegiance, 1804–1823, NA, RG 45:66.

21. McKee, *A Gentlemanly and Honorable Profession,* 43, 62.

22. Clericus, "Biographical Sketch," 127–28.

23. Jones to Secretary of the Navy, 6 May 1806, OL; Secretary of the Navy to Jones, 30 May 1806, OSW.

24. Thomas ap Catesby Jones to Secretary of the Navy, 6 September 1806, 27 June 1807, OL; Secretary of the Navy to Jones, 30 May, 30 September 1806, OSW; ZB File.

25. Secretary of the Navy to Jones, 3 July 1807, OL; Jones to Secretary of the Navy, 25 July 1807, OSW.

26. Stephen Decatur to Robert Smith, 12 July, 27 August 1807, CL.

27. Muster Roll, Gunboat *No. 10,* NA, RG 45:90, misc. vol. 3, 1799–1828; Register of Ships, NA, RG 45:171.

28. Ibid.

29. Secretary of the Navy to Jones, 28 January 1808, OL; Jones to Secretary of the Navy, 5 June 1808, OSW.

Chapter 2. This Inactive, Forlorn Station

1. Jones to Secretary of the Navy, 24 April 1844, Autobiographical Statement.

2. Secretary of the Navy to Jones, 23 January 1808, OSW; David Long, *Nothing Too Daring,* 39–40.

3. Gunboat Letters, NA, RG 45:173; "Data on Gunboats," RG 45:AU box 18; David Porter to John Henley, 10 August 1810, John Henley Letterbook, USNA; Porter to Secretary of the Navy, 26 June 1808, MCL.

4. Porter to Secretary of the Navy, 7 August, 14, 18 November 1808, MCL; Secretary of the Navy to Porter, 7 October 1808, OSW.

5. Porter to Secretary of the Navy, 6 September 1808, MCL; Muster; Samuel Hambleton to Jones, 14 October 1808, Hambleton LB.

6. Samuel Hambleton to Philip Marshall, 1 May 1810, Hambleton LB.

7. Muster; Porter to Secretary of the Navy, 19 February, 16 March 1809, MCL.

8. Porter to Secretary of the Navy, 13 December 1809, 10 January 1810, MCL; Thomas ap Catesby Jones obituary, *Daily National Intelligencer* (Washington, D.C.), 1 June 1858; Jones to Secretary of the Navy, 31 October 1855, CL.

9. Jones to Secretary of the Navy, 31 October 1855, CL; Stanley Faye, "Privateers of Guadeloupe and Their Establishment in Barataria," 16–17.

10. James A. Padgett, ed., "Official Records of the West Florida Revolution and Republic," 719–27; Stanley C. Arthur, *Story of the West Florida Rebellion*, 103–7, 112–15.

11. Shaw to Secretary of the Navy, 3 January 1811, CL; W. C. C. Claiborne to Secretary of the Navy, 14 December 1810, ML.

12. Thomas Cushing to Robert Porter, 1 December 1810, Raymond and Roger Weill Collection, HNOC; Robert Smith to David Holmes, 21 December 1810, Robert Smith Papers, LC; Shaw to Secretary of the Navy, 25 January, 1, 8 February 1811, CL.

13. John Shaw to Joseph Bainbridge, 6 June 1811, ML; Shaw to Secretary of the Navy, 22 June 1811, CL.

14. *Courier of Louisiana*, 10 July 1811; John Shaw to Secretary of the Navy, 26 July 1811, CL; W. C. C. Claiborne to Secretary of the Navy, 9 July 1811, in W. C. C. Claiborne, *Official Letterbooks of W. C. C. Claiborne*, 5:298–300.

15. Shaw to Secretary of the Navy, 13 September 1811, CL.

16. Jones to Secretary of the Navy, 28 November 1811, OL.

17. Shaw to Secretary of the Navy, 17 February 1812, CL.

18. Shaw to Secretary of the Navy, 17 February 1812, CL; Secretary of the Navy to Jones, 15 June 1812, OSW.

19. Daniel Dexter to John Shaw, 24 January 1812, Daniel Dexter Letterbook, NA, RG 45:395, entry 8; John Shaw to Commander of Balize Division, 3 May 1812, and Shaw to Secretary of the Navy, 10 July 1812, John Shaw Papers, NHF-LC.

20. Jones to Secretary of the Navy, 31 October 1855, CL.

21. Shaw to Secretary of the Navy, 10 July, 23 August 1812, CL; W. E. Stackhouse to his brother, 28 June 1812, E. M. Service Papers, SHC-UNC; "Diary Kept by a Hospital Officer at Pass Christian, Mississippi, 5 August to 1 December 1812,"

22, 25 August 1812, HEHL; John Shaw to James Wilkinson, 22 September 1812, Shaw Papers, NHF-LC.

22. Jones to Secretary of the Navy, 25 September 1812, 22 January 1813, OL.

23. Shaw to Secretary of the Navy, 19 April, 12 June 1813, CL; James R. Jacobs, *Tarnished Warrior,* 280–81.

24. Jones to Secretary of the Navy, 31 October 1855, CL.

25. Autobiographical Statement; Shaw to Secretary of the Navy, 28 June 1813, CL.

26. Jones to Secretary of the Navy, 28 May 1813, OL.

27. Patterson to Secretary of the Navy, 20 August 1814, MCL; Arthur P. Hayne to Inspector General Office, Seventh Military District, 17 September 1814, Butler Family Papers, HNOC; *Courier of Louisiana,* 21 September 1814; Edward Nicolls to Monsieur Lafite, 31 August 1814, and William H. Percy to Monsieur Lafitte, 1 September 1814, Edward Nicolls and William H. Percy Letters, HNOC.

28. Patterson to Secretary of the Navy, 10 October 1814, MCL; *Niles' Weekly Register,* 19 November 1814, 7:166–67; George Ross to Andrew Jackson, 3 October 1814, Jackson Papers, LC.

29. Patterson to Secretary of the Navy, 14 October 1814, MCL.

30. Patterson to Secretary of the Navy, 14 October, 18 November 1814, and Jones to Patterson, 11 November 1814, MCL; Andrew Jackson to Patterson, 23 October 1814, in Andrew Jackson, *Correspondence of Andrew Jackson,* 2:80–81.

31. James Monroe to Willie Blount, 10 October 1814, James Monroe Letter, HNOC; Jackson to Monroe, 14 October 1814, 2:73–74; Jackson to Patterson, 23 October 1814, 2:80–81; Jackson to James Winchester, 22 November 1814, 2:104–7, all in Jackson, *Correspondence of Jackson.*

32. Jackson to Patterson, 23 October 1814, in Jackson, *Correspondence of Jackson,* 2:80–81; John Shaw to Daniel Patterson, 21 December 1813, CL.

33. Jones to Patterson, 9 December 1814, OL.

34. Jones Statement.

35. James Stirling to Lord Viscount Melville, 17 March 1813, James Stirling Memorandum, 1813, HNOC; John Shaw to Daniel Patterson, 21 December 1813, CL.

36. Alexander Cochrane to John Wilson Coker, 9 March 1815, *Naval Chronicle* 23 (1815): 337; "Autobiography of Robert Aitchison," 64, manuscript in HNOC.

37. Jones Statement.

38. Memorial of Thomas Shield, Congressional Report no. 66, 4 January 1819, copy in the Andrew Hynes Papers, HNOC; Jones Statement; Lt. Moore to John, 13 December 1814, Kean-Prescott Papers, SHC-UNC.

39. Jones Statement.

40. Ibid.

41. Ibid.; Clericus, "Biographical Sketch," 130–31.

42. John H. Cooke, *Narrative of Events in the South of France and of the Attack on New Orleans*, 162–63; N. H. Claiborne, *Notes on the War in the South*, 56–57; Andrew Jackson to James Monroe, 27 December 1814, *Niles' Weekly Register*, 4 February 1815, 7:357.

43. Patterson to Secretary of the Navy, 16 December 1814, MCL.

44. *Niles' Weekly Register*, 22 July 1815, 8:360; Alexander Walker, *Jackson and New Orleans*, 108–10.

45. Patterson to Secretary of the Navy, 19 December 1814, MCL; Arsène Lacarrière Latour, *Historical Memoir*, 75–77.

46. Alexander Cochrane to Andrew Jackson, 12 February 1815, in Jackson, *Correspondence of Jackson*, 2:163–64.

47. Clericus, "Biographical Sketch," 131; Samuel Wilson, *Plantation Houses on the Battlefield of New Orleans*, 55–60.

48. *Alexandre St. Helme v. Thomas ap Catesby Jones*, 20 April 1815, Records of U.S. District Court, NA, case 801.

49. McKee, *A Gentlemanly and Honorable Profession*, 438–39; Secretary of the Navy to Patterson, 16 May, 11 August 1815, OSW.

50. Secretary of the Navy to Patterson, 16 May, 11 August 1815, OSW; Records of the Court of Inquiry in New Orleans, 15–19 May 1815, Records of General Courts-Martial and Courts of Inquiry of the Navy Department, NA, RG 125:M273.

51. *Niles' Weekly Register*, 15 July 1815, 8:346; ZB File; Clericus, "Biographical Sketch," 131.

CHAPTER 3. AWAITING AN ARDUOUS DUTY

1. *Niles' Weekly Register*, 15 July 1815, 8:346; ZB File; Clericus, "Biographical Sketch," 131.

2. Pension Records of Thomas ap C. Jones, case of Mary W. C. Jones, 24 September 1858, NA.

3. Benjamin W. Crowninshield to John Gaillard, 7 December 1815, *ASP*, 2:366–67; David Porter to Jones, 23 December 1815, Smith Naval Collection, WLCL; Secretary of the Navy to William Bainbridge, 2 January 1816, OSW.

4. Charles O. Paullin, *Commodore John Rodgers*, 314; Secretary of the Navy to Isaac Chauncey, 5 January 1816, OSW.

5. Alfred T. Mahan, *Admiral Farragut*, 54–55; Frank W. Gapp, "Jones and Melville," 4.

6. Muster and Payroll, *Washington*, 1815–25, NA, RG 45:90; Logbook, *Washington*, NA, RG 24.

7. Jones to Secretary of the Navy, 31 May 1816, OL.

8. Logbook, *Washington*, NA, RG 24; Secretary of the Navy to Chauncey, 31 January 1816, OSW.

9. Muster Roll, *Washington,* NA, RG 45; Clericus, "Biographical Sketch," 131.

10. Logbook, *Washington,* NA, RG 24.

11. Robert F. Stockton, *Sketch of the Life of Com. Robert F. Stockton,* 27–28.

12. "Complaints of Subaltern Officers of the Navy and Marine Corps to the Senate, 21 January 1818," *ASP,* 2:453–55.

13. Ibid., 2:455, 500–501.

14. Logbook, *Washington,* NA, RG 24; Charles O. Paullin, *Diplomatic Negotiations of American Naval Officers,* 119–21.

15. Payroll, *Constellation,* NA, RG 45; Logbook, *Constellation,* NA, RG 24; Muster Roll, *Constellation,* NA, RG 45:90.

16. Muster Roll, *United States,* 1809–44, NA, RG 45:90; Donovan Fitzpatrick and Saul Saphire, *Navy Maverick,* 74–78; Jacob Rader Marcus, *Memoirs of American Jews, 1775–1865,* 1:85–86.

17. Marcus, *Memoirs,* 1:86.

18. Fitzpatrick and Saphire, *Navy Maverick,* 79–84.

19. Logbook, *Washington,* 15 July 1815–19 January 1820, NA, RG 24; Muster and Payroll, *Washington,* 1815–25, NA, RG 45:90.

20. *Jones* (co-plaintiff) v. *Roger and Philip de Catesby Jones,* 19 November 1817, Fairfax Court Orders and Minutes Books, FCCA, 284–85.

21. Edmund P. Kennedy to Jones, 29 July 1818, Jones to Secretary of the Navy, 23, 26 July 1818, Benjamin Homans to Jones, 23 July 1818, OL; ZB File.

22. Thomas ap C. Jones, "On the Renovation of Worn-out Lands," 265–66.

23. Ibid., 266.

24. Jones to Secretary of the Navy, 14 April 1820, 3 September, 24 October 1821, MCL; Jones to Secretary of the Navy, 20 June 1821, ML.

25. Taylor Peck, *Round-Shot to Rockets,* 74–75; John Rodgers to Secretary of the Navy, 8 April 1822, Isaac Chauncey to Secretary of the Navy, 12 April 1822, ML; Jones to Secretary of the Navy, 16 April 1822, MCL.

26. Jones to David Porter, 25 September 1822, Jones to John Rodgers, 9 December 1822, "Ammunition Powder," NA, RG 45:BA, box 136, Ammunition Powder.

27. Will of Elizabeth Lee Jones, 16 April 1822, Fairfax County Wills, N1, 48–56, FCCA; Fairfax County Personal Property, 1823, FCL; Jones to Lucius Jones, 1822, drawer X, FCCA.

28. *Jones* v. *Elizabeth and Margaret William,* 1819, Fairfax Court Orders and Minutes Books, 207, 259, 261, FCCA; *Alexandria Gazette,* 28 September 1852, 3 November 1868; Jones to Thomas Chew, 10 October 1822, Chew Papers, WLCL.

29. "Sharon," *Sunday Star,* 8 November 1914; Marriage registered between Jones and Mary Walker Carter, 18 July 1825, Fairfax Court Orders and Minutes Books, 87, FCCA.

30. Map of estate in *Mary W. Jones* case, no. 21,622, Southern Claims Commission Case Files, NA, RG 217:box 353; Balch, "Sharon," 387, 390–91.

31. Samuel Southard, "Report on Traveling and Other Allowances," 1 January 1825, *NASP*, 8:68–73; Fairfax County Personal Property, FCL.

32. George Morgan, *Life of James Monroe*, 14; Jones to Walter Jones, 27 March 1824, Heartman Collection, NYHS.

33. Jones to President of Board of Navy Commissioners, 22 November 1824, "Ammunition Powder," NA, RG 45:BA, box 136, Ammunition Powder.

34. Jones to President of Navy Board, 13 December 1824, ZB File.

35. Naval Register for Year 1825, *ASP*, 2:1080–93; Secretary of the Navy to Jones, 23 March 1825, and Secretary of the Navy to James Nicholson, 30 March 1825, OSW.

CHAPTER 4. THE KIND-EYED CHIEF

1. Secretary of the Navy to Jones, 23, 29 March, 13 April 1825, OSW.

2. Secretary of the Navy to Jones, 29 March, 13 April 1825, OSW.

3. Secretary of the Navy to Jones, 30 March 1825, OSW; "*Peacock*," Register of Ships, Cruises, and Officers, NA, RG 45:179.

4. Logbook/Journal, *Peacock*, Cruise to the Pacific, 1824–26, Harris LB; Logbook, *Peacock*, NA, RG 24; Linda Maloney, *Captain from Connecticut*, 378–79.

5. Jones to Isaac Hull, 12 May 1826, Charles Thomas Harbeck Collection, HEHL.

6. Isaac Hull to Jones, 1 May 1826, Naval Manuscripts, FDRL.

7. Harris LB; Logbook, *Peacock*, NA, RG 24.

8. Harris LB.

9. Samuel L. Southard to Isaac Hull, 24 May 1825, HR 108, 29th Cong., 1st sess., 8–9.

10. Petition to James Monroe, December 1824, Petition to John Quincy Adams, 5 April 1825, HR 108, 9–11.

11. Petition to John Quincy Adams, ca. April 1825, HR 108, 12–13.

12. Hull to Jones, 25 May 1826, HR 108, 13–14; Harris LB; Jones to Samuel Southard, 14 May 1827, Cruise of *Peacock*; Jones to Hull, 9 June 1826, FDRL.

13. Hull to Jones, 25 May 1826, HR 108, 13–14.

14. Hiram Bingham, *Twenty-one Years in the Sandwich Islands*, 303; David Loung, "*Mad Jack*," 66–75, 84; Rufus Anderson, *History of the Sandwich Islands Mission*, 67–68.

15. Harris LB; Jones to Hull, 9 June 1826, FDRL; House Committee on Foreign Affairs, 4 February 1845, 28th Cong., 2d sess., Report no. 92, 2.

16. Jones to Hull, 9 June 1826, FDRL.

17. Harris LB; Cruise of *Peacock*, 2; *Alexandria Gazette*, 3 November 1868, 2.

18. Cruise of *Peacock*, 4; Harris LB.

19. Cruise of *Peacock*, 4–5; Harris LB.

20. Cruise of *Peacock*, 4–6.

21. Ibid., 5–7; Harris LB.

22. Cruise of *Peacock,* 8–9; Harris LB.

23. Cruise of *Peacock,* 10–11.

24. Harris LB; Cruise of *Peacock,* 12–13.

25. C. Hartley Grattan, *The United States and the Southwest Pacific,* 89–90; Harris LB; Cruise of *Peacock,* 13–14; Jean Brookes, *International Rivalry in the Pacific Islands,* 46–47.

26. Cruise of *Peacock,* no. 3; W. Patrick Strauss, "Pioneer American Diplomats in Polynesia," 25.

27. Harris Journal; Cruise of *Peacock,* no. 4, 1–17.

28. Harris LB; Cruise of *Peacock,* no. 1, 16.

29. Harris LB; Cruise of *Peacock,* no. 1, 16, and no. 5, 1–10.

30. Cruise of *Peacock,* no. 5, 1–10.

31. Ibid.

32. Cruise of *Peacock,* no. 1, 18–21.

33. Bernice Judd, *Voyages to Hawaii before 1860,* 21; Cruise of *Peacock,* no. 1, 22; Harris LB.

34. Cruise of *Peacock,* no. 1, 23–24; Harris LB.

35. Ibid.; Jones to Kaikiouli, King of the Sandwich Islands, 17, 31 October 1826, Foreign Office and Executive, Hawaii; Journal of John N. Colcord, 1793–1845, 53, Hawaii.

36. Cruise of *Peacock,* no. 1, 25–26.

37. Harold W. Bradley, "Thomas ap Catesby Jones and the Hawaiian Islands," 23–24.

38. Jones to Southard, 1 November 1826, Cruise of *Peacock,* no. 1, attachment.

39. Agreement signed by Hawaiian Monarchy, 27 December 1826, 28th Cong., 2d sess., House Exec. Doc., Report no. 92, 18–19; John Coffin Jones to William B. Finch, 28 October 1829, Logbook of William B. Finch of *Vincennes,* 1826–30, NA, RG 45:25, subseries 2.

40. Thomas ap C. Jones, "The Sandwich Islands," 286; "Visit of Commodore Thomas AP. Catesby Jones in the U.S. Ship Peacock, to Honolulu in October 1826, to January 1827, . . ." *Hawaiian Gazette,* 17 August 1886; Walter M. Gibson to H. A. P. Carter, 15 June 1885, Hawaiian Legation, Washington, D.C., vol. 1, 1873–87, 461–70, Foreign Office and Executive, Hawaii; "Report of the Minister of Foreign Affairs to the Legislative Assembly of 1886," app. B, xiii–xxii, Foreign Office and Executive, Hawaii.

41. Bradford Smith, *Yankees in Paradise,* 134–35.

42. Bingham, *Twenty-one Years in the Sandwich Islands,* 299–301.

43. Ibid., 300–303; B. Smith, *Yankees in Paradise,* 138–39.

44. Harris LB; Treaty signed by Elisabeta Kaahumanu, Karaimoku, Boki, Hoapili, Lidia Namahana, and Thomas ap Catesby Jones, 22 December 1826, Foreign Office and Executive, Hawaii.

45. Harris LB.

46. Jones to Secretary of the Navy, 29 December 1855, CL.

47. Treaty signed by Kaahumanu, Karaimoku, Boki, Hoapili, Namahana, and Jones, 22 December 1826, Foreign Office and Executive, Hawaii.

48. Harris LB; Cruise of *Peacock,* 27–29.

49. Harris LB; Cruise of *Peacock,* 30–32.

50. Harris LB; Cruise of *Peacock,* 32–36.

51. Harris LB; Log, *Peacock,* NA, RG 24.

52. Cruise of *Peacock,* no. 2, 1–23; J. N. Reynolds to Michael Hoffman, *Explore South Seas,* 20th Cong., 1st sess., House Report no. 209, 1–18.

53. The cape given to Jones by the Hawaiians remained at Sharon until the Civil War. When the estate was overrun by federal forces in 1861 Mary Jones fled south to stay with family. It was reported that the Union Army turned over several exotic items from the Jones house to the Smithsonian Institution, but the museum has no record of the cape being among them.

54. The quotation is Hiram Bingham's. From Mr. Wyllie's comments on extracts from Bingham's History, History and Miscellaneous, 1847, Hawaii.

CHAPTER 5. THE DIE IS CAST

1. Fairfax County Personal Property Records, FCL; Personal Property, Fairfax County Tax Records, Land Tax Books, Fairfax County, Virginia, 1819–1850, Virginia State Library and Archives, Richmond.

2. ZB File; Secretary of the Navy to Jones, 6 November 1827, 26 January, 11 April 1828, OSW.

3. Secretary of the Navy to Jones, 26 January 1828, OSW.

4. Cruise of *Peacock,* 27–29; Secretary of the Navy to Jones, 26 January, 11 April 1828, OSW; Jones to Secretary of the Navy, 26 February 1827, MCL.

5. Deposition of John J. Shipman, 20 May 1875, in *Mary W. Jones* case, no. 21,622, Records of the Southern Claims Commission, 1871–80, NA, RG 217, box 353.

6. Fairfax County Personal Property Records, FCL; Secretary of the Navy to Jones, 18 November 1828, OSW.

7. William Stanton, *Great Exploring Expedition,* 11, 13–18.

8. Jeremiah N. Reynolds to Michael Hoffman, n.d., "Report: The Committee on Naval Affairs," *Explore South Seas,* 1–18 (reference to Jones, pp. 9–10, and letter from Jones to Reynolds, 28 February 1828, p. 15).

9. Jones to Secretary of the Navy, 16 December 1828, Report on Preparations for South Pacific Exploring Expedition, *NASP,* 9:229.

10. Stanton, *Great Exploring Expedition,* 21.

11. John Wilkes to Charles Wilkes, 29 December 1837, Wilkes Family Papers, Duke.

12. Robert E. Johnson to Sarah W. Seaton, 28 November 1828, and Johnson to his grandmother, 13 December 1828, Robert E. Johnson Letters, Duke; Jones to Secretary of the Navy, 16 December 1828, Report on Preparations for South Pacific Exploring Expedition, *NASP,* 9:229.

13. Samuel Jones to Samuel Southard, 26 December 1828, Samuel Southard Papers, PUL; Jones to Charles Wilkes, 2, 11 January 1829, Wilkes Family Papers, Duke.

14. Secretary of the Navy to Jones, 2 May 1829, OSW; ZB File; Marshall D. Haywood, *John Branch, 1782–1863,* 14–15.

15. Jones to President and Directors of the Branch U.S. Bank, Washington City, 15 August 1829, Thomas ap Catesby Jones Papers, VHS; Jones and Mary Walker Carter Jones, deed to trustee Richard Smith for Sharon, 16 March 1829, Fairfax Court Orders and Minutes Books, FCCA.

16. Jones to Secretary of the Navy, 15 June 1829, CL; Secretary of the Navy to Jones, 16 June 1829, OSW; ZB File.

17. Secretary of the Navy to Jones, 21 January 1830, OSW; Jones to Secretary of the Navy, 5 March 1830, *ASP,* 1:568–69; Jones to William P. Lantzing, 29 April 1830, Samuel Southard Papers, PUL.

18. Agreement recorded for division of slaves, 20 August 1829, Fairfax Court Orders and Minutes Books, 114, FCCA; Returns for 1830, Fairfax County Personal Property, FCL; Jones to Edmund Ruffin, 16 February 1838, *Farmers' Register* 6 (1 April 1838): 1; deed, 19 May 1830, Fairfax County Deed Book, D3, 583–85, FCCA; Jones to Mary Love, 28 June 1830, FDRL.

19. Thomas ap C. Jones, "Statements of Particular and General Management and Products in Fairfax," 1–2.

20. Jones, "On the Renovation of Worn-out Lands," 265–66; *Jones v. Bank of the Valley in Virginia,* 26 October 1831, Fairfax Court Orders and Minutes Books, 88, 258, FCCA.

21. Jones to Secretary of the Navy, 21 September 1832, Ins.

22. Jones to Secretary of the Navy, 21 January, 17, 23 April 1833, Ins.

23. Jones to Secretary of the Navy, 23 April, 3 August, 12 November 1833, 20 January 1834, Ins.

24. Jones to Secretary of the Navy, 21 September 1833, Ins.

25. Jones to John Rodgers, 20 January 1834, RNO.

26. Jones to A. Du Pont, 14 November 1833, Samuel F. Du Pont Papers, Hagley Museum and Library, Wilmington, Delaware; Jones to Secretary of the Navy, 12 November 1833, and "Minutes of Weather while Proving Powder at New York between September 12–20, 1833," Ins; Jones to John Rodgers, 10 November 1833, RNO.

27. Jones to John Rodgers, 10 November 1833, RNO.

28. Jones to Secretary of the Navy, 20 January 1834, RNO.

29. Ibid.; Secretary of the Navy to Jones, 14 March 1836, OSW; Jones to Secretary of the Navy, 14, 15 March 1836, CL.

30. Jones to John Rodgers, 20 January 1834, RNO;

31. Jones to John Rodgers, 20 January, John Rodgers to Jones, 29 January, Jones to Rodgers, 10 February 1834, RNO.

32. Jones to Secretary of the Navy, 10 April, 24 September 1834, 5 May 1835, CL; Secretary of the Navy to Jones, 11 April, 2 October 1834, OSW.

33. "Application of Captains and Master Commandant of the Navy for an Increase of Pay and Emoluments," 12 April 1832, 22d Cong., 1st sess., no. 479, *ASP*, 4:134; Jones to Richard Coxe, 8 July 1828, FDRL; Jones to Coxe, 10 July 1828, Thomas ap Catesby Jones Papers, LC; Jones to Samuel L. Southard, Richard Rush, and James Barbour, Board of Commissioners for the Management of the Navy Pension Fund, 14 February 1828, Samuel Southard Papers, PUL; John Branch to Michael Hoffman, 26 February 1831, *ASP*, 10:2.

34. Jones to Samuel L. Southard, Richard Rush, and James Barbour, 14 February 1828, enclosed in Jones to the Senate and House of Representatives, 7 February 1831, "Claim of Master Commandant Thomas ap Catesby Jones, of the Navy, to a Pension, on Account of a Wound Received in Battle," 21st Cong., 2d sess., no. 442, *ASP*, 3:895–96.

35. Michael Hoffman to the House of Representatives, 1 March 1831, "On Claim of a Naval Officer in Service, at Full Pay, to a Pension from the Naval Pension Fund, on Account of a Wound," 21st Cong., 2d sess., no. 452, *ASP*, 4:1.

36. Jones to Samuel Southard, 12 April 1834, Samuel Southard Papers, PUL; indenture, 7 October 1834, Fairfax County Deeds, B3, 351–53, and C3, 381–84, FCCA; "Claim of T. Ap. C. Jones, of the Navy, for Arrears of Pensions, 25 February 1833," 22d Cong. 2d sess., no. 510, *ASP*, 4:298; Thomas ap Catesby Jones, Veterans Administration, RG 15:YL Pensions—Privateers and Navy, War of 1812.

37. "Report on Expediency of Authorizing Exploring Expedition to Pacific and South Seas, 21 March 1836," *NASP*, 9:232–37; W. Patrick Strauss, "Preparing the Wilkes Expedition," 221; Mahlon Dickerson to Jones, 28 June 1836, 25th Cong., 2d sess., H. Exec. Doc. 147, 6.

38. Jones to Mahlon Dickerson, 30 June 1836, 25th Cong., 2d sess., H. Exec. Doc. 147, 7.

39. Stanton, *Great Exploring Expedition,* 35–36.

40. John Boyle to John Rodgers, 25 July 1836, Letters to Board of Navy Commissioners, NA, RG 45:8.

41. Secretary of the Navy to Jones 11, 12, 15 July 1836, OSW; "Board for Testing Ordnance," NA, RG 45:entry 359.

42. Jones to Dickerson, 22 August, 7 November, 15 December 1836, U.S. Exploring Expedition Letters, NA, RG 37:M75.

43. Wilkes to Dickerson, Jones to Dickerson, 22 August, 1836, Exploring Expedition Letters; Charles Wilkes, *Autobiography*, 323–24.

44. Jones to Dickerson, 22 August, 2 September 1836, Dickerson to Jones, 31 August, 12 September 1836, Exploring Expedition Letters.

45. *Army and Navy Chronicle* 3 (1 December 1836): 337–42; Jones to Samuel Southard and copy of undated reply attached, 2 January 1837, Samuel Southard Papers, PUL.

46. *Army and Navy Chronicle* 3 (29 December 1836): 409–10, and 3 (19 January 1837): 35–43.

47. *Army and Navy Chronicle* 4 (26 January 1837): 49–51, and 4 (2 February 1837): 69.

48. *Army and Navy Chronicle* 4 (26 January 1837): 54, and 4 (2 February 1837): 69–71; *North American Review* 45 (October 1837): 389–90; newspaper clipping in Peregrine W. Browning Papers, LC.

49. Jones to Dickerson, 29 August 1836, Letters to the Board of Navy Commissioners, NA, RG 45:8.

50. Jones to Dickerson, 20 April 1837, H. Exec. Doc. 147, 285; Josiah Tattnall to Jones, 2 April 1837, ibid., 312–13; for the exchange of letters, see ibid., 302–15; Dickerson to Van Buren, 3 June 1837, ibid., 317–18; Muster and Payrolls, *Pioneer*, 1837, NA, RG 45:90.

51. Dickerson to Van Buren, 3 June 1837, H. Exec. Doc. 147, 317–18, and Navy Board to Dickerson, 13 July 1837, ibid., 346.

52. Jones to Dickerson, 1 June 1837, Exploring Expedition Letters; Dickerson to Jones, 9 November 1837, H. Exec. Doc. 147, 507–53.

53. Jones to Theodore Bailey, 3 May 1837, Thomas ap Catesby Jones Papers, VHS; Jones to Dickerson, Thomas ap Catesby Jones Papers, LC.

54. Benajah Ticknor Journal, 11 October 1837, Benajah Ticknor Papers, MS Group no. 495, Yale University Library, New Haven, Connecticut; Logbook, *Macedonia*, NA, RG 24; General Order—No. 1, copy of newspaper article in Peregrine W. Browning Papers, LC; *Baltimore American*, 19 October 1837.

55. Pay Roll, *Macedonia*, NA, RG 45:90.

56. Jones to Dickerson, 25 August, 14, 21 November 1837, Exploring Expedition Letters.

57. Dickerson to Jones, 9 November 1837, H. Exec. Doc. 147, 507–53, and Jones to Dickerson, 14 November 1837, ibid., 563–64.

58. Jones to Dickerson, 14 November 1837, ibid., 563–64; quote in Jones to L. U. C., 18 November 1837, Blair and Lee Family Papers, Series: Papers of Samuel Phillips Lee, PUL; Jones to Dickerson, 14 November 1837, 563–64, Jones to Dickerson, 14 November 1837, 586–89, and Dickerson to Jones, 6 December 1837, 601–9, all in H. Exec. Doc. 147; entry for 5 December 1837, Benajah Ticknor Papers.

59. Dickerson Diary, 6 December 1837, Historical Society of New Jersey; Strauss, "Preparing the Wilkes Expedition," 227–32; Joseph G. Clark Journal, U.S. *Vincennes*, 1838–42, LC.

Chapter 6. The Hero of Monterey

1. Secretary of the Navy to Jones, 3 March, 3, 19 May 1838, OSW; Jones to Secretary of the Navy, 2 April, 12 May 1838, CL.

2. American Physician, *Mackenzie's Five Thousand Receipts in all the Useful and Domestic Arts*, 204; Jones to Secretary of the Navy, 22 February 1838, CL; Secretary of the Navy to Jones, 24 February 1838, OSW.

3. ZB File.

4. Jones to Edmund Ruffin, 16 February 1838, *Farmers' Register* 6 (April 1831): 1–2; Patricia Hickin, "Yankees Come to Fairfax County," 100–109.

5. Jones to Edmund Ruffin, 12 February 1839, *Farmers' Register* 7 (March 1839): 153–55; Fairfax County Personal Property, FCL.

6. Sarah Sewell to Jones, 1838, FCCA; Frances C. Robb, "Industry in the Potomac River Valley," 246–48.

7. Virginia, "An Act to Incorporate the Great Falls Manufacturing Company, 11 January 1839," chap. 222; Virginia, "An Act to Establish the Town of South Lowell at the Great Falls of the Potomac River in the County of Fairfax, 6 March 1839," chap. 248.

8. Maskell C. Ewing, *The Water Power at Great Falls*, 6.

9. *Great Falls Manufacturing Company*, 1–2.

10. Alexander Claxton to Francis Sorrel, 13 January 1839, Alexander Claxton Papers, NHF-LC; Samuel E. Morison, *"Old Bruin,"* 123, 126, 171; Jones to S. P. Lee, 10 April 1840, Blair and Lee Family Papers, PUL.

11. Secretary of the Navy to Jones, 24 December 1838, 17 December 1839, OSW; Jones to Secretary of the Navy, 14 December 1839, CL.

12. Jones to Secretary of the Navy, 8 October, 5 December 1840, CL.

13. Jones to Secretary of the Navy, 8 October, 5 December 1840, CL; Secretary of the Navy to Jones, 15 December 1840, OSW.

14. Edward F. Heite, "Virginia Twists the Lion's Tail," 41–44.

15. *Richmond Enquirer*, 25 February 1841.

16. Ibid.; *Niles' National Register* 60 (6 March 1841): 16.

17. *Southern Literary Messenger* 7 (April 1841): 316–20.

18. *Richmond Enquirer*, 23, 25 February 1841.

19. Jones to Secretary of the Navy, 9 March 1841, CL.

20. Secretary of the Navy to Jones, 22 March, 26 April 1841, OSW; Jones to Secretary of the Navy, 25 March, 30 April 1841, CL.

21. "Personal Property," Fairfax County Tax Records, FCCA; "Fairfax County Personal Property," FCL.

22. *Alexandria Gazette*, 30 May 1842; Balch, "Sharon," 386–95.

23. John Quincy Adams, *Memoirs of John Quincy Adams*, 10:163–64.

24. Claude H. Hall, "Abel P. Upshur and the Navy as an Instrument of Foreign Policy," 290, 292; ZB File.

25. Secretary of the Navy to Jones, 10 December 1841, 27th Cong., 3d sess., H. Exec. Doc. 166, no. 5, 46–50; Jones to Secretary of the Navy, 18 June 1842, PSL.

26. Secretary of the Navy to Jones, 10 December 1841, H. Exec. Doc. 166, 46–50.

27. Claude H. Hall, *Abel Parker Upshur*, 177–79; Gene A. Smith, "Thomas ap Catesby Jones and the First Implementation of the Monroe Doctrine," 147–48; William Jay, *A Review of the Causes and Consequences of the Mexican War*, 82–83.

28. Muster Roll, *United States*, NA, RG 45:90; Harold D. Langley, *Social Reform in the United States Navy*, 64–5, 244; William H. Meyers, *Journal of a Cruise to the Pacific Ocean*, 26.

29. Logbook, *United States*, NA, RG 24.

30. Ibid.

31. Secretary of the Navy to Jones, 13 June 1842, OSW; Samuel R. Franklin, *Memoirs of a Rear-Admiral*, 39.

32. Jones to Secretary of the Navy, 18 June 1842, PSL; *Niles' National Register*, 17 December 1842.

33. Jones to Secretary of the Navy, 21 May 1842, H. Exec. Doc. 166, 67; and ibid., 13 September 1842, 68–69.

34. Jones to Secretary of the Navy, 13 September 1842, H. Exec. Doc. 166, 68–69.

35. Jones to James Armstrong, Cornelius Stribling, and Thomas Dornin, 8 September 1842, H. Exec. Doc. 166, 84–85; and Jones to Secretary of the Navy, 13 September 1842, ibid., 68–69; John Parrott to Jones, 22 June 1842, *Army and Navy Chronicle* 1 (April 1843): 481; Circular to the Diplomatic Corps residing in Mexico from José María Bocanegra, 31 May 1842, Bocanegra to Daniel Webster, Secretary of State, 31 May 1842, Bocanegra to Waddy Thompson, 6 June 1842, Thompson to Webster, 20 June 1842, all in Despatches from United States Ministers to Mexico, 1823–1906, NA, RG 59:M97; Meyers, *Journal of a Cruise*, 82–83.

36. Jones to Secretary of the Navy, 13 September, 24 October 1842, H. Exec. Doc. 166, 68–70.

37. Jones to James Armstrong, Cornelius Stribling, and Thomas Dornin, 8 September 1842, H. Exec. Doc. 166, 84–86.

38. Ibid.; Alonzo C. Jackson to Alonzo Paige, 3 November 1842, in Alonzo C. Jackson, *The Conquest of California*, 11; Philo White, *Narrative of a Cruise in the Pacific*, 54.

39. Jones to Secretary of the Navy, 24 October 1842, H. Exec. Doc. 166, 69–73.

40. Jackson, *Conquest of California,* 12; Thomas ap C. Jones, *Visit to Monterey in 1842,* 19; Franklin, *Memoirs of a Rear-Admiral,* 39; Meyers, *Cruise to the Pacific,* 41.

41. General Order, 18 October 1842, H. Exec. Doc. 166, 41–42.

42. Logbook, *United States,* NA, RG 24; Brinton C. Busch, *Alta California,* 326, 351; Jones to Secretary of the Navy, 24 October 1842, H. Exec. Doc. 166, 69–73.

43. Logbook, *United States,* NA, RG 24; Jones to Secretary of the Navy, 24 October 1842, H. Exec. Doc. 166, 69–73.

44. Jones to Secretary of the Navy, 24 October 1842, H. Exec. Doc. 166, 69–73.

45. Ibid.

46. Juan B. Alvarado to Jones, 19 October 1842, H. Exec. Doc. 166, 76; and Jones to Secretary of the Navy, 24 October 1842, ibid., 69–73.

47. Harlan Hague and David J. Langum, *Thomas O. Larkin,* 100; Jones to Secretary of the Navy, 24 October 1842, H. Exec. Doc. 166, 69–73.

48. Jones to Secretary of the Navy, 24 October 1842, H. Exec. Doc. 166, 69–73.

49. Ibid.; and Jones to Juan B. Alvarado and Mariano Silva, 21 October 1842, ibid., 81.

50. Reuben L. Underhill, *From Cowhides to Golden Fleece,* 80; Thomas O. Larkin to Robert J. Walker, 4 August 1844, in Thomas O. Larkin, in *Larkin Papers,* 2:182; Larkin to John C. Calhoun, 18 August 1844, in ibid., 2:205.

51. Thomas O. Larkin to Robert J. Walker, 4 August 1844, in Larkin, *Larkin Papers,* 2:183; Larkin to James G. Bennett, 10 February 1843, in ibid., 2:6.

52. Robert E. Johnson, *Thence around Cape Horn,* 64.

53. Thomas O. Larkin to James G. Bennett, 10 February 1843, in Larkin, *Larkin Papers,* 2:6.

54. Thomas O. Larkin to Secretary of State, 16 April 1844, in Larkin, *Larkin Papers,* 2:97.

55. *El Mosquito Mexicano,* 16 December 1842; *El Eco de la Justicia,* 14 March 1843; J. M. Bocanegra to Waddy Thompson, 19 December 1842, in García, ed., *Material para la historia diplomática de Mexico,* 364–65; Thompson to Bocanegra, 27 December 1842, in ibid., 366.

56. Logbook, *United States,* NA, RG 24; Jones to Upshur, 24 October 1842, H. Exec. Doc. 166, 69–73; Jones to Henry A. Wise, 16 November 1842, Collection of Western America, Beinecke Rare Book and Manuscript Library, Yale University Library, New Haven, Connecticut.

57. José Manuel Micheltorena to Jones, 26 October 1842, H. Exec. Doc. 166, 35–36; Jones to Micheltorena, 1 November 1842, ibid., 37–38; John Marsh to Jones, 25 November 1842, Peregrine W. Browning Papers, LC; Thomas ap Catesby Jones material in the Abel Stearns Papers, HEHL.

58. Jones, *Visit to Los Angeles in 1843,* 11–15.

59. Propositions for a Convention between Micheltorena and Jones, ___ November 1842, H. Exec. Doc. 166, 36–37; Jones, *Visit to Los Angeles in 1843*, 17–18.

60. Jones, *Visit to Los Angeles in 1843*, 18–20; Abel Stearns manuscript in the Abel Stearns Papers, HEHL.

61. Jones, *Visit to Los Angeles in 1843*, 24–27; J. Gregg Layne, "Annals of Los Angeles," 229.

62. Logbook, *United States*, NA, RG 24; Meyers, *Journal of a Cruise*, 45–48.

63. Logbook, *United States*, NA, RG 24; Abel P. Upshur to Jones, 24 January 1843, Mason Family Papers, VHS.

64. Judd, *Voyages to Hawaii before 1860*, 33; Brookes, *International Rivalry in the Pacific Islands*, 131–32.

65. Logbook, *United States*, NA, RG 24.

66. Logbook, *United States*, NA, RG 24; Carroll Storrs Alden, *Lawrence Kearny*, 194–203; Anderson, *History of the Sandwich Islands Mission*, 203–5.

67. Report of Titus Coan on his missionary work at Hilo, in *Missionary Herald* 40 (June 1844): 187; *Friend* (Hawaii), August 1843, 45–46.

68. Logbook, *United States*, NA, RG 24; invitation to King Kamehameha, 9 August 1843, Foreign Office and Executive, 1843, Hawaii; Jones to Secretary of the Navy, 19 August, 21 November 1843, PSL.

69. Anderson, *Melville in the South Seas*, 53–54.

70. Logbook, *United States*, NA, RG 24; Meyers, *Journal of a Cruise*, 60–61.

71. Logbook, *United States*, NA, RG 24; Jones to Alexander Dallas, 22 November 1843, PSL.

72. Logbook, *United States*, NA, RG 24.

73. Dallas to Secretary of the Navy, 23 February 1844, PSL; Johnson, *Thence around Cape Horn*, 68–69.

74. Secretary of the Navy to Jones, 19 September 1844, OSW; obituary clipping in the Jones Family Papers, LC; Abel Upshur to Jones, 24 January 1843, copy in Mason Family Papers, VHS.

75. Hall, *Abel Parker Upshur*, 177–78, 186; Abel Upshur to Jones, 13 June 1842, OSW.

76. 25 March, 4 April 1843, in Adams, *Memoirs of John Quincy Adams*, 11:346–47, 353.

77. *Daily National Intelligencer and Washington Advertiser*, 23 February 1843; Silas Reed to Lyon G. Tyler, 8 April 1885, in Lyon G. Tyler, *The Letters and Times of the Tylers*, 2:698.

78. Secretary of the Navy to Jones, 1 March, 26 May 1845, OSW; notes about Jones's recall by John Y. Mason, 1843, Mason Family Papers, VHS.

79. Seth Ledyard Phelps to Ann B. Towsley Phelps, 9 August 1846, Kate Fowle Collection, LC; James H. Gleason to John Paty, 30 July 1846, in Duncan

Gleason, ed., "James Henry Gleason: Pioneer Journal and Letters—1841–1856," 32.

CHAPTER 7. JONES OVERSTEPPED HIS AUTHORITY

1. *Daily National Intelligencer*, 17 January 1843.
2. Jones to Secretary of the Navy, 28 February 1845, CL; Secretary of the Navy to Jones, 24 December 1844, 1 March 1845, OSW; Jones to Secretary of the Navy, 4 July 1845, and Secretary of the Navy to Jones, 10 July 1845, both in ZB File; Jones to Thomas O. Larkin, 30 July 1845, in Larkin, *Larkin Papers*, 3:286.
3. Thomas ap C. Jones, "Experiments with Bone Manure," 1–2; A New Yorker, "Letters from Virginia. No. 5," 122–23; 1845, 1846, Fairfax County Personal Property, FCL.
4. Secretary of the Navy to Jones, 26 May 1845, OSW; Charles Todorich, *The Spirited Years*, 12, 14; David Henshaw to William W. McKean, 25 January 1844, Bayard Family Papers, LC.
5. Todorich, *The Spirited Years*, 16–17.
6. Jones to Matthew C. Perry, 4 July 1845, Rodgers Family Papers, NHF-LC.
7. Jones to Secretary of the Navy, 3 October 1845, CL.
8. Secretary of the Navy to Jones, 20 October, 6 November 1845, OSW; Jones to Secretary of the Navy, 3, 18 October 1845, CL; Jones to John Marron, 19 December 1845, R. W. Lull Collection, UVA.
9. Jones to Secretary of the Navy, 18 October 1845, CL; Jones to John Young Mason, 19 March 1846, Mason Family Papers, VHS; Secretary of the Navy to Jones, 3 June 1846, OSW.
10. Frank W. Gapp, *The Lewinsville Presbyterian Church*, 9–10; Robert B. Woodworth, *History of the Presbytery of Winchester (Synod of Virginia)*, 212–13.
11. Rev. C. B. McKee Diary, 13, 14 June, 21 October, 13 November 1857, original in possession of Frank W. Gapp, copy in Virginia State Archives; will of Thomas ap Catesby Jones, 5 August 1857, Fairfax County Will Book Z:11, FCCA.
12. Secretary of the Navy to Jones, 19 November 1846, OSW; Jones to Secretary of the Navy, 14 May 1846, CL; Jones to Thomas Ritchie, 14 January 1847, Ritchie Harrison Papers, W & M.
13. Secretary of the Navy to Jones, 30 April, 25 October 1847, CFL; W. Branford Shubrick to John Young Mason, 26 January 1847, John Young Mason Papers, SHC-UNC.
14. Jones to R. Tucker, 3 June 1847, FDRL; "Proceedings of the Board of Naval Examiners, 1847," U.S. Naval Academy Archives, Nimitz Library, Annapolis; Jones to Secretary of the Navy, 1 July 1847, CL.
15. Thomas Ritchie to Jones, 26 August 1847, Ritchie Harrison Papers, W & M; Secretary of the Navy to Jones, 10 August 1847, OSW; Park Benjamin, *The United States Naval Academy*, 72, 89.

16. Secretary of the Navy to Jones, 16 October 1847, OSW; Secretary of the Navy to Jones, 25 October, 30 April 1847, CFL; Jones to Secretary of the Navy, 23 October 1847, CL.

17. Secretary of the Navy to Jones, 16 October 1847, OSW; Jones to Secretary of the Navy, 29 December 1847, 12 February 1848, PSL.

18. Jones to Secretary of the Navy, 11 October 1847, CL; Jones to Secretary of the Navy, circular enclosed with 1 February, 28 February, 11, 24 March 1848, PSL; General Order No. 2, 2 February 1848, Naval History Society Collection, Misc. Jones, NYHS; Jones to Senior Naval Officer in Command at Monterey, 23 March 1848, in Larkin, *Larkin Papers*, 7:206.

19. Logbook, *Ohio*, 3 March 1848, NA, RG 24; Secretary of the Navy to Jones, 21 December 1847, 11 March 1848, CFL.

20. Jones to Thomas O. Larkin, 24 May 1848, in Larkin, *Larkin Papers*, 7:276–77; Jones to Secretary of the Navy, May 1848, Jones to A. Sevier and N. Clifford, 9 May 1848, Jones to H. A. Wise, 9 May 1848, PSL; Logbook, *Ohio*, 13 June 1848, NA, RG 24.

21. Elie A. F. Lavallette to Jones, 14 June 1848, Elie A. F. Lavallette Letterbook, 1847–48, Duke; Secretary of the Navy to Jones, 27 June 1848, Jones to Secretary of the Navy, 15 July 1848, PSL; Henry S. Burton to Jones, 20 July 1848, Thomas ap Catesby Jones Papers, VHS.

22. Jones to Secretary of the Navy, 2 September 1848, Memo to Officers, 30 August 1848, PSL; Logbook, *Ohio*, 9 October 1848, NA, RG 24; Jones to H. S. Burton and C. K. Stribling, 21 August 1848, *Proceedings*, 50–51.

23. Jones to Secretary of the Navy, 19 October 1848, *Proceedings*, 49–50; Secretary of the Navy to Jones, 20 January 1849, PSL.

24. William Stewart to Jones, 20 June 1848, PSL; Ralph P. Bieber, "California Gold Mania," 12–13.

25. Jones to Secretary of the Navy, 15, 28 July, 19 August 1848, PSL; Jones to Elie A. F. Lavallette, 16 August 1848, Smith Naval Collection, WLCL; Jones to Officers and Men of the Pacific Squadron, 21 August 1848, Journal of Midn. Philip C. Johnson, NA, RG 45:392, entry 76.

26. William Stewart to Jones, 20 June 1848, and Jones to Secretary of the Navy, 27 July, 25 October 1848, PSL.

27. Jones to Secretary of the Navy, 28 July 1848, PSL; Secretary of the Navy to Jones, 15 February 1849, CFL.

28. Notice of Bounty for Deserters, 15 October 1848, *NASP*, 8:137; Jones to Secretary of the Navy, 2 November 1848, Secretary of the Navy to Jones, 1 March 1849, PSL.

29. Jones to Officers of Flagship *Ohio*, 17 September 1848, PSL.

30. Jones to Secretary of the Navy, 1 March, 9 April 1849, PSL.

31. Logbook, *Ohio*, 9 October–9 November 1848, NA, RG 24; Jones to Secretary of the Navy, 11 November 1848, PSL; Col. Richard B. Mason to Gen. Roger

Jones, 17 August 1848, in Joseph W. Revere, *Naval Duty in California*, 191; William Rich to General Nathan Towson, 23 October 1848, in ibid., 206.

32. Logbook, *Ohio*, 20 November 1848, NA, RG 24; Dan O'Neil, "From Forecastle to Mother Lode," 73–74; Jones to Secretary of the Navy, 24 November 1848, Lts. J. F. Green and J. B. Marchand to Secretary of the Navy, 9 April 1849, PSL.

33. "Special Orders," 18 October 1848, enclosure marked "B," Lts. J. F. Green and J. B. Marchand to Secretary of the Navy, 9 April 1849, PSL; T. A. M. Craven, *The Journal of T. A. M. Craven, U.S.N.*, 57.

34. Jones to Secretary of the Navy, 25 October 1848, 9 April 1849, PSL; Jones to Charles M. Armstrong, 18 April 1849, Jones to Lts. J. F. Green, J. B. Marchand, and T. A. M. Craven, 20 October 1848, NA, RG 45, ser. 464, box 328, NO-Court Martial Pacific Station; Craven, *Journal of T. A. M. Craven*, 54–55.

35. Craven, *Journal of T. A. M. Craven*, 55.

36. Jones to Secretary of the Navy, 9 April 1849, Stribling to Green, 3 April 1849, Armstrong to Marchand, 8 April 1849, PSL.

37. Jones to Secretary of the Navy, 9 April 1849, PSL; O'Neil, "From Forecastle to Mother Lode," 77–78.

38. Jones to Secretary of the Navy, 5, 9 April 1849, PSL.

39. Fabius Stanly to Secretary of the Navy, 31 March, 9 April 1849, Jones to Stanly, 3 April 1849, NA, RG 45, ser. 464, box 328, NO-Court Martial Pacific Station; A. K. Long to Jones, 7 March 1849, PSL.

40. General Order No. 6, 15 November 1848, Jones to Secretary of the Navy, 21 November 1848, NA, RG 45, ser. 464, box 328, NO-Court Martial Pacific Station.

41. Jones to Secretary of the Navy, 9 April 1849, PSL; Jones to Secretary of the Navy, 24 November 1848, *NASP*, 2:116–19.

42. William H. Ellison, ed., "Memoirs of Hon. William M. Gwin," 4.

43. *California Star* (San Francisco), 26 November 1848; Jones to Secretary of the Navy, 25 November 1848, PSL.

44. Secretary of the Navy to Jones, 25 August 1848, PSL; Records of the General Accounting Office, USS *Ohio*, NA, RG 217, vol. 1255; *Letter from Commodore Thos. ap C. Jones*, 12 February 1853, 32d Cong., 2d sess., House Misc. Doc. 22, 128.

45. Will of Elizabeth Lee Jones, 16 April 1822, Fairfax County Wills, N1, 48–56, FCCA.

46. *Letter from Commodore Thos. ap C. Jones*, 12 February 1853, 128.

47. Green and Marchand to Secretary of the Navy, 9 April 1849, PSL; Gerald Thompson, *Edward F. Beale and the American West*, 30, 34.

48. Jones to Secretary of the Navy, 9 April 1849, PSL; *Review*, 10–15; "Memorandum of California Gold Purchased by Thos. Ap Catesby Jones, . . ." *Proceedings*, 72, and "Memorandum for Mr. Buchanan," 13 March 1849, ibid., 41.

49. James Lawrence Blair to Mary Blair, 29 June 1849, box 2, James Lawrence Blair, Janin Family Collection, HEHL; William T. Sherman, *Personal Memoirs of General William T. Sherman*, 190.

50. Jones to Titus Coan, 2 November 1848, 7 May 1849, Titus Munson Coan Papers, NYHS; Secretary of the Navy to Jones, 16 April 1849, CFL; Jones to Secretary of the Navy, 9 April 1849, PSL; Ten Eyck to Jones, 31 August 1849, in U.S. Congress, *Correspondence of Diplomatic and Naval Officers concerning the Relations of the United States to the Hawaiian Islands*, 313–14.

51. Neal Harlow, *California Conquered*, 324–25; Secretary of the Navy to Jones, 16 April 1849, Jones to Secretary of the Navy, 16 June 1849, PSL; Hubert H. Bancroft, *History of California*, 6:279–80.

52. Jones to T. Butler King, 21 September 1850, *Nashville True Whig*, 6 December 1850; *Daily Journal of Commerce*, 25 March 1850; *Daily Pacific News*, 28 March 1850.

53. Paul Gates, *Land and Law in California*, 109–10.

54. Ibid.; Jones to Larkin, 9 February 1849, Larkin to Jones, 21 May 1849, in Larkin, *Larkin Papers*, 8:134; Jones to Matthew F. Maury, 21 February 1850, in C. Norman Guice, ed., "The 'Contentious Commodore' and San Francisco," 339–40; Sherman, *Personal Memoirs*, 96–97.

55. Louis M. Goldsborough to his wife, 5 April 1849, Louis M. Goldsborough Papers, LC; Secretary of the Navy to Jones, 20 January 1849, CFL; Jones to Matthew F. Maury, 13 July 1850, in Guice, "The 'Contentious Commodore' and San Francisco," 341–42; David Chandler to Jones, indenture of 10 July 1850, Halleck, Peachy, and Billings Papers, Bancroft Library, University of California, Berkeley.

56. Jones to Secretary of the Navy, 14 April, 26 August, 1 September 1849, November 1848, PSL; Secretary of the Navy to Jones, 14 April 1849, CFL.

57. Erwin G. Gudde, "Mutiny on the *Ewing*," 42–43.

58. James E. Valle, *Rocks and Shoals*, 106–8.

59. Ibid.; Leonard Guttridge, *Mutiny: A History of Naval Insurrection*, 116–17.

60. Secretary of the Navy to Jones, 24 April, 10 May 1850, CFL; Jones to Charles McCauley, 21 June 1850, PSL; *New York Daily Tribune*, 23 August 1850.

61. Secretary of the Navy to Jones, 20 January, 22 February, 1 March 1849, PSL.

62. John Coffin Jones to Thomas O. Larkin, 10 June 1847, in Larkin, *Larkin Papers*, 7:34–35; William H. Davis, *Sixty Years in California*, 163; Harlow, *California Conquered*, 313–14.

63. Thompson, *Edward F. Beale*, 26–27, 30, 34; Charles Wilkes to John Wilkes, 1 June, 4 September 1849, Wilkes Family Papers, Duke; *Autobiography*, 636–37.

Chapter 8. The Decision Is Final

1. J. M. Carlisle to John Young Mason, 16 December 1850, "Summons to appear before a Naval General Court Martial," Mason Family Papers, VHS.

2. Millard Fillmore to William A. Graham, 22 July 1850, William A. Graham Papers, North Carolina State Archives, Raleigh.

3. Morison, *"Old Bruin,"* 273–74; John H. Schroeder, *Shaping a Maritime Empire,* 96–99.

4. Myra Glenn, "The Naval Reform Campaign against Flogging," 408–9.

5. Ibid., 418–19; Richard H. Dana, *Two Years before the Mast,* chap. 15: "Flogging"; Herman Melville, *White Jacket,* chap. 6: "The Quarter-Deck Officers"; Melville, *Moby Dick,* chap. 28: "Ahab."

6. Secretary of the Navy to Jones, 7 September 1850, OSW.

7. "Monday, December 16, 1850—12 o'clock, m.," *Proceedings,* 2–11; *Exceptions,* 6–7.

8. *Review,* 10–15; "Invoice of grain gold purchased by order of Commodore Thomas Ap. C. Jones . . . ," 26–27, "Memorandum of California Gold Purchased by Thos. Ap Catesby Jones," 72, "Memorandum for Mr. Buchanan," 13 March 1849, 41, and "Memorandum for my friend Joseph Wilson," 25 November 1848, 27–28, all in *Proceedings.*

9. *Proceedings,* 7.

10. Ibid., 7–8; Jones to Secretary of the Navy, 25 October 1848, PSL.

11. *Proceedings,* 106, 117–18, 120, 125.

12. *Review,* 6–7; Jones to Secretary of the Navy, 25 October 1848, 1, 2, and 25 November 1848, PSL; Jones to the Commissioned and Warrant Officers, Petty Officers, Seamen, and Marines of the Pacific Squadron, 21 August 1848, "Extract from Journal of Midshipman Philip C. Johnson, Jr., *Ohio,* 1847–1848," NA, RG 45:392, entry 76; 11 November 1848, "Notes from the Journal of Lieutenant T. A. M. Craven," 54–55, in *Proceedings.*

13. Jones to Secretary of the Navy, 25 October 1848; Dispatch 34, 64–65; Jones to Lieutenants Green, Marchand, Craven, 20 October 1848, 66–67; and "Cross Examination of T. A. M. Craven," 138–39, all in *Proceedings.*

14. *Proceedings,* 9.

15. Ibid., 10–11; Charles Wilkes to John Wilkes, 1 June 1849, Wilkes Family Papers, Duke; Secretary of the Navy to Jones, 25 June 1849, PSL; 29 January 1849, "Notes from the Journal of Lieutenant T. A. M. Craven," 62, in *Proceedings.*

16. *Proceedings,* 20–21.

17. Jones to Secretary of the Navy, 24 September 1850, *Letter from Commodore Thos. ap C. Jones,* 32d Cong., 2d sess., House Misc. Doc. 22, 125–27; Jones to Secretary of the Navy, 2, 24, and 25 November 1848, PSL.

18. *Proceedings,* 268–69.

19. *Review,* 4–16; *Proceedings,* 268–69.

20. Secretary of the Navy to Jones, 7 September, 1 November 1850, OSW; John Young Mason's handwritten comments on Jones case, in Jones to John Young Mason, 24 November 1852, app. 4, Mason Family Papers, VHS.

21. Jones to John Young Mason, 24 November 1852, app. 4, Mason Family Papers, VHS; Jones to Secretary of the Navy, 22 November 1850, *Proceedings*, 385–86.

22. Jones to Secretary of the Navy, 22 November 1850, 385–86, 18 April 1849, 124–25; "Cross Examination of T. A. M. Craven," 139; and 11 November 1848, "Notes from the Journal of Lieutenant T. A. M. Craven," 55, all in *Proceedings*.

23. Matthew F. Maury to William A. Graham, 7 October 1850, in William A. Graham, *Papers of William Alexander Graham*, 3:408–32; Willie P. Mangum to William A. Graham, 3 December 1850, in Willie P. Mangum, *Papers of Willie Person Mangum*, 5:195–96.

24. *National Intelligencer*, 3 March 1851; Jones to President Millard Fillmore, 13 March 1851, *Review*, 3; Jones to Secretary of the Navy, 8 July 1851, *Exceptions*, 1–17; Secretary of the Navy to Jones, 8 March, 5 June 1852, OSW; John Soney Missroon to Thomas O. Larkin, 30 September 1851, in Larkin, *Larkin Papers*, 9:48–49.

25. Jones to Secretary of the Navy, 12 July 1851, 1 September 1852, CL; John Soney Missroon to Thomas O. Larkin, 30 September 1851, in Larkin, *Larkin Papers*, 9:48–49; Jones to John Young Mason, 24 November 1852, Mason Family Papers, VHS.

26. Secretary of the Navy to Jones, 7 March 1853, OSW; Jones to Stephen R. Mallory, 11 March 1852, Washburn Papers, Massachusetts Historical Society, Boston; congressional investigation is contained in *Letter from Commodore Thos. ap C. Jones*, 1–180.

27. Secretary of the Navy to Jones, 23 February 1853, ZB File; Jones to Secretary of the Navy, 1 March 1853, CL.

28. Memorial of Thomas ap Catesby Jones, 32d Cong., 2d sess., Senate, Committee Report no. 431, 1–4; Thomas ap Catesby Jones, Surety of Walter F. Jones, 33d Cong., 1st sess., House Report no. 226, 1–4; Captain Thomas ap Catesby Jones, 34th Cong., 1st sess., House Report no. 55, 1–3; *Friend* (Honolulu), 1 March 1854.

29. Secretary of the Navy to Jones, 13 September 1855, OSW.

30. Jones to Secretary of the Navy, 31 October, 11 November 1855, CL; U.S. Congress, *Memorial of Commodore Thomas ap Catesby Jones*, 1–15; *Congressional Globe*, 35th Cong. 1st sess., 542, 957, 1000–1002.

31. 1850 Fairfax County, Virginia, Census, Agricultural Schedule; Fairfax County Personal Property, FCL; Fairfax County Deeds, U3, 26–28; V3, 17–25, 113–14; and X3, 111–12, FCCA.

32. Fairfax County Personal Property Assessment, FCL; Fairfax County Deed Book, R3, 126–27, FCCA.

33. Jones, "On the Renovation of Worn-out Lands," 265–73; *Alexandria Gazette*, 28 September 1852, 22, 25 March 1854.

34. Jones to Secretary of the Navy, 27 July 1857, CL; Diary of Rev. Charles B. McKee, 9, 10 October 1857, Lewinsville Presbyterian Church, Vienna, Virginia; *Daily National Intelligencer,* 1 June 1858.

CHAPTER 9. PRECIOUS IN THE SIGHT OF THE LORD
1. Gilbert Workman, "Forgotten Firebrand," 79–87.
2. Obituary, *National Intelligencer,* 1 June 1858.
3. Frank W. Gapp, *The Commodore and the Whale,* 159–61.
4. Gapp, "Jones and Melville," 37–39.
5. "Memorial of Commodore Thomas ap Catesby Jones," 1–15.
6. Morison, *"Old Bruin,"* 430–31; Albert Gleaves, *Life and Letters of Rear Admiral Stephen B. Luce,* 64–65.

~❧ *Bibliography* ❧~

ARCHIVAL SOURCES

College of William and Mary, Williamsburg, Virginia. Manuscripts Department,
Swem Library
    Ritchie Harrison Papers
    Tucker-Coleman MSS
Duke University, Durham, North Carolina. Special Collections Department,
William R. Perkins Library
    Robert E. Johnson Papers
    Elie A. F. Lavallette Papers
    Wilkes Family Papers
Fairfax Circuit Court Archives, Fairfax County, Virginia
    County Tax Records, Personal Property
    Court Orders and Minutes Books
    Deed Books
    Drawer X: Thomas ap Catesby Jones to Lucius Jones, 1822
    Will Books
Fairfax County Public Library, Fairfax County, Virginia
    Fairfax County Census, Agriculture Schedule
    Personal Property Assessment
    Personal Property Records
Hagley Museum and Library, Wilmington, Delaware
    Samuel F. Du Pont Papers
State of Hawaii, Archives Division, Honolulu, Hawaii
    Journal of John N. Colcord
    Foreign Office and Executive Collection
    Miscellaneous Manuscripts
Historic New Orleans Collection, New Orleans, Louisiana
    "Autobiography of Admiral Robert Aitchison"
    Butler Family Papers

Andrew Hynes Papers
Edward Nicolls and William H. Percy Letters
James Monroe Letter
James Stirling Memorandum
Raymond and Roger Weill Collection
Historical Society of New Jersey, Newark
    Mahlon Dickerson Papers
Henry E. Huntington Library, San Marino, California
    "Diary Kept by a Hospital Officer at Pass Christian, Mississippi, 5 August to 1
        December 1812"
    Charles Thomas Harbeck Papers
    Janin Family Papers
    Abel Stearns Papers
Lewinsville Presbyterian Church, McLean, Virginia
    Rev. Charles B. McKee Diary
Library of Congress, Washington, D.C.
    Bayard Family Papers
    Browning Family Papers, Naval Historical Foundation Collection
    Peregrine W. Browning Papers
    Joseph G. Clark Papers
    Alexander Claxton Papers, Naval Historical Foundation Collection
    Kate Fowle Collection
    Louis M. Goldsborough Papers
    Thomas J. Harris Papers
    Andrew Jackson Papers
    Thomas Jefferson Papers
    Jones Family Papers
    Thomas ap Catesby Jones Papers
    James Monroe Papers
    Rodgers Family Papers, Naval Historical Foundation Collection
    John Shaw Papers, Naval Historical Foundation Collection
    Robert Smith Papers
Logbooks of U.S. Navy Ships in the U.S. National Archives
    Constellation, 1817–18. Record Group 24
    Macedonian, 1837–38. Record Group 24
    Ohio, 1846–50. Record Group 24
    Peacock, 1824–25. Record Group 24
    United States, 1841–44. Record Group 24
    Washington, 1815–20. Record Group 24
Maryland Historical Society, Baltimore, Maryland
    Samuel Hambleton Letterbook, in the Hambleton Family Papers

Massachusetts Historical Society, Boston Massachusetts
  Washburn Papers
Muster (M) and Pay (P) Rolls in the U.S. National Archives
  Consort, 1837–43 (M) (P). Record Group 45, 90
  Constellation, 1817 (M). Record Group 45, 90
  Gunboat No. 10 (M). Record Group 45, 90
  Macedonian, 1813–38 (P). Record Group 45, 90
  New Orleans Naval Station (M) (P). Record Group 45, 92, entry 2
  Pioneer, 1836–37 (M) (P). Record Group 45, 90
  United States, 1809–44 (M). Record Group 45, 90
  Washington, 1815–25 (M) (P). Record Group 45, 90
National Archives, United States Congress
  Letters Sent by the Commissioners of Customs Relating to Captured and
    Abandoned Property (Southern Claims Commission Case Files),
    1868–1875. Record Group 17, box 353
National Archives, United States Department of State
  Despatches from U.S. Ministers to Mexico, 1823–1906. Record Group 59, M97
  Letters of Application and Recommendation during the Administration of
    Thomas Jefferson, 1801–1809. Record Group 59, M418
National Archives, United States District Courts
  Records of the United States District Court. Louisiana, Eastern District,
    1806–1859. National Archives–Southwest Region, Fort Worth, Texas,
    Record Group 21, case 801
National Archives, United States Independent Agencies
  Records of Veterans Administration. Record Group 15
National Archives, United States Department of the Navy
  "Ammunition, Powder." Record Group 45, BA, box 136, Ammunition Powder
  "Board for Testing Ordnance." Record Group 45, 359
  Confidential Letters Sent by the Secretary of the Navy. Record Group 45, 14
  Courts-Martial. Record Group 45, 464, box 328
  Cruise of the *Peacock,* 1826—27, Record Group 45, 25, entry 1
  Daniel Dexter Letterbook, Record Group 45, 395, entry 8
  "Extracts from the Journal of Midshipman Philip C. Johnson, Jr., on Board
    the U.S.S. *Ohio,* 1847–1848." Record Group 45, 392, entry 76
  Gunboat Letters. Record Group 45, 173
  Letterbook of William B. Finch of the U.S.S. *Vincennes,* 1826–1830. Record
    Group 45, 5, entry 2
  Letters from Inspectors and Assistant Inspectors of Ordnance. Record Group
    45, 226
  Letters from Officers Acknowledging Receipt of Commissions and Warrants
    and Enclosing Oaths of Allegiance. Record Group 45, 66

Letters from Officers Transmitting Statements of Their Service, June 1842–
    December 1844. Record Group 24
Letters Received by the Secretary of the Navy from Commanding Officers of
    Squadrons, 1841–1886. Record Group 45, M89
Letters Received by the Secretary of the Navy: Captains' Letters, 1805–1861,
    1866–1885. Record Group 45, M125
Letters Received by the Secretary of the Navy: Miscellaneous Letters, 1801–
    1884. Record Group 45, M124
Letters Received by the Secretary of the Navy from Commanders, 1804–1886.
    Record Group 45, M147
Letters Received by the Secretary of the Navy from Officers below the Rank of
    Commander, 1802–1884. Record Group 45, M148
Letters Sent by the Secretary of the Navy to Officers, 1798–1868. Record Group
    45, M149
Letters to the Navy Board of Commissioners. Record Group 45, 8
Records of the General Accounting Office. *Ohio,* vol. 1255, August 1848–Sep-
    tember 1849. Record Group 217
Records of the Office of the Judge Advocate General (Navy). Record Group 125,
    M273
Records of the U.S. Exploring Expedition under the Command of Lt. Charles
    Wilkes, 1836–1846. Record Group 37, M75
Register of Ships. Record Group 45, 171
Register of Ships, Cruises, and Officers. Record Group 45, 179
Report on Naval Ordnance of the United States. Record Group 45, 230
"Statement of Lieutenant Thomas ap Catesby Jones to Daniel T. Patterson, 12
    March 1815." Record Group 45, HJ, box 181, 1814–15
"Statement of Service from Officers." Record Group 45, 72
Naval Historical Center, Washington Navy Yard, Washington, D.C.
    ZB Bibliographic File
New-York Historical Society, New York
    Titus Munson Coan Papers
    Heartman Collection
    Naval History Society Collection
North Carolina State Archives, Raleigh, North Carolina
    William Alexander Graham Papers
Princeton University Library, Princeton, New Jersey, Department of Rare Books and
Special Collections
    Blair and Lee Family Papers; Series: Papers of Samuel Philip Lee; Papers of
        Francis Preston Blair
    Samuel Southard Papers

Franklin D. Roosevelt Library, Hyde Park, New York
    Naval Manuscripts
Southern Historical Collection, University of North Carolina, Chapel Hill,
North Carolina
    Kean-Prescott Papers
    E. M. Service Papers
    John Young Mason Papers
University of California, Berkeley, California, Bancroft Library
    Halleck, Peachy, and Billings Papers
University of Michigan, Ann Arbor, Michigan, William L. Clements Library
    Chew Papers
    Smith Naval Collection
University of Virginia, Charlottesville, Virginia, Alderman Library
    R. W. Lull Collection
U.S. Naval Academy, Annapolis, Maryland, Nimitz Library
    John D. Henley Letterbook
State of Virginia: Petitions to the General Assembly
    Fairfax County Legislative Petition
    "Great Falls Manufacturing Company," chapter 222, 11 January 1839
    "Town of South Lowell," chapter 248, 6 March 1839
Virginia Historical Society, Richmond, Virginia
    Carter Family Papers
    Thomas ap Catesby Jones Papers
    Mason Family Papers
    James Ogilvie Papers
    Peckatone Papers
Virginia State Library and Archives
    Deed Record Book No. 17, Northumberland County
    Personal Property, Fairfax County Tax Records, Land Tax Books, Fairfax
       County, Virginia, 1819–50
Yale University, New Haven, Connecticut, Beinecke Rare Book and Manuscript
Library
    Collection of Western America
    Benajah Ticknor Papers

PUBLISHED SOURCES

Adams, John Quincy. *Memoirs of John Quincy Adams.* 12 vols. Edited by Charles
    Francis Adams. Philadelphia: J. B. Lippincott, 1874–77.
Alden, Carroll Storrs. *Lawrence Kearny: Sailor Diplomat.* Princeton: Princeton
    University Press, 1936.

American Archives. Series 4, vol. 1. Washington, D.C.: M. St. Clair Clark and Peter Force, 1837.

An American Physician. *Mackenzie's Five Thousand Receipts in all the Useful and Domestic Arts.* Philadelphia: James Kay, 1831.

Anderson, Charles Roberts. *Melville in the South Seas.* New York: Columbia University Press, 1939.

Anderson, Rufus. *History of the Sandwich Islands Mission.* Boston: Congregational Publishing Society, 1870.

A New Yorker. "Letters from Virginia. No. 5." *American Agriculturist* 7 (1848): 122–23.

Arthur, Stanley Clisby. *The Story of the West Florida Rebellion.* St. Francisville, La.: St. Francisville Democrat, 1935.

Balch, Thomas Bloomer. "Sharon." *Old Dominion* 6 (1872): 386–95.

Bancroft, Hubert Howe. *History of California.* San Francisco: A. L. Bancroft, 1884–90.

Bauer, K. Jack, ed. *The New American State Papers. Naval Affairs.* 10 vols. Wilmington, Del.: Scholarly Resources, 1981.

Benjamin, Park. *The United States Naval Academy.* New York: G. P. Putnam's Sons, 1900.

Bieber, Ralph P. "California Gold Mania." *Mississippi Valley Historical Review* 35 (1948): 3–28.

Bingham, Hiram. *A Residence of Twenty-one Years in the Sandwich Islands.* 1847. Reprint. Rutland, Vt.: Charles E. Tuttle, 1981.

Booker, J. Motley. "Mt. Zion and Its People." *Bulletin of the Northumberland County Historical Society* 9 (1971): 3–10.

Bosch García, Carlos. *Material para la historia diplomática de México y los Estados Unidos, 1820–1848.* Mexico: Universidad Nacional Autónoma de México, Escuela Nacional de Ciencias Polëticas y Sociales, 1957.

Bradley, Harold W. "Thomas ap Catesby Jones and the Hawaiian Islands, 1826–1827." *Annual Report of the Hawaiian Historical Society* 39 (1930): 17–30.

Bradley, Udolpho Theodore. "The Contentious Commodore: Thomas ap Catesby Jones of the Old Navy, 1788–1858." Ph.D. diss., Cornell University, 1933.

———. "Thomas ap Catesby Jones: A Personality of the Days of Sail." *United States Naval Institute Proceedings* 59 (1933): 1154–56.

Brooke, George M. "The Vest Pocket War of Commodore Jones." *Pacific Historical Review* 31 (1962): 217–33.

Brookes, Jean Ingram. *International Rivalry in the Pacific Islands, 1800–1875.* Berkeley: University of California Press, 1941.

Busch, Brinton Cooper. *Alta California.* Glendale, Calif.: Arthur H. Clark, 1983.

Calendar of Virginia State Papers. 11 vols. Richmond, 1875–93. Reprint. New York: Kraus Reprint Corp., 1968.

Claiborne, Nathaniel Herbert. *Notes on the War in the South; with Biographical Sketches of the Lives of Montgomery, Jackson, Sevier, the Late Gov. Claiborne, and Others.* Richmond: William Ramsay, 1819.

Claiborne, W. C. C. *Official Letterbooks of W. C. C. Claiborne, 1801–1816.* 6 vols. Edited by Dunbar Rowland. Jackson: Miss.: State Department of Archives and History, 1917.

Clericus. "Biographical Sketch of Thomas ap Catesby Jones." *Military and Naval Magazine* (1834): 127–34.

Cooke, John Henry. *A Narrative of Events in the South of France and of the Attack on New Orleans, in 1814 and 1815.* London: T. and W. Boone, 1835.

Craven, T. A. M. *Notes from the Journal of Lieutenant T. A. M. Craven, U.S.N., U.S.S. "Dale," Pacific Squadron, 1846–1849.* Annapolis: Naval Institute Press, 1888.

Dana, Richard Henry. *Two Years before the Mast: A Personal Narrative of Life at Sea.* 1840. Reprint. New York: Bantam Books, 1959.

Davis, Richard Beale. "James Ogilvie: An Early American Teacher of Rhetoric." *Quarterly Journal of Speech* (1942): 289–97.

Davis, William Heath. *Sixty Years in California: A History of Events and Life in California.* San Francisco: A. J. Leary, 1889.

Dudley, William S., ed. *The Naval War of 1812: A Documentary History.* 2 vols. to date. Naval Historical Center. Washington, D.C.: Government Printing Office, 1985–92.

Ellison, William Henry, ed., "Memoirs of Hon. William M. Gwin." *California Historical Society Quarterly* 19 (1940): 1–26.

Eller, E. M., W. J. Morgan, and R. M. Basoco. *The Battle of New Orleans; Sea Power and the Battle of New Orleans.* The Battle of New Orleans, 150th Anniversary Committee of Louisiana, 1965.

Ewing, Maskell C. *The Water Power at the Great Falls of the Potomac.* Washington, D.C.: J. and G. S. Gideon, 1845.

Faye, Stanley. "Privateers of Guadeloupe and Their Establishment in Barataria." *Louisiana Historical Quarterly* 23 (1940): 428–44.

Fitzpatrick, Donovan, and Saul Saphire. *Navy Maverick Uriah Phillips Levy.* Garden City, N.Y.: Doubleday, 1963.

Franklin, Samuel R. *Memoirs of a Rear-Admiral.* New York: Harper and Brothers, 1898.

Gapp, Frank W. *The Commodore and the Whale: The Lost Victories of Thomas ap Catesby Jones.* New York: Vantage Press, 1996.

——. "Commodore Thomas ap Catesby Jones: Naval Hero and Fairfax Farmer." *Northern Virginia Heritage* 5 (June 1983): 15–20.

——. "Jones and Melville: Encounter in the Pacific, 1843." *Yearbook of the Historical Society of Fairfax County, Virginia* 25 (1996): 1–43.

——. "'The Kind-Eyed Chief': Forgotten Champion of Hawai'i's Freedom." *Hawaiian Journal of History* 19 (1985): 101–21.

———. *The Lewinsville Presbyterian Church*. McLean, Va.: Lewinsville Presbyterian Church, 1976.

Gates, Paul W. *Land and Law in California: Essays of Land Policies*. Ames: Iowa State University Press, 1991.

Gleason, Duncan, ed. "James Henry Gleason: Pioneer Journal and Letters—1841–1856." *Quarterly Publication of the Historical Society of Southern California* 31 (1949): 9–52.

Gleaves, Albert. *Life and Letters of Rear Admiral Stephen B. Luce*. New York: G. P. Putnam's Sons, 1925.

Glenn, Myra. "The Naval Reform Campaign against Flogging: A Case Study in Changing Attitudes toward Corporal Punishment, 1830–1850." *American Quarterly* 35 (1983): 408–25.

Gott, John K. "A Genealogy of the Tuberville Family." *Historical Society of Fairfax County Virginia* 11 (1970–71): 49–62.

Graham, William Alexander. *The Papers of William Alexander Graham*. 8 vols. Edited by Joseph Gregorie de Roulhac Hamilton. Raleigh: North Carolina Department of Archives and History, 1957–92.

Grattan, C. Hartley. *The United States and the Southwest Pacific*. Cambridge: Harvard University Press, 1961.

Great Falls Manufacturing Company. *Great Falls Manufacturing Company*. Washington, D.C.: Memorial of the Great Falls Manufacturing Company, n.d.

Gudde, Erwin G., "Mutiny on the *Ewing*." *California Historical Society Quarterly* 30 (1951): 39–48.

Guice, C. Norman, ed. "The 'Contentious Commodore' and San Francisco: Two 1850 Letters from Thomas ap Catesby Jones." *Pacific Historical Review* 34 (1965): 337–42.

Guttridge, Leonard. *Mutiny: A History of Naval Insurrection*. Annapolis: Naval Institute Press, 1992.

Hague, Harlan, and David J. Langum. *Thomas O. Larkin: A Life of Patriotism and Profit in Old California*. Norman: University of Oklahoma Press, 1990.

Hall, Claude H. *Abel Parker Upshur: Conservative Virginian, 1792–1844*. Madison: State Historical Society of Wisconsin, 1964.

———. "Abel P. Upshur and the Navy as an Instrument of Foreign Policy." *Virginia Magazine of History and Biography* 69 (1961): 290–99.

Hanks, Robert J. "Commodore Jones and His Private War with Mexico." *American West* 16 (1979): 30–33, 60–63.

Harlow, Neal. *California Conquered: The Annexation of a Mexican Province, 1846–1850*. Berkeley: University of California Press, 1982.

Hatheway, G. G. "Commodore Jones's War." *History Today* 16 (1966): 194–201.

Haywood, Marshall DeLancey. *John Branch, 1782–1863*. Raleigh: Commercial Printing Company, 1915.

Heite, Edward F. "Virginia Twists the Lion's Tail." *Virginia Cavalcade* 17 (1968): 41–47.

Hickin, Patricia. "Yankees Come to Fairfax County, 1840–1850." *Virginia Cavalcade* 26 (1977): 100–109.

High, James. "Jones at Monterey." *Journal of the West* 5 (1966): 173–86.

The History of the College of William and Mary. Baltimore: John Murphy, 1870.

Jackson, Alonzo C. *The Conquest of California; Reported in the Letters of Alonzo C. Jackson, 1842–1846.* Privately printed, 1953.

Jackson, Andrew. *Correspondence of Andrew Jackson.* 7 vols. Edited by John Spencer Bassett. Washington, D.C.: Carnegie Institution of Washington, 1926–35.

Jacobs, James Ripley. *Tarnished Warrior: Major-General James Wilkinson.* New York: Macmillan, 1938.

Jay, William. *A Review of the Causes and Consequences of the Mexican War.* Boston: Benjamin B. Mussey, 1849.

Johnson, Robert E. "Commodore and Virginia Planter." *Virginia Cavalcade* 16 (1967): 4–11.

———. "A Long Chase." *United States Naval Institute Proceedings* 85 (1959): 144–46.

———. *Thence around Cape Horn: The Story of United States Naval Forces on Pacific Station, 1818–1923.* Annapolis: Naval Institute Press, 1963.

Jones, Lewis H. *Captain Roger Jones of London and Virginia; Some of His Antecedents and Descendants.* Albany, N.Y.: Joel Munsell's Sons, 1891.

Jones, Thomas ap Catesby. *Exceptions to the Illegal Organization, Proceedings, Findings, and Sentence, and etc. of the Naval Court Martial in the Case of Commodore Thomas ap Catesby Jones.* Washington: Gideon and Company, 1851.

———. "Experiments with Bone Manure." *Farmers' Register* 9 (1841): 1–2.

———. "Letter of Com. Jones Relative to the Capture of Monterey." *Army and Navy Chronicle and Scientific Repository* 1 (1843): 480–86.

———. "Profit of Improving Poor Land." *Farmers' Register* 7 (1839): 153–56.

———. "On the Renovation of Worn-out Lands." *American Farmer* 9 (1854): 265–73.

———. "The Sandwich Islands." *Military and Naval Magazine* 6 (1835): 282–88.

———. "Statements of Particular and General Management and Products, in Fairfax." *Farmers' Register* 6 (1838): 1–2.

———. *Summary Statement of Facts, and Etc.* Washington, D.C., 1832.

———. *Visit to Los Angeles in 1843.* Edited by Robert J. Woods. Los Angeles: Cole-Holmquist Press, 1960.

———. *Visit to Monterey in 1842.* Edited by Richard T. Maxwell. Los Angeles: G. Dawson, 1955.

Jones, Walter, Richard S. Coxe, and Joseph H. Bradley. *Review of the Evidence, Findings, and Sentence of the Naval Court Martial in the Case of Commo. Thomas ap Catesby Jones.* Washington, D.C.: Gideon and Company, 1851.

Judd, Bernice. *Voyages to Hawaii before 1860.* 1929. Reprint. Honolulu: University Press of Hawaii for the Hawaiian Mission Children's Society, 1974.

Langley, Harold D. *Social Reform in the United States Navy, 1798–1862.* Urbana: University of Illinois Press, 1967.

Larkin, Thomas O. *The Larkin Papers.* 10 vols. Edited by George P. Hammond. Berkeley: University of California Press, 1951–64.

Latour, Arsène Lacarrière. *Historical Memoir of the War in West Florida and Louisiana in 1814–15.* 1816. Reprint, edited by Gene A. Smith. Gainesville: University Press of Florida, 1999.

Layne, J. Gregg. "Annals of Los Angeles." *California Historical Society Quarterly* 13 (1934): 195–234.

Lewis, James F., and J. Motley Booker. "Catesby Jones of 'Level View': Origin and Descent of an Old Estate." *Bulletin of the Northumberland County Historical Society* 14 (1977): 5–12.

Little, James D. "The Navy at the Battle of New Orleans." *Louisiana Historical Quarterly* 54 (1971): 18–29.

Long, David F. *Gold Braids and Foreign Relations: Diplomatic Activities of U.S. Naval Officers, 1798–1883.* Annapolis: Naval Institute Press, 1988.

———. *"Mad Jack": The Biography of Captain John Percival, USN, 1779–1862.* Westport, Conn.: Greenwood Press, 1993.

———. *Nothing Too Daring: A Biography of Commodore David Porter, 1780–1843.* Annapolis: Naval Institute Press, 1970.

Mahan, Alfred Thayer. *Admiral Farragut.* 1911. Reprint. New York: Chelsea House, 1983.

Maloney, Linda M. *The Captain from Connecticut: The Life and Naval Times of Isaac Hull.* Boston: Northeastern University Press, 1986.

Mangum, Willie Person. *The Papers of Willie Person Mangum.* 5 vols. Edited by Henry Thomas Shanks. Raleigh: North Carolina Department of Archives and History, 1950–56.

Marcus, Jacob Rader. *Memoirs of American Jews, 1775–1865.* Philadelphia: Jewish Publication Society of America, 1955.

Mason, Thomas A. "'The Luminary of the Northern Neck': Walter Jones, 1745–1815." *Northern Neck Historical Magazine* 35 (1985): 3978–83.

McClellan, Edwin N. "The Navy at the Battle of New Orleans." *United States Naval Institute Proceedings* 50 (1923): 2041–60.

McKee, Christopher. *A Gentlemanly and Honorable Profession: The Creation of the U.S. Naval Officer Corps, 1794–1815.* Annapolis: Naval Institute Press, 1991.

Melville, Herman. *Moby Dick.* 1851. Reprint. New York: Oxford University Press, 1999.

———. *White Jacket, or, A World in a Man-of-War.* 1850. Reprint. New York: Quality Paperback Book Club, 1996.

Meyers, William H. *Journal of a Cruise to the Pacific Ocean, 1842–1844, in the Frigate "United States."* Edited by Charles Roberts Anderson. Durham, N.C.: Duke University Press, 1937.

Morgan, George. *The Life of James Monroe.* New York: AMS Press, 1969.

Morison, Samuel Eliot. *"Old Bruin": Commodore Matthew C. Perry, 1794–1858.* Boston: Little, Brown, 1967.

O'Neil, Dan. "From Forecastle to Mother Lode: The U.S. Navy in the Gold Fields." *Southern California Quarterly* 71 (1989): 69–88.

Padgett, James A., ed. "Official Records of the West Florida Revolution and Republic." *Louisiana Historical Quarterly* 21 (1938): 685–805.

Paullin, Charles Oscar. *Commodore John Rodgers.* 1909. Reprint. Annapolis: Naval Institute Press, 1967.

——. *Diplomatic Negotiations of American Naval Officers, 1778–1883.* Baltimore: Johns Hopkins University Press, 1912.

Peck, Taylor. *Round-Shot to Rockets: A History of the Washington Navy Yard and U.S. Naval Gun Factory.* Annapolis: Naval Institute Press, 1949.

Randall, S. S. "Farmers' Club in Fairfax County, Virginia." *Monthly Journal of Agriculture* 2 (1847): 445–47.

Ray, Thomas W. "Late Eighteenth Century Northumberland County: A Brief Glimpse." *Bulletin of the Northumberland County Historical Society* 28 (1991): 49–58.

"Recollections of James Ogilvie, Earl of Finlater." *Southern Literary Messenger* 14 (1848): 534–37.

Revere, Joseph Warren. *Naval Duty in California.* Edited by Joseph A. Sullivan. Oakland, Calif.: Biobooks, 1947.

Reynolds, William. *Voyage to the Southern Ocean: The Letters of Lieutenant William Reynolds from the U.S. Exploring Expedition, 1838–1842.* Edited by Anne Hoffman Cleaver and E. Jeffrey Stann. Annapolis: Naval Institute Press, 1988.

Robb, Frances C. "Industry in the Potomac River Valley, 1760–1860." Ph.D. diss., University of West Virginia, 1991.

Sanchez-Saavedra, E. M. *A Guide to Virginia Military Organizations in the American Revolution, 1774–1787.* Richmond: Virginia State Library, 1978.

Schroeder, John H. *Shaping a Maritime Empire: The Commercial and Diplomatic Role of the American Navy, 1829–1861.* Westport Conn.: Greenwood Press, 1985.

Sherman, William T. *Personal Memoirs of General William T. Sherman.* 4th ed. New York: C. L. Webster, 1890–91.

Smith, Bradford. *Yankees in Paradise: The New England Impact on Hawaii.* Philadelphia: J. B. Lippincott, 1956.

Smith, Gene A. "Thomas ap Catesby Jones and the First Implementation of the Monroe Doctrine." *Southern California Quarterly* 76 (1994): 139–52.

——. "The War that Wasn't: Thomas ap Catesby Jones and the Seizure of Monterey." *California History* 46 (1987): 104–13, 155.

Stanton, William. *The Great United States Exploring Expedition of 1838–1842.* Berkeley: University of California Press, 1975.

Stauffer, Robert. "The Hawai'i–United States Treaty of 1826." *Hawaiian Journal of History* 17 (1983): 40–63.

Stockton, Robert F. *A Sketch of the Life of Com. Robert F. Stockton.* New York: Derby and Jackson, 1856.

Strauss, W. Patrick. "Pioneer American Diplomats in Polynesia, 1820–1840." *Pacific Historical Review* 31 (1962): 21–30.

——. "Preparing the Wilkes Expedition: A Study in Disorganization." *Pacific Historical Review* 28 (1959): 221–32.

Thompson, Gerald. *Edward F. Beale and the American West.* Albuquerque: University of New Mexico Press, 1983.

Todorich, Charles. *The Spirited Years: A History of the Antebellum Naval Academy.* Annapolis: Naval Institute Press, 1984.

Tucker, Spencer. *Arming the Fleet: U.S. Navy Ordnance in the Muzzle-Loading Era.* Annapolis: Naval Institute Press, 1989.

Tyler, Lyon Gardiner. *The Letters and Times of the Tylers.* Richmond, Va.: Whittet and Shepperson, 1884–96.

Underhill, Reuben L. *From Cowhides to Golden Fleece.* Stanford, Calif.: Stanford University Press, 1939.

United States Congress. *American State Papers: Documents, Legislative and Executive of the Congress of the United States: Class VI, Naval Affairs.* 6 vols. Edited by Walter Lowrie and Walter S. Franklin. Washington, D.C.: Gales and Seaton, 1832.

——. *Annals of the Congress of the United States.* 42 vols. Washington, D.C.: Gales and Seaton, 1834–56.

——. "Captain Thomas ap Catesby Jones." 34th Congress, 1st session, House of Representatives Report no. 55, 1–3.

——. "The Committee on Foreign Affairs, to whom was referred the memorial of Captain Thomas ap Catesby Jones, praying renumeration for services. . . ." 28th Congress, 2d session, House of Representatives Report no. 92, 1–24.

——. "The Committee on Foreign Affairs, to whom was referred the memorial of Captain Thomas ap Catesby Jones, praying renumeration for services. . . ." 29th Congress, 1st session, House of Representatives Report no. 108, 1–24.

——. *Correspondence of Diplomatic and Naval Officers concerning the Relations of the United States to the Hawaiian Islands.* 52d Congress, 2d session, Senate Executive Documents 76 and 77, 1893, 1–509.

——. *Explore South Seas.* 20th Congress, 1st session, House of Representatives Report no. 209, 1–18.

———. *Exploring Expedition*. 25th Congress, 2d session, House Document 147, 1–630.

———. *Letter from Commodore Thos. ap C. Jones*. 32d Congress, 2d session, House of Representatives Miscellaneous Documents no. 22, 1–180.

———. *Memorial of Commodore Thomas ap Catesby Jones*. Washington, D.C.: Gideon Printer, 1855, 1–16.

———. "Proceedings of the Board of Naval Examiners, 1847." U.S. Naval Academy Archives, Nimitz Library, Annapolis, Maryland.

———. *The Proceedings of a Court-Martial on Commodore Thomas ap Catesby Jones, and Certain Correspondence between the Secretary of the Navy and Commodore Jones*. 31st Congress, 2d session, Senate Executive Document 45, 1–400.

———. *Taking Possession of Monterey*. 27th Congress, 3d session, House Executive Document 166, 1–117.

———. "Thomas ap Catesby Jones." 29th Congress, 1st session, House of Representatives Report no. 108, 1–24.

———. "Thomas ap Catesby Jones." 30th Congress, 1st session, House of Representatives Report no. 273, 1–7.

———. "Thomas ap Catesby Jones, Surety of Walter F. Jones." 33d Congress, 1st session, House of Representatives Report no. 226, 1–4.

Valle, James E. *Rocks and Shoals*. Annapolis: Naval Institute Press, 1980.

Viola, Herman J., and Carolyn Margolis, eds. *Magnificient Voyagers: The U.S. Exploring Expedition, 1838–1842*. Washington, D.C.: Smithsonian Institution Press, 1985.

Virginia. *Acts of the General Assembly of Virginia*. Richmond: Samuel Shepherd, 1839.

———. *Virginia Tax Records*. Baltimore: Genealogical Publishing Company, 1983.

———. *Virginia Vital Records*. 3 vols. Baltimore: Genealogical Publishing Company, 1982.

Vogel, Robert C. "The Patterson and Ross Raid on Barataria, September 1814." *Louisiana History* 33 (spring 1992): 157–70.

Walker, Alexander. *Jackson and New Orleans*. New York: J. C. Derby, 1856.

White, Philo. *Narrative of a Cruise in the Pacific to South America and California on the U.S. Sloop-of-War "Dale," 1841–1843*. Edited by Charles L. Camp. Denver, Colo.: Old West Publishing Company, 1965.

Wilkes, Charles. *Autobiography of Rear Admiral Charles Wilkes, U.S. Navy, 1798–1877*. Edited by William James Morgan, David B. Tyler, Joye L. Leonhart, and Mary F. Loughlin. Navy History Division, Department of the Navy. Washington, D.C.: Government Printing Office, 1978.

Wilson, Samuel. *The Battle of New Orleans: Plantation Houses on the Battlefield of New Orleans*. 1965. Reprint. New Orleans: Louisiana Landmarks Society, 1989.

Woodworth, Robert Bell. *A History of the Presbytery of Winchester (Synod of Virginia)*. Staunton, Va.: McClure Printing Company, 1947.

Workman, Gilbert. "Forgotten Firebrand." *United States Naval Institute Proceedings* 94 (1968): 79–87.

Wright, Thomas Roane. *Westmoreland County Virginia; 1653–1912, a Short and Bright Day in Its History*. Richmond, Va.: Whittet and Shepperson, 1912.

⌦Further Reading⌫

History has paid surprisingly little attention to Thomas ap Catesby Jones. His role in the gunboat battle on Lake Borgne and his abortive seizure of Monterey, California, have received some coverage, but very little has been written about the rest of his career or his personal life. Perhaps the main reason for this relative obscurity is the lack of a major archival collection of Jones materials. Several holdings pertain to him, but they are generally small and scattered. The most important family collections are the Jones Family Papers and the small collections of Thomas ap Catesby Jones Papers in the Library of Congress and in the archives of the Virginia Historical Society. The papers of the many people associated with him also make a valuable contribution to Jones's story; the most important are cited in the Notes.

Jones appears prominently in the records of the Department of the Navy identified in the Bibliography and in the *American State Papers: Naval Affairs*; the *New American State Papers: Naval Affairs*, edited by K. Jack Bauer; and in *The Naval War of 1812: A Documentary History*, edited by William S. Dudley. Several collections of published papers and memoirs were also very helpful to me, as indicated in the Notes.

Jones wrote a number of interesting treatises that deal with various aspects of his naval career. He described his actions in California in "Letter of Com. Jones Relative to the Capture of Monterey" and his *Visit to Los Angeles in 1843*, edited by Robert J. Woods. He recounted his farming endeavors in "Experiments with Bone Manure," "Profit of Improving Poor Land," "On the Renovation of Worn-out Lands," and "Statements of Particular and General Management and Products, in Fairfax."

There is no serious biography of Thomas ap Catesby Jones. Both Udolpho Theodore Bradley's dissertation, "The Contentious Commodore:

Thomas ap Catesby Jones of the Old Navy, 1788–1858," and Frank W. Gapp's *The Commodore and the Whale: The Lost Victories of Thomas ap Catesby Jones* are of limited use. Bradley and Gapp, however, have written articles that illustrate various aspects of Jones's life, including the former's "Thomas ap Catesby Jones: A Personality of the Days of Sail" and the latter's "Commodore Thomas ap Catesby Jones: Naval Hero and Fairfax Farmer." Robert E. Johnson, "Commodore and Virginia Planter"; and Gilbert Workman, "Forgotten Firebrand," provide cursory introductions to Jones.

Jones's service on the New Orleans station, other than the Battle of Lake Borgne, has not garnered as much attention as it deserves. Robert C. Vogel, "The Patterson and Ross Raid on Barataria, September 1814," is the best prebattle account of the New Orleans Navy Station, but it says little about Jones. E. M. Eller, W. J. Morgan, and R. M. Basoco, *The Battle of New Orleans; Sea Power and the Battle of New Orleans;* James D. Little, "The Navy at the Battle of New Orleans"; and Edwin N. McClellan, "The Navy at the Battle of New Orleans," discuss the navy's—and indirectly Jones's—role during the Battle of New Orleans.

Jones's first cruise in the Pacific has been the subject of several articles, the most important of which are Harold W. Bradley, "Thomas ap Catesby Jones and the Hawaiian Islands, 1826–1827"; Frank W. Gapp, "'The Kind-Eyed Chief': Forgotten Champion of Hawai'i's Freedom"; and Robert Stauffer, "The Hawai'i–United States Treaty of 1826." W. Patrick Strauss, "Preparing the Wilkes Expedition: A Study in Disorganization," examines Jones's unsuccessful planning of the South Seas Exploring Expedition, while Dan O'Neil, "From Forecastle to Mother Lode: The U.S. Navy in the Gold Fields," investigates his missteps while commander of Pacific Squadron during the gold rush.

Jones's abortive seizure of Monterey, California, in 1842 has been the subject of many articles. The most useful include George M. Brooke, "The Vest Pocket War of Commodore Jones"; Robert J. Hanks, "Commodore Jones and His Private War with Mexico"; G. G. Hatheway, "Commodore Jones's War"; James High, "Jones at Monterey"; Robert E. Johnson, "A Long Chase"; and Gene A. Smith's two articles, "The War that Wasn't: Thomas ap Catesby Jones and the Seizure of Monterey" and "Thomas ap Catesby Jones and the First Implementation of the Monroe Doctrine."

Jones appears as a minor character in many works. Lewis H. Jones's *Captain Roger Jones of London and Virginia; Some of his Antecedents and*

Descendants and Christopher McKee's excellent study, *A Gentlemanly and Honorable Profession*, shed light on Jones's background and youth. Arsène Lacarrière Latour, *Historical Memoir of the War in West Florida and Louisiana in 1814–15*, is the first and most complete discussion of the Battle of New Orleans, and it also includes a brief discussion of Jones's service at the Battle of Lake Borgne. Taylor Peck, *Round-Shot to Rockets: A History of the Washington Navy Yard and U.S. Naval Gun Factory*; and Spencer Tucker, *Arming the Fleet: U.S. Navy Ordnance in the Muzzle-Loading Era*, discuss naval ordnance and, indirectly, Jones's work with it, while Herman J. Viola and Carolyn Margolis, eds., *Magnificent Voyagers: The U.S. Exploring Expedition, 1838–1842*; and William Stanton, *The Great United States Exploring Expedition of 1838–1842*, chronicle the events surrounding what became the Wilkes Expedition. Park Benjamin, *The United States Naval Academy*, provides a number of interesting anecdotes that shed light on Jones's reputation within the service, and Charles Todorich, *The Spirited Years: A History of the Antebellum Naval Academy*, offers a good discussion of the founding of the Naval Academy.

There are many books about Pacific affairs, and most include discussions of Jones. Rufus Anderson, *History of the Sandwich Islands Mission*; Hiram Bingham, *A Residence of Twenty-one Years in the Sandwich Islands*; C. Hartley Grattan, *The United States and the Southwest Pacific*; Jean Ingram Brookes, *International Rivalry in the Pacific Islands, 1800–1875*; and Bradford Smith, *Yankees in Paradise: The New England Impact on Hawaii*, all discuss U.S. activities in the Hawaiian Islands. Robert E. Johnson, *Thence around Cape Horn: The Story of United States Naval Forces on Pacific Station, 1818–1923*; David F. Long, *Gold Braids and Foreign Relations: Diplomatic Activities of U.S. Naval Officers, 1798–1883*; and John H. Schroeder, *Shaping a Maritime Empire: The Commercial and Diplomatic Role of the American Navy, 1829–1861*, concentrate on the navy's role in the Pacific and provide insight into Jones's three tours of duty there.

ᏒᏗ Index ᏒᏗ

About the Author

Gene A. Smith is an associate professor of early American history at Texas Christian University in Fort Worth. He has written two other books on naval history: *"For the Purposes of Defense": The Politics of the Jeffersonian Gunboat Program,* and *Iron and Heavy Guns: Duel Between the* Monitor *and the* Merrimac. He has also edited Arsène LaCarrière Latour's *Historical Memoir of the War in West Florida and Louisiana in 1814–15,* and co-authored *Filibusters and Expansionists: Jeffersonian Manifest Destiny, 1800–1821.* Currently he is working on several projects dealing with the War of 1812.

The Naval Institute Press is the book-publishing arm of the U.S. Naval Institute, a private, nonprofit, membership society for sea service professionals and others who share an interest in naval and maritime affairs. Established in 1873 at the U.S. Naval Academy in Annapolis, Maryland, where its offices remain today, the Naval Institute has members worldwide.

Members of the Naval Institute support the education programs of the society and receive the influential monthly magazine *Proceedings* and discounts on fine nautical prints and on ship and aircraft photos. They also have access to the transcripts of the Institute's Oral History Program and get discounted admission to any of the Institute-sponsored seminars offered around the country.

The Naval Institute also publishes *Naval History* magazine. This colorful bimonthly is filled with entertaining and thought-provoking articles, first-person reminiscences, and dramatic art and photography. Members receive a discount on *Naval History* subscriptions.

The Naval Institute's book-publishing program, begun in 1898 with basic guides to naval practices, has broadened its scope in recent years to include books of more general interest. Now the Naval Institute Press publishes about one hundred titles each year, ranging from how-to books on boating and navigation to battle histories, biographies, ship and aircraft guides, and novels. Institute members receive discounts of 20 to 50 percent on the Press's more than eight hundred books in print.

Full-time students are eligible for special half-price membership rates. Life memberships are also available.

For a free catalog describing Naval Institute Press books currently available, and for further information about subscribing to *Naval History* magazine or about joining the U.S. Naval Institute, please write to:

Membership Department
U.S. Naval Institute
291 Wood Road
Annapolis, MD 21402-5034
Telephone: (800) 233-8764
Fax: (410) 269-7940
Web address: www.usni.org